Workhouses
of London
and the
South East

WORKHOUSES OF LONDON AND THE SOUTH EAST

PETER HIGGINBOTHAM

First published 2019
Reprinted 2019

The History Press
The Mill, Brimscombe Port
Stroud, Gloucestershire, GL5 2QG
www.thehistorypress.co.uk

British Library Cataloguing in Publication Data.
A catalogue record for this book is available from the British Library.

ISBN 978 0 7509 8777 6

Typesetting and origination by The History Press
Printed and bound in the UK by TJ International Ltd.

CONTENTS

1

INTRODUCTION

In a roundabout way, the workhouse owes its existence to Henry VIII. His dissolution of England's religious houses from 1536 onwards removed a major source of support for the nation's poor. Over the following decades, a variety of legislative measures were tried which gradually established the principle that the relief of the poor should come from the public purse rather than through a reliance on charitable endeavours.

The 1552 Act for Provision and Relief of the Poor required that 'collectors of alms' be appointed in each parish, with every parishioner giving whatever their 'charitable devotion' suggested. When the funds raised by such voluntary donations proved inadequate, compulsory contributions were instituted by the Vagabonds Act of 1572, which introduced a local property tax, the poor rate, administered by parish officials known as overseers. The money raised was to be used to relieve 'aged, poor, impotent, and decayed persons'.

Publicly managed institutional provision for the poor was also starting to make its appearance. In 1546, one of the religious establishments previously confiscated by Henry, Greyfriars Monastery, on London's Newgate Street, was handed over to the City of London to be used for the relief of the poor. By 1552, the buildings had been refurbished and 340 poor, fatherless children were admitted into what became known as Christ's Hospital.

The city was also given Bridewell Palace, a former residence of Henry VIII on the banks of the River Fleet. At the end of 1556, Bridewell adopted a role somewhere between that of a prison, a workhouse and a reformatory. Its inmates were primarily adults – vagrants, idlers and prostitutes – who, for a period ranging from a few weeks to several years, could be placed under its regime of daily labour and strict discipline. Bridewell's intake also included

The river frontage of Bridewell about 1660. As well as providing a tough regime for vagrants, idlers and prostitutes, Bridewell also housed the orphaned and destitute.

the young, however. The orphaned sons of city freemen were received there, parish officials sent destitute children, and the establishment's own beadles directed others from the streets to its doors.[1]

In 1576, the Act for Setting the Poor on Work stated a principle that was to influence the administration of poor relief for centuries to come – that the able-bodied were not to have 'any just excuse in saying that they cannot get service or work and be then without means of livelihood'. To achieve this, every town was enjoined to provide 'a stock of wool, hemp, flax, or other stuff by taxation of all; so that every poor and needy person, old or young, able to work and standing in need of relief, shall not fear want of work, go abroad begging, or committing pilfering, or living in idleness.'

Further institutional provision featured in the 1598 Act for the Relief of the Poor. The Act, which brought together various elements of earlier legislation, required every parish to appoint overseers of the poor, whose responsibility it was to collect and distribute the poor rate, find work for the able-bodied, and to set up 'houses of dwelling' for those who were incapable of supporting themselves. In the same year, the Hospitals for the Poor Act encouraged the founding of hospitals or 'abiding and working houses' for the poor. Providing accommodation for those in need through no fault of their own – often referred to as the 'impotent' or 'deserving' poor – coupled with premises and work for the able-bodied, formed the basis of what would eventually evolve into the workhouse.

THE 1601 POOR RELIEF ACT

The year 1601 saw the passing of another Act for the Relief of the Poor which, although essentially a refinement of the 1598 Act, marked the foundation of what became known as the Old Poor Law. The main elements of the 1601 Act were: the parish being the administrative unit responsible for poor relief, with its overseers collecting poor rates and allocating relief; the provision of materials to provide work for the able-bodied poor, with able-bodied paupers refusing to work liable to be placed in a Bridewell-like 'house of correction'; the setting to work and apprenticeship of pauper children; and the relief of the impotent poor, including the provision of 'houses of dwelling'.

The assistance given to the poor through the parish poor rates was predominantly dispensed as 'out-relief' – what might now be referred to as hand-outs. Out-relief could be given as a cash payment, either for one-off specific purposes, such as the purchase of clothing or shoes, or as a regular weekly pension. Alternatively, it could be dispensed in kind, most commonly in the form of bread or flour.

At the heart of all this activity was the parish's governing body, the vestry, which comprised the priest, churchwardens, and other respected householders of the parish.

EARLY WORKHOUSES

Although the 1601 Act talked about 'work' and 'houses', it made no mention of the word 'workhouse' – a term which seems to have come into general use in the 1620s. These early workhouses were often non-residential establishments where work, usually related to the production of textiles, was provided for the willing able-bodied.

In 1627–28, the towns of Reading and Newbury in Berkshire constructed premises to provide work for unemployed clothiers. Apart from a few supervisory staff who had accommodation on the premises, these workhouses were more like workshops in character, with their workers living elsewhere. In Guildford, a workhouse was established in 1630 where unemployed clothworkers were occupied in spinning hemp and flax for cloth-making.[2] In 1631, the Mayor of Abingdon reported that 'wee haue erected wthn our borough a workehouse to sett poore people to worke.'[3] During the 1620s and 1630s, workhouses also appeared at places such as Taunton, Sheffield, Halifax, Leeds, Exeter, Plymouth and Cambridge.[4]

The remaining section of Newbury's first workhouse, opened in 1628 and one of the oldest surviving workhouse buildings in England, now home to a local museum.

A similar role could be performed by houses of correction of this period, such as that erected at London's Tothill Fields in 1622, which also functioned as 'a house to set the poor of the parish on work'.[5]

CORPORATIONS OF THE POOR

London's first workhouses proper were set up by the city's Corporation of the Poor, a body created by the 1647 Ordinance for the Relief and Employment of the Poor. The Ordinance's provisions included the erection of workhouses – one of the earliest legislative uses of the word. The Corporation was given two confiscated royal properties – Heydon House in Minories and the Wardrobe building in Vintry – in which it established workhouses. By 1655, up to 100 children and 1,000 adults were receiving relief through the scheme, although residence was not a prerequisite. Adults could perform out-work in their own homes or carry it out each day at one of the workhouses.

As well as basic literacy, children in Corporation care were taught singing. A verse of one of their songs paints a very rosy picture of their treatment:

In filthy rags we clothed were
In good warm Raiment now appear
From Dunghill to King's Palace transferred,
Where Education, wholesome Food,
Meat, drink and Lodging, all that['s] good
For Soul and Body, are so well prepared.[6]

The Corporation's activities were halted with the Restoration in 1660, when Charles II reclaimed his properties.

The 1662 Act for the Better Relief of the Poor provided for Corporations to also be created in the City of London, Westminster, and parts of Middlesex and Surrey. These Corporations were empowered to erect workhouses, and in 1664, Middlesex spent £5,000 on setting one up in Clerkenwell, at the east corner of the junction of Corporation Lane (now Corporation Row) and Bridewell Walk (now Northampton Road). The workhouse supplied materials for the poor to work with in their own homes and was also used for 'the reception and breeding up of poor fatherless or motherless infants'. The Middlesex workhouse was not a success and closed in 1672.[7]

SETTLEMENT AND REMOVAL

Other parts of the 1662 Act, which is often referred to as the Settlement Act, had a far-reaching effect on the poor relief system. The Act decreed that a parish was required to give poor relief only to those who were legally established or 'settled' there. Unless they were able to rent a property for £10 a year or more, any new arrivals deemed 'likely to be chargeable' to the poor rates could be forcibly removed back to their own parish.

A child's settlement at birth was taken to be the same as that of its father. At marriage, a woman took on the same settlement as her husband. Illegitimate children were granted settlement in the place they were born and thus became the responsibility of that parish. This sometimes led parish overseers to try and get rid of an unmarried pregnant woman before her child was born, for example by forcibly transporting her to another parish just before the birth, or by paying a man from another parish to marry her.

Over the years, the settlement laws were much amended. From 1691, settlement could be obtained by serving an apprenticeship in a new parish or by a year's continuous employment there. From 1697, newcomers with settlement certificates from their own parish were protected from removal until they actually became chargeable on the poor rates.

The settlement laws were to govern the administration of poor relief for almost three centuries and it was only in 1948 that their final remnants were repealed.

SETTING THE POOR TO WORK

The last quarter of the seventeenth century was an era of experimentation in how best to provide useful work for the needy poor. The Chief Justice, Sir Matthew Hale, proposed that small groups of parishes should combine to establish premises where the poor could be supplied with materials for work and where children could be taught a trade. The chairman of the East India Co., Sir Joshua Child, suggested a similar scheme across the whole of London, run by a body he proposed calling 'The Fathers of the Poor'.[8]

A different approach was taken by philanthropist Thomas Firmin who, in 1676, set up a workhouse at Little Britain near Smithfield. More than 1,700 carders, combers, spinners and weavers were employed to manufacture linen from flax, much of which was done in their own homes. The establishment 'was at once school and factory, wholesale warehouse and retail shop'.[9] Children were admitted from the age of 3 and taught to read and spin. However, the scheme, which was financed from Firmin's own pocket, lost upwards of £200 each year.

A similar strategy was adopted in 1680 by the Society of Friends, or Quakers. Stocks of flax were bought and given to the Quaker poor to spin up at home or in prison. The scheme's treasurer, John Bellers, later developed plans for a 'College of Industry' – a co-operative, self-sufficient, humanitarian community where up to 200 labourers and 100 of the impotent poor would live and work together. The college building was planned to consist of four wings: one for married people, one for single young men and boys, one for single women and girls, and one for sick and invalid members.[10]

Although Bellers' plans were never implemented, their influence can be seen in the workhouse opened by the Quakers in 1702 at Clerkenwell. The establishment occupied the former Middlesex Corporation workhouse premises and housed up to fifty-six 'decayed Friends and orphans'. The elderly occupied one section of the house, with the children in another where they were employed in spinning mop-yarn. The girls made and mended the inmates' clothing, while the boys learned to read, write and cast accounts. The inmates brewed their own beer and were provided with cold baths 'for their health or cleanliness'.[11]

THE BISHOPSGATE STREET WORKHOUSE

The London Corporation of the Poor was revived in 1698 and opened a workhouse at the west side of Bishopsgate Street in 1700. Its aim was 'to employ all the poor children, beggars, vagrants, and other idle and disorderly persons' in the city. The children, up to 400 in number, were taught to read and write, and given work to do until they were apprenticed, sent to sea, or 'otherwise disposed'.[12]

The premises were divided into the Steward's Side and the Keeper's Side. The Steward's Side, at the rear of the building, housed the children, who were occupied in spinning wool or flax, or in sewing or knitting. They were also given religious instruction and taught to read, write and cast accounts

The frontage of London's Bishopsgate Street workhouse in 1819.

'whereby they are qualify'd for Services, and honest Ways of Livelihood'. The Steward's Side was three storeys high and contained the boys' work-room on the ground floor, the girls' work-room on the first floor, and two wards for lodging the boys on the top floor. The girls' ward was located over the chapel which separated the two sides of the establishment. The Keeper's Side, facing onto Bishopsgate Street, housed 'vagabonds, beggars, pilferers, lewd, idle, and disorderly persons' who were employed in beating hemp and doing the children's laundry.[13]

The reluctance of the city's parishes to fund the workhouse forced it to drastically reduce its intake of children, and from 1713 it mainly operated as a house of correction for beggars and vagrants. By 1829, the decaying building had fallen into disuse and was disposed of. The area was redeveloped in the 1870s with the construction of Liverpool Street Station.

THE WORKHOUSE TEST ACT

By the start of the eighteenth century, a few parishes had begun to provide residential accommodation for their poor. Early establishments in London included St Martin in the Fields (1665), St Giles in the Fields (1675), St James Piccadilly (1688), St Anne Soho (1697) and St Paul Covent Garden (1703). Examples elsewhere in the South East included Ashford (1705), Enfield (1719) and Maidstone (1720). Some, such as St Martin's and Maidstone, occupied purpose-built premises, while others hired a building for the purpose.

Establishments varied as to whether they required inmates to perform work in return for their accommodation and maintenance. Those where labour was not demanded, often referred to as poorhouses, typically housed only the elderly and infirm, who received little or no supervision. At Willesden, for example, cottages in the churchyard were being used by 1704 to house the old and widows.[14] Those where work was required, at least from those capable of it, were usually referred to as workhouses. As well as the work element, a work-house typically had a resident governor, strict rules relating to the behaviour of the inmates, and a restricted and plain diet. However, use of these terms was not always consistent and two words could be used almost interchangeably. The character of any particular establishment could also change over time.

A major impetus to the use of parish workhouses came from the Workhouse Test Act of 1723, also known as Knatchbull's Act. The Act gave a legal frame-work for workhouses to be set up by parishes either singly, or in combination with a neighbour. Premises could be hired or purchased for the purpose, and

St Margaret's parish workhouse, Rochester, now used by the town's King's School.

workhouse operation could be contracted out – a system that became known as 'farming' the poor. The Act also provided for the use of the workhouse 'test' – that the prospect of the workhouse should act as a deterrent and that poor relief could be restricted only to those prepared to accept its regime.

The development of the workhouse test is often credited to Matthew Marryott, a workhouse contractor from Buckinghamshire. He opened his first establishment at Olney in 1714 and over the next fifteen years was involved in the setting up and management of many others in the East and South Midlands and around London. Marryott became an advisor to the Society for Promoting Christian Knowledge (SPCK), an organisation which encouraged the use of workhouses. His activities were brought to prominence in the SPCK's book *An Account of Several Workhouses for Employing and Maintaining the Poor*, published in 1725 with a second edition in 1732. The *Account* described the operation of more than 100 workhouses and extolled the financial benefits to parishes of their use by reducing the number of poor relief claimants.

Although the 1723 Act was permissive, many parishes made use of its provisions. In the City of London, just over a third of the parishes opened workhouses in the eighteenth century, among the earliest being St Alban Wood Street and St Giles Cripplegate, both in 1724. Outside the city's walls, workhouses appeared at Wapping (1723), Ratcliff (1723), Whitechapel (1724), Limehouse (1725), Mile End Old Town (1725), St Giles in the Fields (1725) and Kensington (1726). Early adopters in Kent were Cranbrook, Ramsgate, Meopham, Rochester, Tenterden and St Lawrence in Thanet (all 1723–24). A workhouse was in use by about 1725 at Faringdon, Berkshire. In Surrey, Kingston had a workhouse by 1725, and Chertsey by 1727. In Sussex, workhouses were in use at Rye from 1724 and at East Grinstead from 1725.

The 1723 Act's provision for the joint use of workhouse premises was taken up by a number of parishes in Kent. In 1748, Davington began to send paupers to the Lenham workhouse, making an annual payment of £6 plus a weekly sum for each pauper. From 1749, Birling, Luddesdowne, Snodland and Halling shared the use of a workhouse in Halling. In 1774, Darenth and Horton Kirby began sharing a building in Darenth.[15]

THE PARISH WORKHOUSE REGIME

Parish workhouses varied in matters such as the inmates' diet and the tasks given to those able to work. A typical establishment of the period was that run by the City of London parish of St Dunstan in the West:

> A new house was built 1728, wherein there are now 30 men and women, and 26 children, of which 21 are daily sent to the parish charity-school, and work only out of school hours. These and the grown persons, who are not employed in keeping the house clean, and nursing the old and young, card wool, and spin mop yarn for a turner in the parish, who furnishes the wool for this purpose, and the turner pays 2d. for the carding and spinning every pound so returned. They have roast or boiled beef 4 days in the week for dinner, and other days, rice-milk, or dumplins. Breakfasts of broth, or milk-porridge, and suppers of bread and butter, or cheese. Prayers are read in the house every day, and they that are able, go to church every Sunday.[16]

Workhouses often had extensive rules covering matters such as the daily routine, prohibitions on smoking or the use of distilled liquors, and punishments for behaviour such as swearing, lying, malingering or disobedience. Despite the ban on strong drink, parish workhouses usually served 'small' or weak beer to their inmates – it was often healthier than the local water supply.

Even with all its restrictions, the workhouse could actually prove a tolerable or even attractive place. Robert Blincoe, an orphan inmate of St Pancras workhouse in the 1790s, later wrote that he had been 'well fed, decently clad, and comfortably lodged, and not at all overdone as regarded work'.[17] Some workhouses were positively enticing – at Chatham in 1832, the inmates ate best white bread and were allowed gin and porter.

As well as simply housing the poor, workhouses often performed other roles such as providing a parish with emergency wards and casual night shelters, orphanages and crèches, lying-in wards, a dispensary, fire engine station and a feeding station for paupers still living at home.[18]

OUT-RELIEF VERSUS THE WORKHOUSE

By the mid-1770s, across England and Wales, there were almost 2,000 workhouses in operation, with around one in seven parishes making use of this option. Berkshire was close to the national average, with just over 14 per cent of its parishes having a workhouse. In Kent, however, the figure was around 30 per cent, while in Surrey and Sussex it was nearly 40 per cent.

Despite the growing use of the workhouse, out-relief remained the dominant means for supporting the poor. In 1804, expenditure on out-relief in England and Wales, excluding the metropolis, was three times that spent on indoor (i.e. workhouse) relief. In the metropolis, however, out-relief expenditure was a little over half of that on indoor relief. The capital's indoor-relief expenditure accounted for almost a fifth of the £1.2 million spent nationally each year.[19] In terms of numbers relieved, 36.1 per cent of claimants in the metropolis received indoor relief, compared to 11.4 per cent across the rest of the country. London's disposition towards workhouses partly reflected its generally buoyant labour market – work was usually available for those willing to do it – and also the transient nature of much of its population. The ease of moving between parishes made the tracking of claimants difficult and so gave ample opportunity for fraudulent claims. Offering relief in a workhouse helped to reduce such pressures.

FARMING THE POOR

The use of private contractors or 'farmers' such as Matthew Marryott became particularly popular in the City of London where, by 1777, the number of workhouses being run by city parishes had fallen to seventeen. Factors such as the cost of running a workhouse or the lack of suitable premises had led the majority to contract out the accommodation of their poor, either to a neighbouring parish which had a workhouse or to a commercial operator based outside the city. The 1723 Act contributed to this trend because of its requirement that where a parish had a workhouse beyond its own boundary, it had to be run by a contractor.

By the early 1800s, the city parishes of All Hallows the Less, St Augustine and St Alban were paying a contractor in Hoxton 4*s* a head per week to house their indoor poor. In 1815, the establishment run by James Robertson at Hoxton could house up to 300 paupers coming from as many as forty different parishes in the city. Thomas Tipple's pauper farm at 12 Queen's Street, Hoxton, had 230 places and served seventeen city parishes, while Edward Deacon's two houses at Mile End and Bow accommodated a total of 520 paupers from more than forty city parishes.[20] In some cases, parishes that still had a workhouse of their own, such as St Sepulchre Newgate, used a contractor's establishment for inmates who misbehaved or were troublesome.

INFANT POORHOUSES

In 1766, the high mortality rate of young children in the capital's workhouses led to the passing of Hanway's Act, which required that pauper children below the age of 6 from metropolitan parishes should be sent to school in

A view from Barnet Hill of a row of cottages (right) which formerly housed the 'infant workhouse' operated by the London parish of St Andrew's, Holborn.

the countryside at least 3 miles from London or Westminster. To satisfy this requirement, parishes placed their children in a variety of out-of-town establishments, sometimes known as 'infant poorhouses' or 'baby farms', many of which were privately run. In 1832, the parish of St Luke reported that its infant paupers were put out to nurse at Southgate where an average of fifty children were under the care of three nurses. Similarly, St James Westminster put its infant poor out to nurse at Wimbledon. Shoreditch had its own establishment at Baker Street in Enfield, with a resident master, matron and 'suitable assistants'. St George, Southwark, had an infant poorhouse that stood opposite to Lewisham's workhouse, while that used by Islington was at Fords Green, Lower Edmonton. Other establishments were located at Hendon (used by St Clement Danes), Merton (St Mary Magdalen, Bermondsey), Heston (St Giles in the Fields & St George, Bloomsbury) and Barnet (St Andrew Holborn & St George the Martyr). One of the largest such institutions was Mr Aubin's school at Norwood which served a number of London's parishes.

LOCAL ACT ADMINISTRATIONS

Even with the options provided by the Workhouse Test Act, the administrative framework laid down in 1601 did not suit everyone. This was particularly the case in towns and cities that contained a number of small parishes. In 1696, Bristol's eighteen parishes obtained a Local Act of Parliament to create the Bristol Incorporation of the Poor. The Act enabled the Incorporation to manage poor relief across the whole city, including the appointment of paid officers and the setting up of workhouses. By 1712, more than a dozen other towns had followed Bristol's example and formed Incorporations under Local Acts. This route was taken by Canterbury in 1727, Chichester in 1753 and Brighton in 1810.

ANNO TRICESIMO QUINTO

Georgii III. Regis.

●●

C A P. LXI.

An Act for repealing an Act, passed in the Twelfth Year of the Reign of His present Majesty, intituled, *An Act for the more effectual assessing and collecting of the Rates for the Relief of the Poor in the Parish of* Saint Botolph Bishopsgate, *in the Liberties of the City of* London ; for providing a Workhouse for the Reception of the Poor of the said Parish ; and for the Employment, Maintenance, and Regulation, of the said Poor therein.
[5*th May* 1795.]

WHEREAS an Act was passed in the Twelfth Year of the Reign of His present Majesty, intituled, *An Act for the more effectual assessing and collecting of the Rates for Relief of the Poor in the Parish of* Saint Botolph Bishopsgate, *in the Liberties of the City of* London : And whereas the Powers of the said Act have been found defective and insufficient, and it is necessary the same should be wholly repealed, and new Powers granted : And whereas the Poor of the said Parish of *Saint Botolph Bishopsgate,* in the Liberties of the City of *London,* are very numerous, and are maintained and supported at a very great Expence by the said Parish : And whereas the granting of proper Powers for

The front page of the Local Act obtained by the City of London parish of St Botolph Bishopsgate in 1795.

From the 1740s onwards, around twenty London parishes obtained Local Acts relating to poor relief and the operation of workhouses. Such single-parish Acts commonly provided for the setting up of a new body, typically styled as Guardians, Governors or Directors of the Poor. Its members were usually elected periodically by the vestry and required to own a property of above a certain rateable value.

Despite the considerable legal expenses involved in obtaining a Local Act, parishes usually judged that the benefits would justify the cost. Care was needed in drafting the legislation, however, and parishes sometimes ended up needing a further Act when a previous one was later found to be inadequate or defective in some respect. Wapping obtained a Local Act in 1817 allowing it to raise £10,000 for the erection and furnishing of a workhouse. However, the cost of the scheme was miscalculated and a second Act was required in 1819 to provide additional funds.

GILBERT'S ACT

In 1782, MP Thomas Gilbert successfully promoted his Act for the Better Relief and Employment of the Poor. Under Gilbert's Act, the use of work-houses could be restricted to the old, the sick and infirm, and orphan children, while able-bodied paupers were to be found employment near their own homes, with landowners, farmers and other employers receiving allowances from the poor rates to bring wages up to subsistence levels. The Act also allowed parishes to form groups or 'unions' and operate a common workhouse. The administration of Gilbert Unions was through a Board of Guardians, one from each member parish, elected by the ratepayers and appointed by local magistrates. Around eighty Gilbert Unions were eventually established, some comprising more than forty parishes. Having a share in a large Gilbert Union workhouse could prove financially attractive for a parish compared to running its own institution. Gilbert's Act could also be adopted by an individual parish.

Gilbert administrations were particularly popular in Kent, where sixteen were eventually formed.[21] Seven Gilbert Unions were created in West Sussex,[22] while Arundel and Petworth adopted Gilbert's Act as single parishes. In Surrey, three Gilbert Unions were formed, together with seven Gilbert Parishes.[23] Just one Gilbert Union and one Gilbert Parish were formed in Berkshire,[24] while none appear to have been set up in East Sussex. The Act was also ignored in the metropolis, where many parishes already had Local Acts in place. In addition, the Act's prohibition on the use of the workhouse for able-bodied paupers went against the general practice in metropolitan parishes.

THE OLD POOR LAW IN CRISIS

The early nineteenth century saw a time of increasing financial problems for the poor relief system. The national cost of poor relief rose enormously – from around £2 million in 1784 to a peak of £7.87 million in 1818.[25] In 1803, around three-quarters of the poor rates were spent on out-relief.[26]

In many parts of the country, the supplementing of labourers' wages from the poor rate recommended by Gilbert's Act had become common. The practice had become formalised in allowance systems such as that introduced in 1795 at Speenhamland in West Berkshire, which linked wage supplements to the price of bread and size of family. The Napoleonic Wars (1803–15) also contributed to an increase in the number of relief claimants, while the introduction of the Corn Laws in 1815 led to higher food prices and the cost of feeding the poor.

A few places, however, managed to buck the national trend of rising poor rates. In the early 1820s, the Nottinghamshire parish of Southwell virtually abolished out-relief and claimants were instead offered only the workhouse. The workhouse was strictly and economically run, with males and females segregated, work required of the inmates and a restricted diet imposed. As a result, the parish's poor relief expenditure fell from £1,884 in 1821–22 to £811 in the following year. In 1824, a much larger workhouse run on similar lines was opened nearby by the Thurgarton Incorporation, again achieving significant financial savings.[27]

Elsewhere in the country, growing discontent among the labouring classes reached a climax in the autumn of 1830 with the so-called Swing Riots. Beginning in Kent and rapidly spreading across Surrey, Sussex, Middlesex and Hampshire, agricultural labourers engaged in increasingly violent protest against low wages, expensive food and the growing mechanisation of farms. Attacks on workhouses featured among their activities.

A Royal Commission, appointed in 1832 to review the operation of the Poor Laws, highlighted the deficiencies of the poor relief administration in many parishes. The report characterised the typical parish workhouse as containing:

> a dozen or more neglected children, twenty or thirty able-bodied adults of both sexes and probably an equal number of aged and impotent persons who are proper objects of relief. Among these the mothers of bastard children and prostitutes live without shame, and associate freely with the youth, who also have the example and conversation of the inmates of the county gaol, the poacher, the vagrant, the decayed beggar, and other characters of the worst description. To these may be added a solitary blind person, one or two idiots, and not infrequently are heard, from among the rest, the incessant ravings of some neglected lunatic.

The Royal Commission criticised allowance systems, which were said to be particularly prevalent in the south of England, particularly in towns, and also documented numerous examples of inefficiency or corruption in the local administration of poor relief. Eradicating this state of affairs was the main thrust of their report's proposals.

THE 1834 POOR LAW AMENDMENT ACT

The Royal Commission published its report in 1834 and its main recommendations were implemented in the Poor Law Amendment Act of that year. The Act, which formed the basis of what became known as the New Poor Law, aimed to create a national, uniform and compulsory system of poor relief administration under a new central authority, the Poor Law Commissioners (PLC). New groupings of parish areas known as Poor Law Unions were created, each managed by a Board of Guardians elected by local ratepayers. (Very populous parishes could be constituted as single Poor Law Parishes.) Funding of the new system continued to be from local poor rates. A plural voting system was adopted for Guardians' elections, with ratepayers having as many as six votes depending on the value of their property. Each union was expected to provide a workhouse which was to be the only form of relief available to the able-bodied and their families, although out-relief would still be available in certain situations.

Although the 1834 Act had an enormous impact, it did not overturn the existing principles of poor relief – the financial responsibility of the parish, the use of a workhouse test, the administrative grouping of parishes, local management by ratepayer-elected bodies, settlement qualifications, and plural voting all featured in Old Poor Law legislation. What the 1834 Act did change was the administrative structure through which poor relief was dispensed. Details of exactly how the new system would operate were left for the PLC to devise.

One of the commissioners, George Nicholls, later noted two significant deficiencies in the Act. First, it allowed Local Act Incorporations and Gilbert Unions to continue operating. The latter continued to hinder the formation of new Poor Law Unions in some areas until all remaining Gilbert Unions were abolished in 1869. Second, the PLC could not compel a union to provide a workhouse without the support of a majority of its ratepayers or its Board of Guardians, although the alteration or enlargement of existing workhouse premises could be demanded.[28]

RESISTANCE TO THE 1834 ACT

The implementation of the 1834 Act in the South East of England was not entirely trouble-free. One of the earliest incidents, at the end of April 1835, was in the newly formed Milton Union in Kent. The introduction of a new poor relief policy – giving out-relief in vouchers for goods rather than in cash – led to a riot in the Kent village of Bapchild, when a Guardian and a Relieving Officer were assaulted. Guardians leaving a board meeting at Milton were also stoned by protestors. A week later, the Guardians and a Relieving Officer were besieged in a church at Rodmersham after confronting angry demonstrators and were only saved from the mob by the arrival of troops. In September 1835, there was a riot in Steyning, Sussex, when the Guardians decided to house parents and their children at separate workhouses. The following month at Abingdon, the Master of the newly erected workhouse was shot at through one of its windows.

The 1834 Act received a hostile reception in many parts of London. Some of the proposed unions were criticised as being too large. Some richer parishes complained that being joined in a union with a poorer parish would result in them suffering an unfair financial burden. The Act's adoption of plural voting was another source of antipathy. Particularly strong resistance came from Local Act parishes who believed the 1834 legislation did not extend to their existing administrations. Foremost among these was St Pancras, which in January 1837 obtained a legal ruling in its favour. A number of other Local Act parishes successfully claimed exemption, in some cases, such as Islington, forcing the PLC to rescind orders it had already issued for the holding of Guardians' elections. By the late 1830s, thirty-five separate poor relief authorities were in operation in the metropolis. They comprised fifteen Poor Law Unions, eight Poor Law Parishes and twelve Local Act administrations.[29]

The widespread antagonism to the 1834 Act in London was evident not only in the refusal of parishes such as St Pancras to give up their Local Act status, but also in a general reluctance to build new workhouse accommodation. Many parishes had existing premises which, although often quite old, they considered perfectly adequate without the expense of erecting new buildings. In the first decade of the 1834 Act's operation, only five new workhouses were erected in the metropolis: Greenwich (1840), Wandsworth & Clapham (1840), Whitechapel (1842), Bethnal Green (1842) and Chelsea (1843). Outside the capital, it was a rather different story, with the majority of the newly formed unions in the South East deciding to build new workhouses.

WORKHOUSE DESIGN

The operation of New Poor Law workhouses was based on a principle known as 'less eligibility' – that the regime they provided would always be less attractive than that enjoyed on the outside by even the lowliest independent labourer. Inmates in union workhouses had plain, repetitive food, were required to work according to their ability, and were separated into a number of groups – the aged and infirm, the able-bodied, children aged 7–15, and those under 7. The first three groups were further divided by gender, creating seven classes in total. Additional classes could be locally designated by the Guardians, such as East Ashford's 'women with illegitimate children'.[30]

A fundamental requirement of workhouse accommodation was the segregation of the various classes of inmate. This could be achieved in two ways: by housing different groups in separate premises, or by partitioning a single building. Many unions initially adopted the former option, but only while they erected a large, new, single-site workhouse. The single 'general mixed workhouse' invariably proved a simpler and cheaper option and rapidly became the standard style of workhouse provision.

In 1835, the PLC published a number of model plans to assist unions in the construction of new workhouse buildings. The most widely adopted in the South East was the 'courtyard' plan devised by Sir Francis Bond Head, a baronet, author and former soldier, who in 1834 was appointed Assistant Poor Law Commissioner for East Kent. Although apparently lacking any architectural credentials, Head had clear views about the design of the new workhouses to be constructed in the area. They should, he believed, be 'low, cheap homely' buildings, modelled on poor labourers' cottages.[31] His proposed design, housing up to 500 inmates, was effectively a long terrace of such dwellings wrapped around three sides of a large quadrangle. The inmates' accommodation, arranged on two storeys, consisted of a large number of small dormitories, each around 15ft by 10ft, with eight inmates accommodated in four double beds. A dayroom and a single lavatory or privy were provided on each floor on each side of the workhouse. The administrative offices, boardroom, master's quarters, kitchens, dining halls, etc. were placed on two floors at either side of an entrance archway on the fourth side of the quadrangle. The large inner courtyard contained a high wall dividing the male and female sides. Metal staircases from the courtyard led up to a gallery which gave access to the upper rooms. The building had no outward-facing windows, leading to suggestions that it was influenced by the military barracks with which Head was familiar. Deficiencies in the original design were the absence of a chapel and

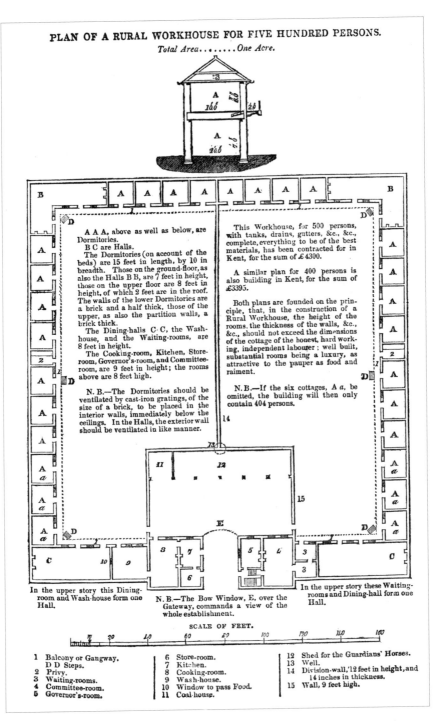

PLAN OF A RURAL WORKHOUSE FOR FIVE HUNDRED PERSONS.

Total Area........One Acre.

A A A, above as well as below, are Dormitories.

B C are Halls.

The Dormitories (on account of the beds) are 15 feet in length, by 10 in breadth. Those on the ground-floor, as also the Halls B B, are 7 feet in height, those on the upper floor are 8 feet in height, of which 2 feet are in the roof. The walls of the lower Dormitories are a brick and a half thick, those of the upper, as also the partition walls, a brick thick.

The Dining-halls C·C, the Wash-house, and the Waiting-rooms, are 8 feet in height.

The Cooking-room, Kitchen, Store-room, Governor's-room, and Committee-room, are 9 feet in height; the rooms above are 8 feet high.

N. B.—The Dormitories should be ventilated by cast-iron gratings, of the size of a brick, to be placed in the interior walls, immediately below the ceilings. In the Halls, the exterior wall should be ventilated in like manner.

This Workhouse, for 500 persons, with tanks, drains, gutters, &c., &c., complete, everything to be of the best materials, has been contracted for in Kent, for the sum of £4300.

A similar plan for 400 persons is also building in Kent, for the sum of £3395.

Both plans are founded on the principle, that, in the construction of a Rural Workhouse, the height of the rooms. the thickness of the walls, &c., &c., should not exceed the dimensions of the cottage of the honest, hard working, independent labourer ; well built, substantial rooms being a luxury, as attractive to the pauper as food and raiment.

N. B.—If the six cottages, A a, be omitted, the building will then only contain 404 persons.

In the upper story this Dining-room and Wash-house form one Hall.

N. B.—The Bow Window, E, over the Gateway, commands a view of the whole establishment.

In the upper story these Waiting-rooms and Dining-hall form one Hall.

SCALE OF FEET.

1	Balcony or Gangway.	6	Store-room.	12	Shed for the Guardians' Horses.
	D D Steps.	7	Kitchen.	13	Well.
2	Privy.	8	Cooking-room.	14	Division-wall,'12 feet in height, and 14 inches in thickness.
3	Waiting-rooms.	9	Wash-house.	15	Wall, 9 feet high.
4	Committee-room.	10	Window to pass Food.		
5	Governor's-room.	11	Coal-house.		

Sir Francis Head's model courtyard plan. The rooms were based on the size of a typical labourer's cottage.

A rear view of the Bridge Union's courtyard-plan workhouse. The inmates' quarters had no outward-facing windows.

infirmary, and inadequate provision for segregation. The latter was remedied by adding a diagonal wall across each half of the courtyard.

In all, twelve courtyard-plan workhouses were erected in Kent based on Head's design, with other architects sometimes involved in customising the layout for a particular site. Head responded to objections about the use of double beds by suggesting that the men's dormitories be fitted with two-tier bunks or his own design of hammocks slung from iron rings in the ceiling.[32]

The rest of the PLC's model plans were by a young architect called Sampson Kempthorne. His radial layouts, influenced by prison designs of the period, consisted of either three or four wings for different classes of inmate, which radiated from a central hub. The space between the wings provided segregated exercise yards which could be supervised from the central hub, where the master and matron had their quarters. An entrance block at the end of one of the wings contained a porter's lodge and waiting room on the ground floor, with the Guardians' boardroom above. The perimeter buildings housed stores, workshops, laundry, stables, mortuary, etc. The footprint of the three-wing 'Y-plan' design formed a hexagon, while that of the four-wing cruciform layout was a square. The rooms in Kempthorne's plans occupied the full width of the building, with windows at each side providing light and ventilation.

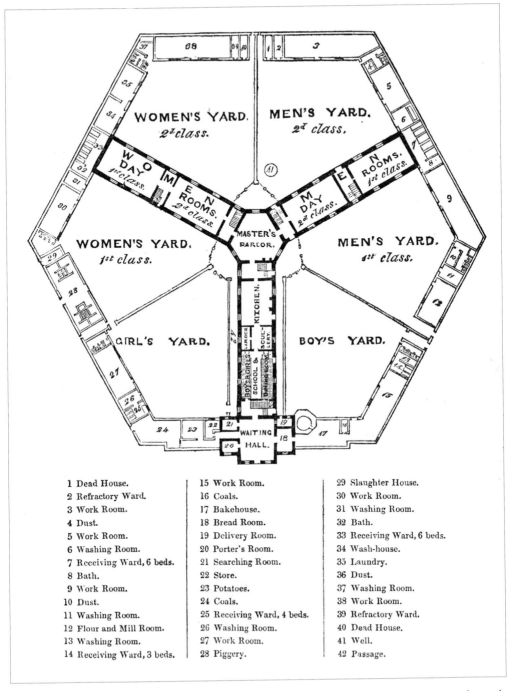

1 Dead House.
2 Refractory Ward.
3 Work Room.
4 Dust.
5 Work Room.
6 Washing Room.
7 Receiving Ward, 6 beds.
8 Bath.
9 Work Room.
10 Dust.
11 Washing Room.
12 Flour and Mill Room.
13 Washing Room.
14 Receiving Ward, 3 beds.
15 Work Room.
16 Coals.
17 Bakehouse.
18 Bread Room.
19 Delivery Room.
20 Porter's Room.
21 Searching Room.
22 Store.
23 Potatoes.
24 Coals.
25 Receiving Ward, 4 beds.
26 Washing Room.
27 Work Room.
28 Piggery.
29 Slaughter House.
30 Work Room.
31 Washing Room.
32 Bath.
33 Receiving Ward, 6 beds.
34 Wash-house.
35 Laundry.
36 Dust.
37 Washing Room.
38 Work Room.
39 Refractory Ward.
40 Dead House.
41 Well.
42 Passage.

The ground-floor layout of Sampson Kempthorne's model hexagonal plan. '1st Class' inmates were the aged and infirm, and '2nd Class' the able-bodied.

A bird's-eye view of Kempthorne's model cruciform design.

Kempthorne himself designed nine workhouses in the area covered by this volume, including the first New Poor Law institution to be erected, at Abingdon in 1835.[33] His influence is also apparent in the work of other architects of the period, such as H.E. Kendall's design at Uckfield, and those of William Mason at Epsom and Kingston.

Other prominent workhouse architects of the period included the partnership of George Gilbert Scott (previously an assistant to Kempthorne) and William Bonython Moffatt, who designed over forty workhouses and evolved their own distinctive layout, which was used at Guildford. It featured a long single-storey block at the front, which contained the porter's lodge, boardroom, receiving wards and chapel. A central entrance archway led through to an inner courtyard either side of which were boys' and girls' yards. The long main building, running parallel to the entrance block, was usually three storeys high and again featured a central hub containing the master's quarters, with kitchens and scullery behind. The male and female accommodation wings to each side contained day rooms and dining halls on their ground floor with dormitories above and sometimes had cross-wings at their ends. A separate infirmary was placed at the rear, parallel to the main block.

Although Scott and Moffatt's later designs, such as those at Windsor and Edmonton, did away with a separate entrance building, their use of parallel blocks became a popular workhouse layout, a good example being at Greenwich. Such designs increasingly featured deeper blocks where the rooms

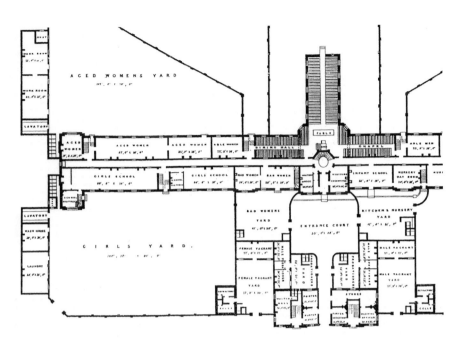

Part of the ground-floor layout of Greenwich's corridor-plan workhouse. The female side included sections for able women, aged women, girls, female vagrants and 'bad' women.

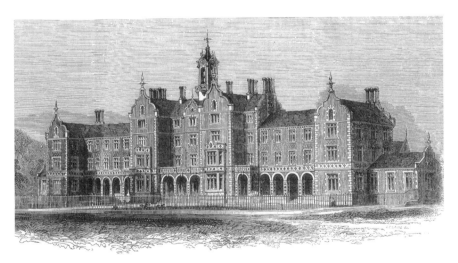

The St Mary Abbots workhouse, later St Mary Abbots Hospital, Kensington. After his death in 1970, rock guitarist Jimi Hendrix was placed in the former workhouse mortuary.

were placed off a corridor running along the centre or one side of the building. Corridor-plan workhouses in the region included Bethnal Green (1842), Bromley (1844), Kensington (1848), City of London (1849), Fulham (1849), Hampstead (1850), East London (1855), Medway (1859), West London (1864) and Shoreditch (1865).

WORKHOUSE LIFE

On entry to a union workhouse, new inmates were given a bath, had their own clothes taken away for disinfection and storage, and were issued with workhouse clothing – the term 'uniform' was never officially used. For men, this typically consisted of a jacket and trousers made in rough cloth, a cotton shirt, cloth cap and shoes. A common women's uniform was a long blue-and-white-striped cotton shift, with a smock over. Old women wore a long gown, apron, shawl and bonnet or mop-cap. New arrivals usually spent some time in a receiving ward, where they had a medical inspection in case they were carrying any infectious disease such as smallpox.

Daily life in a workhouse was conducted to a fixed timetable, punctuated by the ringing of the workhouse bell. On Sundays, no work was performed except for essential domestic chores. Below is the typical routine for able-bodied inmates:

	Rise	Breakfast	Start work	Dinner	End work	Supper	Bedtime
Summer	6 a.m.	6.30–7 a.m.	7 a.m.	12–1 p.m.	6 p.m.	6–7 p.m.	8 p.m.
Winter	7 a.m.	7.30–8 a.m.	8 a.m.	12–1 p.m.	6 p.m.	6–7 p.m.	8 p.m.

Communal prayers were read before breakfast and after supper every day and Divine Service was performed on Sunday, Good Friday and Christmas Day. The PLC's rules originally required that during meals 'silence, order and decorum shall be maintained', though from 1842 the word 'silence' was dropped.

The work demanded from the able-bodied inmates was at the discretion of the local Guardians. Some workhouses had workshops for sewing, spinning and weaving or other local trades. Others had vegetable gardens where the inmates worked to provide food for the workhouse. Women chiefly performed the domestic tasks of cooking, cleaning and laundry. In some London workhouses, they did 'slop work' – making cheap clothing. Able-bodied men were given heavy manual work such as breaking stone, pumping water from a well, turning a large capstan-style mill, or picking oakum (teasing apart the fibres of old ropes, known as 'junk').

Some concessions were made for 'elderly' inmates (a precise age was never formally specified but they were usually taken as being the over-60s). From 1847, elderly married couples could request a shared bedroom.

Workhouse discipline distinguished two classes of offence. Disorderly conduct, which included swearing, failing to wash, refusing to work, or feigning sickness, could be punished by withdrawal of foods such as cheese or tea. The more serious category of refractory conduct, such as disobeying or insulting a workhouse officer, being drunk, or damaging workhouse property, could earn a period of solitary confinement. More serious misdemeanours could be referred to a magistrate – an act such as deliberately breaking a window could result in two months' prison and hard labour.

Inmates could discharge themselves from the workhouse at any time – workhouses were not prisons. However, leaving the premises without permission while wearing workhouse clothing could result in a charge of stealing union property. A few hours' notice had to be given for an inmate's own clothes to be retrieved from storage.

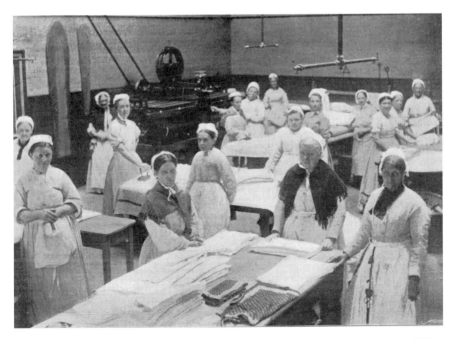

Female inmates at work in the laundry at the Holborn Union workhouse at Mitcham in 1896.

If an inmate died, their next of kin were given the opportunity to arrange a funeral. Otherwise, there were two possibilities. The first was a pauper's burial, usually in the local parish churchyard, in an unmarked multiple-occupancy grave. The second, from 1832, was for the body to be sold or donated for use in medical training or research. From the 1850s, when many London parish graveyards had become full, many metropolitan workhouses buried their dead in one of the new privately operated cemeteries such as that at Brookwood in Surrey, to which special funeral trains ran from Waterloo.

WORKHOUSE FOOD

In 1835, the PLC published a set of six model 'dietaries' or menu plans. Their intention was that the workhouse diet should on no account be 'superior or equal to the ordinary mode of subsistence of the labouring classes of the neighbourhood'.[34]

The dietaries prescribed repetitive meals of basic foods such as potatoes, bread, cheese, suet pudding, gruel and broth, with meat and vegetables two or three times a week. The uptake of the dietaries by unions varied around the country. Those most often adopted in southern counties largely consisted of bread and cheese, while northern unions had a preference for those based on potatoes and oatmeal porridge.

Men received, on average, around 25 per cent more food than women. The elderly could usually enjoy a ration of butter, sugar and tea. Children under 9 were given a locally decided proportion of the adult amount. Contrary to the impression given by Charles Dickens, no workhouse inmates – not even children – ever existed just on watery gruel.

Alcohol was prohibited in union workhouses except for medical or sacramental purposes. An exception was added in 1847, when it was allowed to be provided along with other treats on Christmas Day. Some workhouses also provided a ration of beer to able-bodied inmates engaged in certain types of heavy labour such as laundry or nursing work.

An overhaul of workhouse food in 1900 allowed Guardians to compile their own weekly dietary from a list of about fifty dishes approved for the purpose. These included items such as Irish stew, fried fish, pasties and roley-poley pudding, with a specially compiled cookbook being issued to each workhouse.[35]

No. 3.—DIETARY for ABLE-BODIED PAUPERS.

		BREAKFAST.		DINNER.					SUPPER.	
		Bread.	Gruel.	Cooked Meat.	Potatoes or other Vegetables.	Soup.	Bread.	Cheese.	Bread.	Cheese.
		oz.	pints.	oz.	lb.	pints.	oz.	oz.	oz.	oz.
Sunday	Men	8	1½	..	..	..	7	2	6	1½
	Women	6	1½	..	..	..	6	1½	5	1½
Monday	Men	8	1½	..	..	..	7	2	6	1½
	Women	6	1½	..	..	..	6	1½	5	1½
Tuesday	Men	8	1½	8	¾	..	..	..	6	1½
	Women	6	1½	6	¾	..	..	..	5	1½
Wednesday	Men	8	1½	..	..	..	7	2	6	1½
	Women	6	1½	..	..	..	6	1½	5	1½
Thursday	Men	8	1½	..	..	1½	6	.	6	1½
	Women	6	1½	..	..	1½	5	.	5	1½
Friday	Men	8	1½	..	..	..	7	2	6	1½
	Women	6	1½	..	..	..	6	1½	5	1½
				Bacon.						
Saturday	Men	8	1½	5	¾	..	..	..	6	1½
	Women	6	1½	4	¾	.	..	..	5	1½

Old people, of sixty years of age and upwards, may be allowed one ounce of tea, five ounces of butter, and seven ounces of sugar per week, in lieu of gruel for breakfast, if deemed expedient to make this change.

Children under nine years of age, to be dieted at discretion; above nine, to be allowed the same quantities as women.

Sick to be dieted as directed by the medical officer.

One of the six weekly meal plans issued by the PLC in 1835. The majority of the meals were either bread and gruel or bread and cheese.

The dining hall of the Holborn Union workhouse at Mitcham in 1896. Women are seated at the front and men at the rear.

CAMPAIGN FOR CHANGE

By the 1850s, the frequently poor conditions inside metropolitan workhouses were beginning to attract criticism. This was particularly the case in those that occupied old premises, often dating from the previous century.

Typical of these was the Strand Union workhouse on Cleveland Street, in Fitzrovia, erected in the 1770s for the parish of St Paul Covent Garden. In 1853, Louisa Twining (of the family of tea and coffee merchants) visited a Mrs Stapleton, a former nurse of her acquaintance who was an inmate of the workhouse. Such visits required a special letter of permission from the Strand Guardians. After witnessing the neglect experienced by the inmates, Twining began to press for better access for visitors to workhouses, later founding the Workhouse Visiting Society.[36]

In 1856, Dr Joseph Rogers was appointed as the Strand workhouse's medical officer and was appalled at the cramped and dirty conditions he discovered. Nursing of the sick was performed by elderly female inmates who were often drunk.[37] The Strand was not unusual in this respect – at this date there were only seventy paid workhouse nurses in the whole of London.[38] Rogers became a leading light in a campaign to improve workhouse medical facilities and also founded the Association of Metropolitan Workhouse Medical Officers, which campaigned for the cost of workhouse drugs to be met from the poor rates rather than the doctor's own salary, as was usually the case at that time.

A highly influential contribution to the cause was made by the medical journal *The Lancet*, which in 1865 published detailed reports about the frequently abysmal conditions in London workhouses and their infirmaries. At Bethnal Green, for example, it found that: no running water was available from 5 p.m. until 7 a.m.; lighting and ventilation were inadequate, with many windows 6ft from the floor to prevent the inmates from seeing out; there was overcrowding, with each patient having only a quarter of the official space recommendation; washing facilities were severely lacking – in one children's ward, seventeen children were washed daily in one pail, several in the same water, and dried with sheets; in the male wards, forty-five men were served by two latrines which were flushed only twice a day; up to 600 sick inmates were nursed by a staff of two paid but untrained nurses, assisted by forty pauper nurses and helpers 'whose tendencies to drink cannot be controlled'.[39]

As well as Rogers and *The Lancet*, the campaign to reform workhouse medical provision was supported by a number of prominent people of the day such as Charles Dickens. Its most influential advocate was Florence Nightingale, who personally lobbied the Prime Minister and the President of the Poor Law Board.[40]

THE METROPOLITAN POOR ACT

Eventually, the campaigners' efforts bore fruit in the shape of the 1867 Metropolitan Poor Act, which aimed to take the care of the sick poor away from individual unions and parishes. An initial scheme to divide the capital into six Sick Asylum Districts, each with its own large hospital, was subsequently judged to be too impractical and expensive, although two did survive – the Central London and the Poplar & Stepney Asylum Districts. Instead, some existing unions such as Holborn were enlarged, and Boards of Guardians were pressed to separate the administration of their workhouses and infirmaries, which ideally would be sited at separate locations. The Local Act status of many of London's parishes, which had allowed them to escape most of the strictures of the New Poor Law, was also abolished.

In the years that followed, some authorities acquired new sites on which to erect infirmaries, such as Holborn (at Archway in 1879) and St Marylebone (at Ladbroke Grove in 1881). Whitechapel built a new workhouse on South Grove in 1871, with its existing workhouse on Baker Street then becoming the union infirmary. Similarly, when the Wandsworth & Clapham Union opened a new workhouse on Garratt Lane in 1886, its old premises on St John's Hill became its infirmary. Unions already possessing multiple workhouse sites could concentrate their medical facilities at a particular location, such as St Olave's new infirmary on the old Rotherhithe workhouse site in 1876. Finally, a new infirmary could be opened at an existing workhouse site but run separately from it, as happened at Fulham, Hackney, Kensington and Paddington.

The St Marylebone workhouse infirmary opened in 1881 at Rackham Street, Ladbroke Grove.

THE METROPOLITAN ASYLUMS BOARD

In addition to the changes in workhouse medical provision, the Metropolitan Poor Act led to the creation of a new body, the Metropolitan Asylums Board (MAB), which took over the provision of care for the London's sick poor in respect of infectious diseases and mental incapacity. The MAB went on to set up institutions for the care of those suffering from smallpox, fever, 'imbecility', tuberculosis and venereal diseases.

Between 1867 and 1930, the MAB played an increasing role in the care of London's sick poor, eventually providing around forty general and specialist care establishments, many purpose-built and staffed by well-trained personnel. The institutions set up by the MAB came to be accessible by all the capital's inhabitants, not just the poor, allowing it the credit to have provided the nation's first state hospitals and to have laid the foundations of what in 1948 became the National Health Service.[41] This trend was followed by provincial unions. From the 1870s, those too poor to pay for medical treatment were increasingly able to make use of their union's infirmary without first needing to be an inmate of the workhouse.

PAVILION PLAN INSTITUTIONS

New workhouse buildings erected from the 1870s onwards were increasingly based on the approach of placing different departments in separate blocks or pavilions. This concept had its roots in the principles espoused by Florence Nightingale in her 1859 *Notes on Hospitals*. What became known as 'Nightingale' wards were long and narrow, with pairs of opposing windows allowing a through draught. Beds, typically between twenty-eight and thirty-two per ward, were placed along each wall either singly or in pairs between the windows. Sanitary facilities were placed in towers at the outer ends of the blocks, which were typically two or three storeys high. Infirmaries incorporating 'Nightingale' wards began to appear in the mid-1860s. They usually comprised a number of men's and women's ward blocks, all linked by a corridor or covered walkway to an administrative block, which was often placed between the men's and women's sides.

Most of the MAB's hospitals were pavilion-block designs, as were many of the separate workhouse infirmaries built to comply with the 1867 Act, such as those at Islington (1870), St Pancras (1870), St George's (1878), Fulham (1884) and St Saviour (1887). New workhouses built entirely on pavilion principles

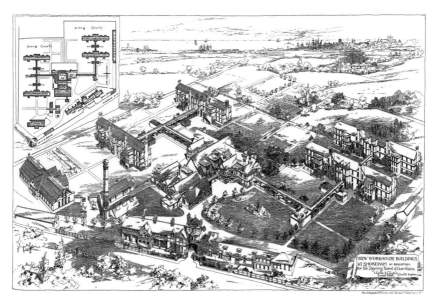

A bird's-eye view of the Steyning Union's pavilion-plan workhouse opened in 1901 at Kingston-by-Sea.

included Lambeth (1874), Holborn (1886), Wandsworth & Clapham (1886), Camberwell (1892) and St Olave's (1900). The St Olave's workhouse was the only such institution in London designed specifically for elderly inmates.

Outside the metropolis, pavilion-plan workhouse infirmaries were erected at Epsom (1882), Croydon (1885), Guildford (1893) and Edmonton (1910), while complete workhouses were opened at Steyning (1901), Brentford (1902), Willesden (1902–08) and Hastings (1904).

CASUAL WARDS

From 1837, workhouses were obliged to provide temporary overnight shelter for any destitute person at their door. At first, the 'casual' poor, as they were officially known, were often housed in stables and outhouses. Eventually, however, most workhouses had a purpose-built casual ward, an institution which became popularly known by tramps and vagrants as the 'spike'.

In London and other large towns, casual wards were sometimes erected on sites separate from the main workhouse. The more usual arrangement, though, was for the casual ward to be placed at the edge of the main workhouse site, often with its own separate access gate. The wards were sometimes superintended by the workhouse porter, perhaps with his wife attending the female casuals. Some spikes were in the charge of a 'Tramp Major', usually a former tramp himself, and now informally employed by the workhouse.

The routine for those entering a casual ward began in the late afternoon by joining the queue for admission – the number of beds was limited and latecomers might find themselves turned away. Casual wards had separate entrances for males and females – as in the main workhouse, segregation of the sexes was strictly observed.

At opening time, usually 5 or 6 p.m., new arrivals would be admitted and searched, with any money, tobacco or alcohol confiscated. It was common practice for vagrants to hide such possessions in a nearby hedge or wall before entering the spike, although the items were often in danger of being removed by local children. Contraband such as cigarettes could also be smuggled in by various means. One ploy was to hide such items under the armpit, held there by sticking plaster.

Entrants were required to strip and bathe – in water that might already have been used by a number of others. They were then issued with a blanket and nightshirt, with their own clothes being dried and fumigated or disinfected. Each was given a supper, typically 8oz of bread and a pint of gruel

A line of men await admission to the Whitechapel workhouse casual ward on Thomas Street. A porter stands on the steps outside the women's entrance off to the right.

(or 'skilly', as it was colloquially known), before being locked up until 6 a.m. the next morning. Until the 1870s, the norm was for casual wards to have communal association dormitories where the inmates either slept on the bare floor or in rows of low-slung hammocks.

The following morning, a breakfast of bread and gruel would be served. From 1842, casuals were required to work for up to four hours before being released. For male casuals, stone breaking and oakum picking were widely used. For females, labour tasks included oakum picking and domestic work such as scrubbing floors. Once vagrants had done their stint of work, they were given a lump of bread and released to go on their way. Even with an early start to the work, this meant that only half the day remained to tramp to another workhouse. From 1882, casuals were detained for two nights, with the full day in between spent performing work. They could then be released at 9 a.m. on the second morning, allowing more time to search for work or to travel to another workhouse. From 1871, return to the casual ward of the same union was not allowed within thirty days, the whole of metropolitan London counting as a single union for this purpose. Tramping circuits evolved linking a progression of spikes, eventually returning to the first a month later.

A woman (centre) engaged in oakum picking, thought to be at Lambeth workhouse in about 1907. Short chunks of old rope had to be picked apart into their raw fibres.

A cell at the former Guildford workhouse 'spike'. At the rear is a stone-breaking area where broken stone was passed through a grille to the outside.

From around 1870, a new form of vagrants' accommodation was developed by the architect Henry Saxon Snell. It consisted of individual cells, much like those in a prison, usually arranged along both sides of a corridor. Sleeping cells contained a simple bed, while work cells were usually fitted out for stone breaking. This usually included a hinged metal grille which could be opened from the outside to allow unbroken lumps of stone to be deposited in the cell. The inmate had to break up the stone into lumps small enough to pass back through the holes in the grille. The broken stone could then be collected on the outside. Sometimes sleeping cells and work cells were separated, sometimes one led through to the other.

In 1912, the MAB took over the running of London's casual wards. A few were closed or disposed of, with twenty-one still in use in 1914. By 1921, the number had been reduced to six, but a rise in demand during the 1920s led to an increase in provision.[42] By 1929, nine were in operation, at Chelsea, Hackney, Lambeth, Paddington, Poplar, St Pancras, Southwark, Wandsworth and Woolwich.[43]

CHILDREN'S ACCOMMODATION

In 1838, almost half the total workhouse population were children under 16.[44] In the same year, Dr James Kay (later known as Sir James Kay-Shuttleworth) put forward his proposals for housing pauper children in separate accommodation away from the workhouse. His scheme envisaged the creation of a number of District Schools, each serving a group of unions. Kay argued that such establishments would give children a much better education, together with 'industrial training' – practical skills to equip them for later life, such as manual trades for the boys and domestic training for the girls. Kay also believed that such schools would protect pauper children from what he saw as the 'polluting association' with adult workhouse inmates.[45]

Kay tested out his ideas at two privately run schools still being used to house pauper children from the metropolis under Hanway's Act: Mr Drouet's at Lower Tooting and Mr Aubin's at Norwood. Although Hanway's Act was repealed in 1844, it was only after a disastrous outbreak of cholera at Drouet's in 1849, when 180 children died, that the use of such institutions was prohibited. Three School Districts were then formed (Central London, South Metropolitan and North Surrey) which covered ten of the capital's thirty Poor Law authorities. Each district opened a large school – the Central London at

The Central London District School at Hanwell where Charlie Chaplin was once an inmate. Now a community centre, much of the main building still survives.

Hanwell, the South Metropolitan at Sutton, and the North Surrey at Upper Norwood. By the 1890s, two further districts were in operation – the West London, with a school at Ashford, near Staines, and the Kensington & Chelsea, with a site at Banstead. The districts then covered fifteen London unions or parishes, with eleven individual schools being run by the Boards of Guardians at Bethnal Green, St George in the East, Hackney, Holborn, Islington, Lambeth, St Marylebone, Mile End Old Town, St Pancras, Strand and Westminster.

The School Districts formed by Farnham & Hartley Wintney and by Reading & Wokingham were among the few ever created outside London. Separate schools were set up by a number of non-metropolitan administrations, such as Brighton's Warren Farm establishment.

Separate and District Schools, or 'Barrack' Schools as they were disparagingly known, became the subject of growing criticism. They were too impersonal and were also a breeding ground for various infectious conditions such as ringworm and ophthalmia.

In the late 1870s, an alternative form of accommodation became popular. Cottage homes, as they were known, typically comprised a 'village' of small houses, often erected in a rural location. In each house, fifteen to twenty girls or boys of varying ages lived under the supervision of a house mother or house parents. As well as houses and a school, larger cottage home sites could include

Children stand at the entrance to 'The Hollies' – the Greenwich Union's cottage homes site at Lamorbey, near Sidcup, opened in 1902.

One of Camberwell's first scattered homes at 9–11 Matham Grove in about 1903.

workshops, an infirmary, chapel, bakehouse, laundry, gymnasium, and even a swimming pool. Boys were taught practical trades such as shoemaking, tailoring and joinery, while girls learned household skills such as sewing, cooking and cleaning, to equip them for domestic service. Cottage homes often had a boys' military band which could lead to a career as a musician in the army or navy. Metropolitan Guardians erecting major cottage home sites included Bermondsey, Greenwich, Hackney, Poplar, Shoreditch, Stepney, Whitechapel and Woolwich. Those elsewhere in the region included Croydon, Elham, Isle of Thanet, Medway and Milton.

Cottage homes were criticised by some as isolating children from the real world, and in the 1890s another system, known as scattered homes, was devised by the Sheffield Union. Like cottage homes, these were based on family-style groups of children under the care of a resident house mother. Scattered homes, however, were distributed around the suburbs of a town or city and their inmates attended ordinary local schools. London's first scattered homes were opened by Camberwell in 1898. They were eventually employed by more than twenty Poor Law authorities in the region.[46]

From 1904, to help avoid disadvantage in later life, the birth certificates for those born in a workhouse gave the location as an anonymous-sound-ing street address. For example, Lewisham workhouse was identified as 390 High Street Lewisham.

In 1913, the Local Government Board decreed that no healthy child over the age of 3 should be living in a workhouse after 1915.[47]

ENTERTAINMENT

Life for workhouse inmates, especially the elderly and children, was not devoid of entertainment. In 1867, Bethnal Green inmates were given a concert by the Delaware Minstrels, an amateur company of blacked-up clerks from a Lombard Street bank. In June 1871, 400 aged inmates from St Pancras workhouse had a day's outing at Crystal Palace, conveyed there in twenty covered vans.

From 1891, Camberwell workhouse residents had an annual excursion to the seaside. For their 1896 day out to Bognor Regis, a 650-seat train was chartered for the inmates, most aged 60 to 90. However, many of the group had apparently obtained money from friends and visited a public house before boarding the train. On arrival at Bognor, they continued drinking, then went for their dinner at the town hall, at which beer was also served. Afterwards, there were more visits to local inns. It was later reported that a number of cases of disorderly conduct and indecent behaviour had occurred on secluded parts of the beach.

Workhouse inmates could also make their own entertainment. A former inmate of Poplar workhouse in 1885 recorded the proceedings of a lengthy informal concert of songs and stories in one of the men's dormitories after 'lights out'.

By the 1920s, radios were starting to appear in some workhouses. At Abingdon, some workhouse inmates even had weekly trips to a local cinema.

WARTIME

During the First World War, many workhouses were given over, entirely or in part, to war-related use. Those used as military hospitals included Brighton, Eastbourne, East Preston, Elham, Greenwich Grove Park, Guildford, Hampstead, Lewisham and Richmond. Existing inmates were usually dispersed among other workhouses in the area. Staff, however, generally stayed on to assist with the institution's new role. Unions housing military patients in only part of their premises included: Blean, Brentford, Edmonton, Faversham,

The Greenwich Union workhouse at Grove Park, Lewisham, during its First World War
occupation as a barracks for the Army Service Corps.

The Strand Union workhouse at Edmonton during the First World War, when it was used to
house Belgian refugees.

Hastings, Hollingbourne, Kingston, Maidstone, Reigate, Steyning, Thanet and Tonbridge. A few unions in Sussex and Kent provided venereal clinics and maternity centres. Some, such as Tenterden, received 'mental defectives' who would have otherwise gone into county asylums, many of which were also being used for war purposes. Several housed refugees, including Holborn's Endell Street workhouse and the Strand's workhouse and children's home at Edmonton. Westminster's Poland Street workhouse became a centre for Jewish refugees. The Willesden workhouse and the Dartford Union's workhouse and children's homes housed munitions workers.

THE END OF THE WORKHOUSE

A Royal Commission set up in 1905 to examine the operation of the poor relief system had been divided in its conclusions. The majority of its members recommended the creation of a new Public Assistance Authority in each county or county borough, together with the replacement of workhouses by more specialised institutions catering for separate categories of inmate such as children, the old, the unemployed and the mentally ill. A minority group, which issued its own report, was more radical and advocated the complete abolition of the Poor Laws.

No new legislation resulted from the 1905 Commission, but by the 1920s the ever-growing role of local councils in public administration and service provision was making the role of Boards of Guardians look increasingly anachronistic. The end for the road for the Guardians came in the 1929 Local Government Act. The following year, the Boards were abolished and responsibility for poor relief (or public assistance, as it then became known) was transferred to county and borough councils. Each council set up a new Public Assistance Committee, although its members were often former Guardians.[48]

Outside the London County Council (LCC) area, most workhouse sites continued in operation as Public Assistance Institutions (PAIs), providing accommodation for a similar range of inmates except that the able-bodied were no longer received. Many casual wards also continued in use. The 1929 Act gave councils the power to 'appropriate' part or all of their former workhouse premises for use as municipal hospitals. Councils taking advantage of this option included Reading, Croydon and Brighton.

A few workhouse sites were converted to other uses such as Chertsey (a home for the 'mentally defective'), Hoo (council offices) and Romney Marsh (housing). Children's establishments taken over by local councils in 1930 generally continued in operation with little change. In 1948, most PAIs either joined the new National Health Serviced (NHS) or became council-run old people's homes.

In 1930, the LCC took over the work of the metropolitan Poor Law unions and parishes and also that of the MAB. The majority of these establishments became either general hospitals or hospitals for the chronic sick. In cases such as Hackney, Hammersmith and St Mary Abbots, where a workhouse and its infirmary had been on the same site, the workhouse department was used for the chronic sick. Most of these hospitals became part of the NHS in 1948.

Fourteen workhouse sites were originally designated by the LCC for use as PAIs: Bethnal Green, Bromley, Camberwell, Chelsea, Christ Church (Southwark), Fulham, Islington, Ladywell (St Olave's), Newington, Poplar, St Marylebone, Southern Grove (Whitechapel), Wandsworth and Woolwich. The Bethnal Green and Christchurch premises were subsequently closed as being unsuitable. Most of the PAIs were mixed but as there were more male than female inmates overall, the Fulham, Southern Grove and Woolwich premises housed only men. A gradual programme of modernisation was carried out during the 1930s and over half of these institutions were still in use in the 1960s.

THE LONG VIEW

Today, the workhouse is invariably portrayed as a grim and inhumane institution. Much of the blame for this image can be laid at the door of Charles Dickens. Although *Oliver Twist* was set in an early-1830s parish workhouse, it still shapes most people's view of the entire workhouse system.

Over the centuries of its existence, the workhouse changed enormously. By the start of the twentieth century, workhouse inmates were generally well fed and had good healthcare. Many workhouses were provided with books and newspapers and had occasional musical concerts or outings. The majority of workhouse children lived in their own accommodation and received education and training to make them employable as adults. Any evaluation of workhouse conditions needs to be made against those experienced by the poor of the time, rather than modern-day standards. It is all too easy to judge workhouse 'uniforms', for example, as deliberately dehumanising, rather than a practical solution to clothing large numbers of people who might be arriving in filthy rags.

The workhouse system was not without its faults, of course. To some degree, it acted as a poverty trap. Adults leaving a workhouse rarely received any kind of help in finding accommodation or employment in order to escape from pauperism.

Perhaps the most significant legacy of the workhouse era comes from the widespread improvement in its medical facilities from the 1870s onwards, which established the principle of free publicly funded treatment for those in need. A large proportion of the real estate inherited by the new National Health Service in 1948 came from former workhouse sites. It was significant that when Health Minister Nye Bevan officially launched the NHS on 5 July 1948, the location chosen for this momentous occasion was a former workhouse infirmary.

The stigma of the workhouse was to leave a long-lasting mark, however. For decades afterwards, many elderly people adamantly refused to enter the doors of an NHS hospital that had once been a workhouse, convinced that they would only leave in a coffin. That belief was actually founded on reality. The elderly poor did frequently die in workhouses, though not because they were such terrible places, but because in their day they were generally the only source of medical care available to those approaching the ends of their lives.

WORKHOUSE CATALOGUE

The rest of this book provides more detailed information on the hundreds of workhouses that existed in London (also referred to as the metropolis) and the counties of Berkshire, Middlesex, Kent, Surrey and Sussex. London's institutions are covered in two chapters, namely the City of London and the County of London. The latter includes the City of Westminster, the Borough of Southwark, and a number of parishes historically belonging to the counties of Middlesex, Surrey and Kent. The separate chapters covering those counties relate only to their non-metropolitan parts.

Each chapter is divided into sections relating to the post-1834 Poor Law administrations in that area. There is a slight deviation to the general pattern in the chapter on the City of London, whose numerous parishes and their workhouses are generally better documented than elsewhere.

It should be noted that Poor Law administrative areas in London continued to evolve after 1834 and maps only provide snapshots at a particular date. Outside the capital, union borders were largely static. However, they sometimes strayed across county boundaries. Details of the various parish workhouses will always be placed under the relevant Poor Law Union, even though that may occasionally seem to place them in the wrong county chapter.

Details for many pre-1834 workhouses come from major UK Parliamentary reports published in 1776, 1777 and 1834 (the latter largely based on data

A map of Poor Law Unions in Berkshire, Kent, Middlesex, Surrey and Sussex, in about 1880. (Reproduced by kind permission of GB Historical GIS Project.)

A map of Poor Law administrative areas in the metropolis in about 1880. (Reproduced by kind permission of GB Historical GIS Project.)

collected in 1832). Except where noted, references in the text to these dates come from the reports listed below:

1776   Abstracts of Returns concerning the Relief and Settlement of the Poor
1777   Abstract of Returns made by the Overseers of the Poor
1832   Report into the Administration and Practical Operation of the Poor Laws

Abbreviations frequently used in the text are listed below:

LGB   Local Government Board
LCC   London County Council
MAB   Metropolitan Asylums Board
NHS   National Health Service
PAI   Public Assistance Institution
PLB   Poor Law Board
PLC   Poor Law Commissioners

Many building locations are identified by a UK National Grid Reference (e.g. TQ123456), which indicates the bottom left-hand corner of a 100-metre-square map area. Map websites which accept such references include the National Library of Scotland's historical maps collection (maps.nls.uk/geo) which allows the development of workhouse and other sites to be tracked from the 1850s onwards.

2

CITY OF LONDON

CITY OF LONDON PARISHES

The old City of London comprised more than a hundred parishes, the majority of which were tiny and lay inside its ancient walls. At least a third of the within-the-walls parishes operated workhouses or poorhouses prior to 1834, as did most of those lying just outside ('without') the walls.

Allhallows Barking by the Tower
Allhallows Barking by the Tower had a workhouse by 1737. In 1776, it could house up to seventy inmates. The building was located at Cooper's Row, Tower Hill (TQ335808).

Allhallows Bread Street
Allhallows, Bread Street, opened a workhouse in December 1730. It occupied a former tavern on Fish Street, in the nearby parish of St Nicholas Cole Abbey. All the poor pensioners from Allhallows were dieted and lodged there under the care of a mistress. There were prohibitions on leaving the workhouse without permission, bringing distilled liquors onto the premises, and swearing, cursing or quarrelling. Repeat offenders could be expelled from the establishment. All 'healthful and strong' inmates were to rise in summer at 5 or 6 a.m. and go to bed at 9 p.m. In winter, they were to be up by 8 a.m. and in bed by 8 p.m. to save on fires and candles. The able-bodied poor went to church twice on Sundays and anyone coming home drunk on such occasions was to be severely punished. If an inmate died, their clothing was placed in the store

for the use of the parish; the nurse who attended them while sick was to safely deliver up all the other possessions and money of the deceased or be severely punished if she purloined any.[1]

In 1776, a maximum of fourteen of the parish poor were farmed out, with six children and two lunatics provided for in that number.

Allhallows the Great
Allhallows the Great was operating a workhouse in 1746.[2] By 1776, the poor were being farmed out.

Allhallows Honey Lane
Allhallows Honey Lane had a workhouse from 1731.[3] By 1776, the parish poor were farmed out at Hoxton.

Allhallows Lombard Street
Allhallows Lombard Street had a workhouse from 1736.[4] By 1776, the parish was farming out its poor with a contractor at Blackfriars.

Allhallows London Wall
Allhallows London Wall had a workhouse from 1736.[5] By 1776, the poor were farmed out at Mile End.

Allhallows Staining
Allhallows Staining had a workhouse from 1736.[6] By 1776, the poor were being farmed by a contractor at Little Bartholomew Close.

Christchurch Greyfriars / Newgate Street
In 1729, Christchurch Greyfriars (also known as Christchurch Newgate Street) erected a workhouse at Town Ditch, on the north side of Christ's Hospital (TQ319814). In September 1731, the establishment had forty-four inmates, of whom about twenty were children. The children attended the charity school of Farringdon Ward Within. All those who were able, both old and young, were employed in spinning mop yarn.[7]

The parish obtained a Local Act in 1753, amended in 1778 and 1784, enabling it to purchase, hire or erect a workhouse. In 1776, the workhouse housed up to eighty inmates. By 1804, however, the parish farmed out its poor with Mr Overton at Mile End.

Holy Trinity Minories

From around 1692 to 1749, the parish provided accommodation for its poor in two houses rented from Lord Granderson. Thereafter, they were largely farmed out.[8]

St Alban Wood Street

The parish established a workhouse around 1724.[9] In 1731, it was located in a hired house in Merchant Taylor's Rents, at the upper end of Moor Lane, in the parish of St Giles Cripplegate.[10] By 1776, the parish was farming out its poor with a contractor at Hoxton.

St Andrew Holborn Below the Bars

St Andrew Holborn comprised three Liberties, one falling within the City of London, the other two in the county of Middlesex (see page 86).

In June 1727, the London Liberty opened a workhouse in a rented property adjoining the churchyard on the east side of Shoe Lane (TQ315815). In September 1730, there were sixty-two inmates who were occupied as follows:

7 old Men and Women pick Ockam.
4 Women and Boys spin Noyl.[11]
9 knit Noyl Yarn into Caps for Seamen.
2 make the Woollen Cloaths.
2 make Linnen Cloaths.
2 Cooks constantly attend the Kitchen.
4 get up the Linnen and wash for the House.
2 make Beds, clean, and wash the House.
2 mend Cloaths, Linnen and Woollen.
3 nurse those that are in the Infirmary.
1 School-Mistress.
21 Children at School, in Rotation as they can be spared from their Work.
1 Child nursed.
2 Lunaticks.[12]

The workhouse's weekly 'bill of fare' was as follows:

	Breakfast	Dinner	Supper
Saturday	Milk Pottage or Water-gruel	Suet Puddings Baked & Beer	Bread & Cheese or Bread & Butter with Beer
Sunday	Bread & Beer	Beef Broth & Beer	Beef Broth & Beer
Monday	Milk Pottage or Water-gruel	Rice Milk and Beer in Summer, Pease Pottage of Sunday's Broth in Winter	Bread & Cheese or Bread & Butter
Tuesday	Ditto	Broth Beef and Beer	Broth Beef and Beer
Wednesday	Ditto	Rice Milk and Beer	as Monday
Thursday	Ditto	Broth Beef Bread and Beer, as Sunday	as Tuesday
Friday	Ditto	Frumetty & Beer at three o'clock	Bread & Cheese or Bread & Butter with Beer

The workhouse had extensive rules governing its operation and the behaviour of the inmates. New inmates had to hand over all their household goods and also their clothes, which were cleaned and added to the general stock of the house. Prayers were read before breakfast and supper each day, and grace said before and after each meal. Anyone not attending prayers forfeited their next meal. Those that were able were required to attend church every Sunday morning and afternoon. Anyone found loitering or begging en route again lost their next meal. Drunkenness, cursing or swearing were punished by the stocks and confinement to the workhouse until further notice. Bringing strong drink onto the premises, brawling, quarrelling, fighting or abusive language resulted in the loss of one day's meat, with second offenders put into the dungeon for a day. The hours of work, meal times apart, were 6 a.m. till 6 p.m. in summer and 7 a.m. till 5 p.m. in winter. Adults refusing to work were put on bread and water or expelled from the house. Anyone found to be feigning sickness or infirmity in order to avoid work was taken before a magistrate. All beds were to be made by 9 a.m. while every room and passage was to be swept and cleaned by 10 a.m. and washed three times a week in summer or once in winter. Anyone found smoking in bed, or in any room of the house, was put in the dungeon for six hours. Any person proved to have been telling lies was placed on a stool in the dining room at dinner-time with a paper fixed on their breast, bearing the words 'Infamous Lyar', and also lost that meal. All the rules were publicly read each week so that no one could plead ignorance.[13]

In 1832, the Shoe Lane workhouse had 100 inmates, twenty-four of whom were men, forty-six women, and the rest all children under the age of 14. The adults were nearly all former journeymen mechanics and domestic servants. Those considered 'improper objects of relief' were farmed, with an order to pick oakum.

St Andrew Undershaft / St Mary Axe
St Andrew Undershaft (also known as St Mary Axe) had a workhouse from 1733.[14] In 1776, it could house up to fifty inmates. By 1804, the parish's poor were being farmed out with Jonathan Tipple at Hoxton.[15]

St Andrew Wardrobe
In 1776, the parish had a workhouse housing ten inmates, although most of its poor were boarded out.

St Ann Blackfriars
St Ann Blackfriars had a workhouse from 1734.[16] By 1776, the parish poor were being farmed out.

St Anne and St Agnes within Aldersgate
The parish of St Anne and St Agnes erected a workhouse in 1730. In 1776, it housed up to twenty-eight inmates who were said to be the aged and infants. By 1804, the parish was farming out its poor with Jonathan Tipple at Hoxton.[17]

St Augustine Watling Street
St Augustine Watling Street had a workhouse from 1732.[18] The parish was farming out its poor by the 1750s.[19]

St Bartholomew the Great
St Bartholomew the Great had a workhouse from 1737.[20] By 1776, its poor were being farmed out.

St Botolph without Aldersgate
By 1777, St Botolph without Aldersgate had a workhouse for up to 240 inmates. In 1820, the workhouse was at 129 Aldersgate Street (TQ321817).[21] In 1832, the inmates typically comprised thirty men, sixty women and about forty children.

St Botolph without Aldgate
The parish of St Botolph without Aldgate lay partly in the City of London and partly in Middlesex. The City portion, known as the Freedom part, and

the Middlesex portion, also called the Lordship part (see page 142), operated independently with regard to matters such as poor relief.

By 1734, the Freedom part had a workhouse on Seven Steps Alley, off Gravel Lane, Houndsditch (TQ335813). In 1767, after obtaining a Local Act, it erected a workhouse at Cock and Hoop Yard, Gravel Lane (TQ335813). In 1776, the building could house up to 300 paupers, who were occupied in winding silk, spinning worsted and picking oakum.[22]

In 1832, the inmates numbered around 180, three-quarters of whom were adults, mainly servants and labourers plus a few 'decayed tradesmen'.

In October 1828, the workhouse master attended a hearing at the Mansion House with a bandage around his head after being beaten by a male inmate. After discovering a female pauper in the men's quarters, drunk on gin smuggled into the workhouse and 'in close conversation' with a male inmate, the master had ordered her back to her proper place but had then been violently attacked by her paramour.[23]

In 1832, the average number of inmates at Houndsditch was about 190, comprising fifty men, ninety women, twenty girls and thirty boys. The women were employed in needlework and the men in general labour.

St Botolph without Bishopsgate

In 1730, St Botolph without Bishopsgate erected a large workhouse on Rose Alley, near 34 Bishopsgate Street (TQ332817). In September 1731, there were 129 inmates. The old people picked oakum and the young spun worsted and mop yarn. On Sundays, the inmates attended the parish church, where the old people sat in the middle and the children in the gallery so that the parishioners could see their good order.[24] In 1776, the workhouse could house up to 300 inmates, who were employed in winding silk and spinning mop yarn.

In 1795, a Local Act enabled the parish to provide a workhouse for the employment, maintenance and regulation of its poor. By 1810, a workhouse was in operation at Dunning's Alley, near 151 Bishopsgate Street (TQ333815), where up to 200 inmates were accommodated.[25]

In 1832, the workhouse had 200 residents, aged from one month to 90 years. The men were employed in picking oakum and hair, the women in needlework and winding silk. Few of the inmates were capable of productive labour, however.

St Bride Fleet Street

St Bride opened a workhouse in 1727 in Peterborough Court, Fleet Street. In September 1731, there were eighty-two inmates, old and young. About thirty were children under 9 years of age, who were occupied in spinning mop yarn and yarn for stockings for the house. Inmates who had previously been 'housekeepers in repute' were lodged in the best apartments and ate at a separate table, so that they would not be 'incommoded by the noise of the common poor, who are clamorous, and unaccustomed to good manners'. Those in good health were allowed out to church on Sunday mornings, and in the afternoon attended prayers and scripture reading in the workhouse 'to prevent their gossiping and coming home late in the evening'.[26]

St Bride subsequently farmed out its paupers at Hoxton, but in 1796 obtained a Local Act allowing it to raise money for a workhouse which was then established at the southern end of Shoe Lane, at the rear of the present-day Express building (TQ315811). The premises were rebuilt or extended around 1831 and were later described as 'superior brick Gothic … with a frontage of 45 feet by a depth of 74 feet, and six lofty rooms 36 feet by 16 each, numerous bedrooms, committee room, parlour, store-rooms, kitchens, larders, pantries, laundry, cellars, vaults, open yard, and side entrance.'[27]

In 1832, the average number of inmates was 200. There were also twenty children at nurse in the country. To encourage them to work, the inmates were allowed to keep a portion of their earnings.

St Dunstan in the East

In February 1730, a parish-owned house near the church on St Dunstan's Hill (TQ330806), formerly let to a wine merchant, was adapted to receive the poor of the parish, together with twelve children belonging to Tower Ward charity school in Harp Lane. In August 1731, the inmates comprised twenty-six women, two elderly men and sixteen children. A Premier Inn now occupies the site.[28]

In 1776, the workhouse could house seventy inmates, who were employed in winding silk. In 1832, the inmates comprised: two men, both aged 69; twenty-six women, aged from 16 to 80; and seven boys and nine girls.

St Dunstan in the West

St Dunstan in the West built a workhouse in 1728 adjoining the burial ground in Fetter Lane (TQ312813). In August 1731, there were thirty men and women in residence, together with twenty-six children, of whom twenty-one attended the parish's charity school each day, performing their workhouse chores outside school hours. The children and those adults not employed in keeping the house clean or nursing the old and young were occupied in carding wool and spinning mop yarn. The inmates made and mended their own clothes and, when required, spun a quantity of finer wool, which was woven into serge. Dinners on four days a week included roast or boiled beef, with rice-milk or dumplings on the other days. Breakfast consisted of broth or milk-porridge, and suppers of bread and butter or cheese.[29]

In 1767, the *London Chronicle* reported that a male inmate aged 105 had died in the workhouse. In 1776, the establishment could house seventy-eight inmates.

In 1832, the inmates typically comprised about fourteen men and fifty to sixty women, mostly old and infirm, and generally former mechanics and servants. The women were employed at needlework or as nurses, and the men in picking oakum and bristles.

St Ethelburga Bishopsgate
St Ethelburga had a workhouse by 1745. In 1776, it could house forty-six inmates, who were occupied in winding Turkey cotton.

St Faith under St Paul's
St Faith under St Paul's had a workhouse from 1745.[30] By 1776, the parish farmed out its paupers at Mile End. In 1804, the contractor was Mr Overton at Hoxton.[31]

St Giles without Cripplegate
St Giles without Cripplegate had two parts. Its Freedom Liberty fell within the City of London, while its Lordship Liberty was in Middlesex. In 1733, the latter became the parish of St Luke Old Street (see page 113).

In 1726, a workhouse was set up in the Freedom Liberty at Sugar Loaf Court, Moor Lane (TQ325816). In September 1731, there were sixty-five adults in residence and thirty-five children. The inmates were originally employed in picking oakum then were moved onto spinning mop yarn. Although an easier occupation for the elderly, it generated less income for the workhouse.[33]

The Moor Lane premises were rebuilt on a larger scale in 1758, and in 1776 could accommodate 260 inmates. In 1832, the residents comprised 143 males and 175 females, ranging in age from birth to 80 years or more. The men who were capable were employed in picking oakum, the boys in winding cotton, and the women and girls in needlework.

In February 1832, the bodies of an aged man and woman were stolen from the workhouse mortuary. A few months after this incident, the 1832 Anatomy Act attempted to end the illegal trade in bodies by giving surgeons and their students legal access to corpses that were unclaimed after death in institutions such as workhouses and prisons.

The building was demolished in 1843 and St Bartholomew's Church erected on the site.

St Gregory by St Paul's
St Gregory by St Paul's had a workhouse from 1732.[34] By the 1750s, the parish poor were being farmed out with a contractor.

St Helen Bishopsgate
St Helen Bishopsgate had a workhouse from 1741 in a property leased from St Olave's parish on Gunpowder Alley, Crutched Friars (TQ335809).[35]

In 1744, the wife and children of William Carvell were in the workhouse after he had left them to live with another woman. A vestry meeting agreed that he should be immediately taken into custody and carried to the Compter that night as a vagrant.[36]

In 1760, the site was vacated to make way for a new road (now Crosswall) linking Crutched Friars and the Minories. The parish poor were then farmed out at Hoxton by Mr Solomon Pepper.[37] By 1804, Messrs Robertson and Simpson were the contractors.[38]

St Katherine by the Tower
St Katherine by the Tower had a workhouse from 1725.[39] In May 1729, it was occupied by about thirty men, women and children. In 1776, the premises housed up to sixty inmates who were employed in making and mending clothing for the establishment.

St Katherine Coleman
St Katherine Coleman had a workhouse from 1728.[40] In 1740, the parish began farming out its poor.[41] A new workhouse was built in 1775 at Northumberland Alley, Fenchurch Street (TQ334810).[42] It housed up to forty inmates who were mostly occupied in household work.

St Katharine Cree

In 1776, the parish had a workhouse accommodating up to forty-five inmates. In 1832, nine males and thirty-three females were in residence, their ages ranging from under 10 to over 90.

St Lawrence Jewry with St Mary Magdalen, Milk Street

The parish of St Mary Magdalen, Milk Street, was joined with St Lawrence Jewry (or Jury) following the destruction of the former's church in the Great Fire of London. In 1728, the united parishes leased a large old house in Grub Street, St Giles without Cripplegate (TQ324817), and fitted it up for the reception of all the poor receiving parish relief. In September 1731, there were four adults and eight children in residence.[43] By 1776, the parish poor were being farmed out at Hoxton.

St Leonard Foster Lane

In 1776, the parish had a workhouse in leased premises. It housed up to 100 inmates who were occupied in spinning mop yarn and winding silk. By 1804, the poor were being farmed by Mr Overton at Mile End.[44]

St Martin Ludgate

In October 1731, the parish took a twenty-one-year lease on six old houses in Holiday Yard, Creed Lane (TQ318810), in which to receive all its pensioners.[45] By 1776, the poor were being farmed out at Hoxton.

St Martin Vintry

In 1727, the parish hired a house in Brickhill Lane, off Thames Street (TQ324807), for the reception of all its poor. In September 1731, the inmates comprised six adults and four children. The latter attended the charity school at Cordwainers Ward.[46] The parish was farming its poor at Mile End by 1776.

St Mary Aldermanbury

St Mary Aldermanbury had a workhouse from 1730.[47] From 1750, the parish farmed out its poor at Mile End.

St Mary le Bow Cheapside

In November 1731, it was reported that the parish vestry had agreed to hire premises for maintaining the poor and setting to work those who were able.[48] By 1746, the workhouse was at George Yard at the east side of Bow Lane (TQ324811).[49] In 1776, the parish poor were being farmed out at Norton Falgate.

St Michael Cornhill
St Michael Cornhill had a workhouse from around 1732.[50] From 1745, the parish poor were farmed out.[51]

St Olave Hart Street
St Olave Hart Street had a workhouse from 1737.[52] In 1776, it housed up to fifty-six inmates who were occupied in making, mending and washing their own linen, etc. In 1832, the establishment, located at Gunpowder Alley, Jewry Street (now Crutched Friars, TQ335809), was confined to the aged and infirm 'of decent habits and situations in life', together with children aged from 3 to 14 years. The inmates then comprised thirteen women, two men and seven children.

St Pancras Soper Lane
St Pancras Soper Lane had a workhouse from around 1731.[53] By 1776, the parish poor were being farmed out.

St Peter Cornhill
St Peter Cornhill had a workhouse from around 1737.[54] By 1776, the parish poor were being farmed out.

St Sepulchre Newgate
St Sepulchre had two districts, or Liberties. One, St Sepulchre without Newgate, belonged to the City of London. The other lay in Middlesex (see page 129).

St Sepulchre Newgate erected a workhouse, 'a good commodious Brick-House', in 1727 on land adjoining the parish burial ground on Chick-Lane (later renamed West Street) near Smithfield (TQ316816). In October 1729, its inmates comprised: fourteen men, who were mostly sick or lame; fifty-six women, many of whom were old and infirm; twenty-five boys and nineteen girls. Adults who were not capable of other work were employed in picking oakum. The rest, if they were not occupied in keeping the house clean, or nursing, spent their time in spinning Jersey, with about a dozen spinning-wheels in constant use.[55]

In 1777, the workhouse could house up to 279 inmates. In 1798, a Local Act was obtained for rebuilding the workhouse, which was said to be old, ruinous and too small. A further Act in 1806 raised additional money to complete the rebuilding.

In 1832, the workhouse had ninety-eight inmates aged from 5 to 90 years. The few able to work were employed in feather-picking, paper-bag-making and needlework.

In 1837, St Sepulchre Newgate became part of the West London Poor Law Union and its West Street premises remained in use by the union until 1865, when the building was demolished and the Metropolitan Railway was extended.

CITY OF LONDON UNION

Following the 1834 Act, the PLC initially planned to create a single City of London Union comprising 108 parishes. Many of the parishes within the old city walls were tiny and, by 1834, none were operating a work-house. However, some City parishes outside the walls had ample workhouse accommodation which could serve the new union. To keep the size of the proposed union's Board of Guardians within reason, the commissioners sought Parliamentary approval for a scheme allowing a guardian to represent more than one parish. When this was not forthcoming, the commissioners set up three separate unions: the City of London Union (which included ninety-six parishes inside the city walls and two outside), the East London Union (with four parishes, all outside), and the West London Union (seven parishes, all but one outside).

The City of London, formed in March 1837, was a wealthy union and was initially extremely reluctant to build a union workhouse. Most of its paupers received outdoor relief, largely in cash, supplemented by generous allowances of food and drink. Its indoor paupers were farmed out, at con-siderable expense, in accommodation run by private contractors and located miles away from the union's offices at the Mansion House. Children were placed at Mr Aubin's school at Westow Hill, Norwood (TQ335705), women went to Edward Deacon's establishment at Stepney Green (TQ357817), and able-bodied males were sent to Marlborough House on Peckham High Street (TQ343768), run by William Richards.

Conditions at Peckham were the subject of regular complaint. In December 1838, the Lord Mayor visited the establishment after receiving a petition from

Situated where Mile End Road continues as Bow Road, the City of London Union workhouse (later St Clement's Hospital) was opened in 1849.

176 of the inmates. Although he found the premises in an excellent state of cleanliness, the inmates appeared to be receiving less than their regulation allowance of bread. They also complained of overcrowding and being only allowed out once a month.[56]

Marlborough House was also used for casuals, numbering up to 300 a night, which was just enough in summer but wholly inadequate in winter. In January 1841, more than 1,000 casuals besieged it every night and were crammed three to a bed in temporary wooden huts.[57]

Eventually, the union agreed to build its own workhouse on Bow Road (TQ367826). The new premises, housing up to 800 inmates, opened in December 1849. The palatial design by Richard Tress cost over £55,000 to construct and boasted central heating, a dining hall measuring 100ft by 50ft, Siberian marble pillars, and a chapel with stained-glass windows and a new organ. However, the new workhouse had room only for casuals deemed to be sick and helpless – healthy ones were to be refused admittance.[58]

The entrance block, facing onto Bow Road, contained the porter's lodge and receiving wards for new inmates. The main building was H-shaped with males accommodated on the east side and females on the west. Chapel and dining-room blocks were located at the front and rear centre of the main building. A large infirmary block was situated at the south-east of the site.

In 1869, the City of London Union, the East London Union, and the West London Union were amalgamated to form an enlarged City of London Union. The new union took over the former East London Union workhouse at Homerton, and the former West London Union workhouse at Upper Holloway. The Bow Road site became the union's infirmary. By the 1870s, the union also had a casual ward at Robin Hood Court, Shoe Lane, Holborn (TQ314814).

In March 1897, the City of London Union Guardians received unwelcome publicity over the refreshments that were served at their weekly meetings. The proceedings began with a light luncheon of bread and cheese, beer, spirits, etc. After the main business of the meeting, the Guardians were served a repast of fish (salmon for preference), fowl, roast mutton and beef, and sundry other dishes followed by a selection of puddings and sweets. The food was accompanied by champagne and other wines as well as spirits. Then, after a long series of well-lubricated toasts, the members rounded off their meal with tea, coffee, biscuits, cakes, and other dainties and delicacies.[59]

From 1904, the birth certificates for those born at the Bow Road site gave its address simply as 2a Bow Road.

In 1909, the Bow Road site was vacated by the City of London Union, who had decided to concentrate their work at Homerton. After a period of standing empty, the premises were reopened on 1 March 1912 as Bow Institution. Although still managed by the City of London Board of Guardians, it now provided medical and nursing care for workhouse inmates from other unions. By October 1912, nearly 300 paupers from the Poplar Union were in residence, including many who had previously been in Poplar's Forest Gate branch workhouse. Subsequently renamed the City of London Institution, the west wing of the main building was destroyed by a fire in January 1935. The following year, it became St Clement's Hospital, which continued in operation until 2005.

In recent years, the buildings have been redeveloped for a mixture of community, cultural, commercial and residential use.

EAST LONDON UNION

The East London Poor Law Union was created in December 1837 from the parishes of St Botolph without Aldersgate, St Botolph without Aldgate, St Botolph without Bishopsgate, and St Giles Cripplegate.

The union took over the existing parish workhouses on Aldersgate Street (TQ321817) and Dunning's Alley, Bishopsgate Street (TQ333815).

The Aldersgate Street workhouse, which housed 210 male inmates, was badly damaged by a major fire in the area in June 1855. The Dunning's Alley premises, said to be one of the worst workhouses in London, accommodated 396 women and children.

In November 1853, the foundation stone was laid for a new workhouse on a 6-acre site to the south of Clifden Road at Homerton. The new premises, which were certified to house up to 834 inmates, were opened at Christmas 1855. A porter's lodge, with casual wards to its rear, lay at the south of the site. The main building had a T-shaped layout with its entrance at the eastern side. Administrative offices and the master's quarters were placed at the centre of the block, with males housed in the south wing and females in the north. A dining hall with a chapel above lay to the rear. An insane ward and infirmary were located in a separate block to the north of the workhouse. On the female side, a nursery and a laundry lay towards the western side of the site.

The East London Union was wound up in 1869 and its parishes were transferred to the City of London Union, which also took over the Homerton workhouse.

In 1908, the City of London Union decided to concentrate its facilities at Homerton. The existing Homerton workhouse was substantially enlarged with a new administrative block, nurses' home and 320-bed infirmary.

The land to the east of the workhouse was acquired in 1868 by the MAB for its new Eastern Fever and Smallpox Hospital. After the workhouse closed in 1921, it was absorbed into the MAB's premises. In 1930, both sites were taken over by the LCC and continued to operate as the Eastern (Fever) Hospitals, and then as the Eastern Hospital for general cases.

The hospital closed in 1982 and most of the buildings were demolished soon after. In 1987, the new Homerton Hospital was erected on the old workhouse site.

WEST LONDON UNION

The West London Poor Law Union, formed in December 1837, included the parishes of St Andrew Holborn below the Bars, St Bartholomew the Great, St Bartholomew the Less, St Bride, St Dunstan in the West, and St Sepulchre without Newgate.

Initially, the union took over two former parish workhouses. That of St Sepulchre Newgate, on West Street, near Smithfield Market (TQ316816), was used for males, while that of St Bride, on Shoe Lane (TQ315811), housed females. Following enlargement of the West Street premises in 1840, the females were transferred there and Shoe Lane was closed.

In February 1857, the Lord Mayor of London made an unannounced visit to inspect the West London Union's casual ward. He arrived at the West Street workhouse, only to be told that the casual ward was some 2½ miles away at Battlebridge (now King's Cross). After making their way through the city's streets, the mayor and his party found that the men's accommodation consisted of a twelve-stall stable, while women were housed on the floor of an adjoining cattle-shed.

In July 1865, the union opened a new workhouse for 500 inmates at the west side of Cornwallis Road in Upper Holloway (TQ301867). The Italianate design by Searle, Son and Yelf had a T-shaped layout with administrative offices and master's quarters at the centre, above which rose a lofty tower containing a large water tank. Males were housed in the south wing and females in the north, while a dining hall with a chapel above it lay to the rear.

The West London Union was wound up in 1869 and its constituent parishes became part of the City of London Union. The Cornwallis Road workhouse was subsequently taken over by Islington Board of Guardians. The building was used to house prisoners of war during the First World War. The premises were subsequently used as a storage depot for telephone equipment. The site is now occupied by the modern housing of Cornwallis Square.

Up until 1850, the West London Union also operated a separate school housing 150 children on Meeting House Lane (now Church Road), Edmonton (TQ340921).

The West London Union workhouse on Cornwallis Road in Upper Holloway was erected in 1864.

3

COUNTY OF LONDON

BERMONDSEY

In 1725, St Mary Magdalen, Bermondsey, opened a workhouse on Salisbury Street, now known as Wilson Grove (TQ345795). In May 1729, the inmates consisted of forty-seven adults and eleven children, who were under the care of a steward. Those able to work were employed in picking oakum and spinning mop yarn.[1] In 1777, the workhouse could house 291 inmates.

A new workhouse was erected in 1791 on Russell Street (now Tanner Street, TQ333797). In 1832, there were 164 male inmates and 265 female, described as being of all ages, and mostly of the class of labourers. Males were employed in picking oakum and the females in slop-work. The sexes had separate quarters but shared an outdoor yard. The children, then numbering 232, were in a separate establishment at Merton and occupied in weaving, shoemaking and making clothing.

In March 1836, Bermondsey was designated as a single Poor Law Parish. Alterations and additions were made to the Russell Street workhouse to satisfy the PLC's requirements. The buildings roughly formed a square, with the Russell Street side containing the workhouse entrance, porter's lodge, dining hall, kitchens and Guardians' boardroom. Male inmates were accommodated along the west side of the building.

In 1865, a report in *The Lancet* made a number of serious criticisms about the establishment. The infirm wards were described as a 'fever-nest' and likely to foster epidemics. The sanitary arrangements of the infirm department were 'scandalously bad' – two of the wards were very dirty, with their occupants 'herding together in a miserable manner … their water closet and urinal (abutting on the deadhouse) stink so offensively as to poison the whole atmosphere of their airing-court.' The accommodation for tramps was 'not fit for a dog'. The beds consisted of bunks, or long orange-boxes, with a wooden log for a pillow and a blanket and rug to cover the sleeper, and not even a bit of straw to lie on.[2]

In the wake of the Metropolitan Poor Act, Bermondsey became part of the St Olave Union in October 1869. The Tanner Road workhouse continued in use until 1922. After its closure, the building became a laundry. It was demolished in 1928 and the site cleared to create the Tanner Street recreation ground.

BETHNAL GREEN

St Matthew Bethnal Green had a workhouse by 1751, in Jorey's house at the east side of the green. From 1757, the workhouse was run by a contractor who was paid 2*s* 4*d* per head per week. An inmate's daily rations were two pints of beer and a pound of bread together with 4oz of cheese, 2oz of butter, 7oz of meat or ¾lb of suet dumpling and broth or pottage.[3]

A Local Act in 1763 allowed the parish to raise £2,000 by the sale of annuities to provide a workhouse where children were to be educated, the idle corrected, and the able-bodied given work by master weavers. The new building, housing up to 400 inmates, was completed in 1766 on a site to the south of Hare Street (TQ342823). Four sick wards were added at the south of the building in 1802.[4]

In 1826, overcrowding in the workhouse led to its expansion into an adjacent property containing a large house and outbuildings. Inmate numbers continued to rise, however, and in October 1831 there were just fourteen beds between ninety-nine boys. Deaths among the children were also resulting from a lack of air or from disease caused by rubbish in the workhouse yard. In February 1832, the premises contained 1,044 inmates sleeping up to five in a bed and producing 'indecent scenes'. In the same year, the high level of pauperism in the parish was blamed on the stagnation in the silk-weaving trade and 'miserably low' wages.

In March 1836, Bethnal Green became a single Poor Law Parish. It took over the existing workhouse at 50 Hare Street but failed to improve conditions, which in 1837 were criticised as 'totally unfitted to act as an efficient test of indigence … on account of the deficiency both in the extent and nature of the accommodation provided for the inmates.'[5]

Following pressure from the PLC to provide new premises, the Guardians acquired a 5-acre site at Bonner's Hall Fields, to the west of what became

Waterloo Road, now Waterloo Gardens (TQ351835). The new building, designed by Mr Bunning, could house 1,000 inmates. On its completion in August 1842, it was said to be the 'most complete in its character' of any workhouse in the metropolis. The corridor-plan building had a frontage of 440ft, a depth of 50ft, and contained separate wards for the aged, the young, the children, and the disorderly of each sex. A large chapel occupied the centre of the building. All the rooms were lit by gas.[6]

In 1866, *The Lancet* reported on the state of the medical facilities at the workhouse. Lighting and ventilation were said to be inadequate – many windows were 6ft from the floor to prevent inmates from seeing out. Each patient had only 300 cubic feet of space, a quarter of official recommendations. There was a lack of water-closets and floors were soaked with urine. Washing facilities were insufficient – in one ward, seventeen children were washed daily in one pail, several in the same water, and dried with sheets. There were only two paid nurses, both untrained, to nurse up to 600 sick. They had forty pauper helpers 'whose tendencies to drink cannot be controlled'.[7]

In 1908, the building was remodelled with the provision of new casual wards, enlargement of the dining hall, new kitchens, a new wing for 100 female inmates, new bath and lavatory buildings, and modern padded rooms.

Bethnal Green's Waterloo Road workhouse, completed in 1842, was home to over 1,000 inmates.

In 1914, the workhouse adopted the name Waterloo House. In October of that year, 235 Belgian refugees were given emergency accommodation at the premises.

In 1930, Waterloo House became an LCC PAI. After its closure in the mid-1930s, the building was demolished and flats were erected on the site.

Between 1891 and 1900, Bethnal Green operated a second workhouse at Well Street, Hackney (TQ353842). It housed the 'aged respectable poor' – those who had demonstrated good behaviour at the Waterloo Road workhouse.

In March 1900, the parish opened a 750-bed infirmary on Cambridge Heath Road (TQ350832). Designed by Giles, Gough and Trollope it comprised eleven pavilion ward-blocks, arranged in pairs either side of a corridor running from east to west across the site. An administrative block and laundry block were at the centre.

During the First World War, the infirmary became Bethnal Green Military Hospital. In 1930, the LCC took over the site, then in 1948 it became part of the NHS as Bethnal Green Hospital, providing geriatric care. After its closure in 1992, the buildings were demolished apart from the entrance block on Cambridge Heath Road.

In 1867, the parish purchased Leytonstone House and its 9 acres of grounds on Whipps Cross Road (TQ397878) for use as a residential school which eventually housed 664 children. In 1930, the LCC took over the establishment, which continued in use as Leytonstone Children's Home until 1937. It subsequently became Leytonstone House Hospital for people with learning difficulties. Following its closure in 1994, the site was redeveloped for residential and commercial use with some of the original buildings surviving.

From around 1910, the parish operated a casual ward at Hollybush Gardens, Bethnal Green Road (TQ349827).

CAMBERWELL

Camberwell erected a workhouse in 1728 near St Giles' Church on Peckham Road.[8] By 1777, the establishment housed up to 100 inmates.

In 1813, the parish obtained a Local Act for repairing or rebuilding the workhouse. In 1818, a new workhouse was opened at Havil Street (TQ332769). It was a long, narrow two-storey building.[9] Inmates grew vegetables in the garden.

Camberwell was constituted as a Poor Law Parish in October 1835 and took over the Havil Street workhouse. It was extended in 1847 and then accommodated 550 inmates. In 1865, the institution was the subject of a report in *The Lancet*. Despite concluding that the infirmary urgently needed to be rebuilt and that the lying-in ward was entirely unfit for its purpose, the report was relatively complimentary.[10]

In 1873, a large infirmary was erected at the north of the site. Its five-storey central block contained offices, staff quarters and special wards. At each side was a three-storey ward wing, with men at the north and women at the south. In 1889–90, a circular ward tower, a design then in vogue, was added. Its four storeys each had twenty-four beds placed around a central shaft containing heating and ventilation services.[11]

In 1930, the site was taken over by the LCC and renamed St Giles' Hospital. Many of the original buildings have now been demolished.

In 1878, the Guardians erected a new workhouse at Gordon Road, Camberwell (TQ346764), designed by Berriman & Sons. A central administrative block was linked by covered walkways to two dormitory pavilions. The workhouse was originally intended only for able-bodied inmates. Men performed stone-breaking and wood-chopping, while women did laundry work. In 1930, under LCC control, the site became the Camberwell Reception Centre. It continued in use into the 1980s, housing homeless, single men.

In 1895, an additional workhouse was opened at Constance Road, East Dulwich (TQ333752). The buildings, designed by Thomas Aldwinckle, housed around 1,000 inmates, mostly aged and infirm, plus some lunatics. A central

Camberwell's former Gordon Road workhouse, now converted into flats.

two-storey administration block was flanked at each side by four four-storey dormitory pavilion ward-blocks. There was also a small block for married couples and a chapel. After the site was taken over by the LCC in 1930, it became St Francis Hospital. It joined the NHS in 1948 as Dulwich Hospital North Wing and was linked to its parent hospital (the former St Saviour's Union infirmary) by a subway under the railway that lay between them. The hospital closed in 1991 and housing was built on the site.

In 1894–95, the Guardians used the former Birkbeck Schools premises on Willowbrook Road, Peckham (TQ338776), as a temporary workhouse. Camberwell also operated a casual ward at Albert Road, Peckham (TQ345764).

CHELSEA

In 1737, the parish of St Luke, Chelsea, erected a workhouse on land donated by Sir Hans Sloane at the north of the King's Road, at the corner of Arthur Street (now Dovehouse Street) and Britten Street (TQ271781). The premises were gradually extended and by 1829 included a committee room, school rooms, nursery room, room for infirm women, dining room, kitchen, bakehouse, wash-house, laundry, dormitories, men's infirmary, two rooms for insane men and five rooms for insane women. Two rooms over the gateway were used for 'receiving houseless strangers in an evening'. There was also a dispensary which could be attended by anyone having a ticket from a churchwarden or overseer.[12]

In 1832, the workhouse had 450 inmates. The men were employed in cutting firewood for sale, and the women in needlework. The aged and sick were allowed tea and other indulgences.

From 1837 until 1841, Chelsea was part of the Kensington Union, then became a separate Poor Law Parish. Major building work was carried out at the Arthur Street site in 1843–44 including a new central range, master's house, vagrants' ward, and mortuary. In the 1860s, Bennet's Yard, a narrow thoroughfare at the east of the workhouse, was incorporated into the site and three new buildings were erected, including offices facing King's Road. In 1903–05, all the 1860s blocks were extended eastwards to Sydney Street. The northernmost two, each five storeys high, housed aged women and infirm women. The extended offices building included the Guardians' committee room and boardroom, previously located in the infirm and aged women's blocks.

Under LCC control from 1930, the workhouse became a PAI, later King's Mead old people's home. Apart from the King's Road offices and the women's

The surviving part of the Chelsea workhouse formerly contained offices for the Guardians and Relieving Officer, with an infirm women's ward block to the rear.

block to its rear, the buildings were demolished in 1965 and replaced by a new care home on Dovehouse Street.

In 1872, a new infirmary was erected on a narrow site between Britten Street and Cale Street (TQ270782) and was linked to the workhouse by an underground tunnel. The infirmary was renamed St Luke's Hospital in 1925. Under LCC control from 1930, it became the main acute general hospital for Chelsea. In June 1941, a direct bomb hit caused considerable damage to the buildings. The hospital joined the NHS in 1948 and closed in 1974, with the subsequent demolition of the building.

Casual wards were erected in 1894 on Milman's Street, Chelsea (TQ268775).

CLERKENWELL

In May 1727, St James, Clerkenwell, opened a workhouse at the west of Coppice Row (now 143–157 Farringdon Road, TQ313822). In September 1731, the 'large, plain, commodious brick-house' had eighty-nine inmates, those able to work being employed in spinning mop-yarn and picking oakum.

The children were taught to read and say their catechism, worked at the spinning wheel, and were obliged to keep themselves clean. In 1729, an infirmary was built at one end of the workhouse.[13]

In 1775, the parish obtained a Local Act allowing poor relief to be administered by a committee of Guardians of the Poor and for it to erect or enlarge a workhouse. The latter course was taken in 1790 when the Coppice Row premises were substantially enlarged. The building then comprised three storeys plus a basement, with apartments for the master and a handsome committee room for the Guardians. There was also a large separate block at the rear.[14]

In November 1797, it was reported that since the passing of an Act that year for levying a duty on clocks and watches, over 300 watchmakers had received relief from the Clerkenwell workhouse. The Act had led to a massive drop in the number of new timepieces being bought and was repealed shortly afterwards.[15]

In 1832, the workhouse had 481 inmates, mostly elderly. Aged men, and boys after school hours, sorted bristles, while 'incorrigible' men picked oakum. The women did washing, needlework and nursing. The parish housed pauper infants in an establishment at Enfield and lunatics at Bethnal Green.[16]

Clerkenwell's Local Act status allowed its poor relief administration to continue outside the 1834 Act.

The Clerkenwell parish workhouse on Coppice Row (now Farringdon Road), erected in 1727.

In 1865, a *Lancet* report revealed Clerkenwell as having some of the worst medical provision of any London workhouse. The building was described as a tall, gloomy brick edifice, consisting of two long parallel blocks, both four storeys in height, separated by a flagged courtyard about 20ft wide. The rear block had 'an aspect of squalid poverty and meanness'. There was no separate infirmary, and the sick, infirm, insane and able-bodied wards were jumbled side by side, echoing to the shrieks and laughter of noisy lunatics. The 560 inmates comprised about 250 sick and 280 infirm (including about 80 insane), about sixty more than the PLB would have allowed. In several of the infirm wards, inmates washed in their chamber pots. In the casual wards, inmates lay on straw beds, spread on a wooden grid-iron framework, and had to huddle so close as to be almost in contact with each other. Finally, the parish dead-house was located in a corner of the central courtyard from where 'reminiscences' of departed parishioners wafted to the windows of the nearby wards.[17]

In 1869, Clerkenwell was added to the Holborn Union, which also took over the Farringdon Road workhouse. Although the building became increasingly dilapidated and suffered from vibration caused by the construction of the nearby Metropolitan Railway, it continued in use until 1879 and was subsequently demolished.

FULHAM

In 1732, Fulham opened a workhouse on the east side of the High Street (then Bear Street). Prior to 1754, when silk winding was introduced, the inmates were occupied in picking oakum.[18]

A new workhouse, a substantial brick building, was erected in 1774, at what is now the site of 13–17 Fulham High Street (TQ243762). The inmates had meat for dinner on four days a week, and bread and cheese on other days. There was milk-porridge for breakfast on five days, and bread and cheese on the other two, with the children receiving bread and butter.[19] In 1777, the establishment housed up to ninety inmates. From 1790, the inmates were occupied in carding and spinning wool.[20] In 1802, Dr Henry Bunnett, who acted as the workhouse surgeon, apothecary and midwife, offered to inoculate the parish's paupers against smallpox.

In 1832, there were eighty-eight inmates, the men were mostly worn-out labourers, the women chiefly widows, and the children orphans or illegitimate.

In February 1837, Fulham became part of the Kensington Poor Law Union and its workhouse was used to house pauper girls. When the Kensington

The main entrance to the Fulham workhouse on Fulham Palace Road.

Union was dissolved in 1845, Fulham and Hammersmith joined to form the Fulham Poor Law Union. This arrangement continued until 1899 when the two became separate Poor Law Parishes.

In 1848–50, the Fulham Union erected a new workhouse for up to 450 inmates at the east side of Fulham Palace Road (TQ236780). The inmates of Fulham's old workhouse moved to the new premises in November 1850. The old building was demolished in 1860.

The new workhouse was an Italianate-style design by Alfred Gilbert, constructed in red brick. It had a corridor-plan layout with an entrance block, T-shaped main block and infirmary placed parallel to one another.[21] In 1884, a pavilion-plan infirmary was added facing St Dunstan's Road. A casual ward at the east of the site had its entrance on Margravine Road.

From 1915–18, the workhouse and infirmary were taken over for use as Fulham Military Hospital. In 1925, the site became Fulham Hospital, now Charing Cross Hospital. All the former workhouse buildings have been demolished.

In 1908, Fulham took over the former South Metropolitan District School at Sutton, which became known as the Belmont workhouse. It housed 'inmates from any metropolitan union who are capable of taking their meals in the dining hall'.[22]

Trouble hit Belmont in December 1910 when a riot broke out in the dining hall over complaints about the porridge being served to the inmates. The staff telephoned for police assistance, and a force of forty constables arrived on the scene. The police soon gained control and eighty-six prisoners were conveyed to Sutton in cabs. The two ringleaders later received prison sentences.

In 1916–19, the Belmont site served as a military hospital. It was again in the news in January 1926 when a major fire occurred at the institution. Despite considerable panic among the 1,000 or so inmates, no lives were lost. The building's huge central bell tower collapsed during the blaze. The total cost of the damage was estimated at £20,000.

In the 1920s, a training programme was introduced to improve the employability of Belmont inmates. This was further developed by the LCC who took over the establishment in 1930 and renamed it the Sutton Training Centre. Subjects of instruction included bricklaying, plastering, motor repair work and hairdressing.

The site later became Belmont Hospital, renamed the Henderson Hospital in 1958. The buildings no longer exist and housing now occupies the site.

GREENWICH

Greenwich's first workhouse was erected in 1724 next to St Alfege's Church on Church Street. Its construction and operation were based on advice from workhouse contractor, Matthew Marryott. All weekly allowances in the parish were halted and the workhouse offered instead. In August 1724, there were around ninety inmates who were employed in picking oakum, winding silk and spinning jersey. Breakfast on Sundays was bread and cheese, with either beef broth or milk porridge on other days. Dinner on three days was beef and broth, with plum pudding, rice milk or hasty pudding on other days. Supper every day was bread and cheese.[23]

The premises eventually proved inadequate and in 1766 a new workhouse was erected at the north side of Maidenstone Hill (TQ381768). The large brick building housed up to 350 inmates who were employed in spinning mop-yarn. In 1776, the staff included a mistress, a superintendent of spinning yarn, his assistant who also read prayers, a superintendent of spinning jersey, her assistant, and a beadle.

Deptford erected a workhouse in 1726 on the site of Sayes Court, an old manor house, just north of what is now Dacca Street (TQ36977). By May 1729, it had seventy inmates, including twenty-six children, all 'decently lodged, fed, cloathed, and taught'.[24] In 1730, Deptford was divided into two parishes: St Nicholas (which included the old town and workhouse) and St Paul. In 1776, the St Nicholas workhouse was said to be 78ft long, 36ft deep, two storeys high, and to contain fifteen 'apartments' housing up to 130 inmates, who picked oakum for the Royal Dockyard. The St Paul workhouse, at the east side of Deptford Church Street where Castell House now stands (TQ374772), was a brick building, 122ft long, 20ft deep, and housed 125 inmates who were occupied in picking oakum.

Woolwich built a workhouse in 1731 at Rope Yard Rails, a street now covered by Maribor Park (TQ435791).[25] The building was U-shaped and three storeys high. Following a bequest in 1754, a schoolhouse was added where pauper girls could be taught reading, needlework and knitting.[26] In 1777, the building housed up to 100 inmates. By 1820, two further houses had been purchased, taking the total accommodation to over 300.

Greenwich Poor Law Union was formed in November 1836 and included Woolwich, despite efforts by the Woolwich vestry to form a separate body. The union took over the old workhouses at Greenwich, Woolwich and St Paul, Deptford.

A large new union workhouse, housing 1,025 inmates, was opened in September 1840 at the junction of Woolwich Road and Vanbrugh Hill (TQ395782). The architect, Robert Browne, later described his design as

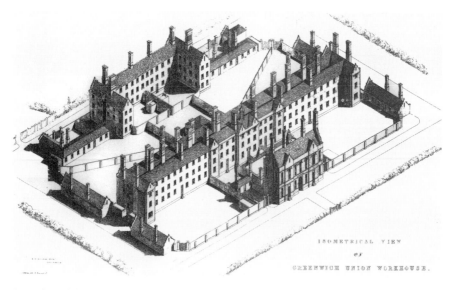

An architect's bird's-eye view of the Greenwich Union workhouse, the largest in the metropolis when it opened in 1840.

'plain but cheerful and almslike'. The two-storey entrance block contained the boardroom, porter's lodge, probationary wards, refractory wards and vagrants' wards. The main block, three storeys high, was an early example of a corridor-plan design. A central corridor ran the whole length of each floor giving access to rooms for children at the front and for adults at the rear. Males were housed at the west of the building and females at the east, including a section for 'bad women'. The master's quarters were at the centre, with a chapel/dining hall behind. Separated from the main block by inmates' yards was the infirmary which also contained the laundry, work-rooms and mortuary.[27]

In 1865, a *Lancet* report made a number of criticisms of the establishment. The infirmary was overcrowded, badly ventilated and insanitary, with the excreta from wet and dirty cases soaking through their straw beds and collected in a pan below. The nursing was carried out by pauper inmates, who were given daily allowances of tea, sugar, meat and beer, and occasionally gin. There were defects in the workhouse water supply, which was drawn from an artesian well.[28]

In 1868, Woolwich separated from the union to become a separate Poor Law Parish (see page 145).

In 1875–76, a new 250-bed infirmary was erected south of the workhouse with its entrance on Vanbrugh Hill. Designed by William Wallen, it had a four-storey central administrative block connected by corridors to three-storey male and female ward pavilions. Additions in the 1880s included two further pavilions at the west of the infirmary providing 250 beds, and two workhouse blocks for 300 chronically sick patients. After being taken over by the LCC in 1930, the site became St Alfege's Hospital. The buildings were demolished in the late 1960s to make way for a new Greenwich District Hospital. It closed in 2001, and the buildings were demolished in 2006.

In 1897, a site for a second workhouse was acquired at Grove Park (TQ410727). It was designed by Thomas Dinwiddy to house 815 inmates. The institution had its entrance and receiving wards on Marvels Lane. An administration block at the centre of the site included kitchens, dining hall and stores. To its rear were a 400-seat chapel, laundry block and water tower. Around the central buildings were eight three-storey pavilions, with males accommodated at the north and females at the south. The aged were placed at the front of the site and the able-bodied at the rear. Each pavilion housed up to 100 inmates, with one for elderly married couples having individual bedrooms. The pavilions and central blocks were linked by covered arcades. When construction was completed in 1902, a significant fall in numbers applying to enter the workhouse led to the new premises standing empty for two years.

The press made much of the situation, especially as the building was one of the most luxurious in the country with 'mosaic flooring, beautiful panelling, a dining hall fit for royalty, and a church which any rector would envy'.[29]

In 1914–19, the Grove Park site was used by the Army Service Corps as a barracks for training recruits. From 1926–77, it operated as a TB and chest hospital, then became a residence for the mentally handicapped. The site has now been redeveloped for residential use but the entrance and administration blocks survive.

In 1902, the Greenwich Guardians opened a large cottage homes development at Burn Oak Lane, Sidcup (TQ460734). In 1930, the homes were taken over by the LCC and renamed Lamorbey School, then became The Hollies in 1950. In 1965, Southwark Council took over the site which continued in use until the 1980s. The buildings have now been converted to residential use. The union also operated a children's home at 9–19 Calvert Road, adjacent to the Vanbrugh Hill workhouse. It acted as a reception home for Sidcup.

HACKNEY

The parish of St John, Hackney, set up a workhouse in the winter of 1728/9 at the north side of Homerton High Street, where fifteen paupers could be housed.[30]

In 1741, the workhouse moved to a Tudor cottage at the south of the High Street, with space for thirty inmates. In 1750, a room was reserved for sick paupers with a matron and a nurse appointed. Richard Charles was contracted in 1755 to run the workhouse and was required to provide 'wholesome meat and drink', a weekly clean shirt for men and a clean shift for women.

Rising pauper numbers led the parish to obtain a Local Act in 1764, placing management of poor relief in the hands of a board of trustees. The workhouse was enlarged several times and by 1813 could hold 280 inmates. At the front of the site, facing the High Street, were the master's house and inmates' dining rooms. Behind the men's ward was a stone-breaking yard where up to 1,000 tons of Blue Guernsey granite were broken each a month. Combing and knitting rooms were placed next to the women's ward. Boys' and girls' schoolrooms lay next to the infirmary.[31]

An 1822 report noted that many illegitimate children had been born in the house and recommended a wall be built to prevent communication between the sexes.[32]

In 1832, the workhouse had 393 inmates including 140 children. Men were employed in the workhouse garden or in beating flax. Women were occupied in needlework, spinning or washing. The children did spinning as well, with the boys also weaving and basket-making.

Stoke Newington set up a workhouse in 1733 but later farmed out its poor.[33]

Hackney Poor Law Union, comprising Hackney and Stoke Newington, was formed in January 1837 and took over the High Street workhouse. By 1842, the front block of the workhouse had been replaced by a U-shaped three-storey building. At the front, a boardroom was on the ground floor, the master's quarters on the first floor, and servants' accommodation on the top floor. Male and female inmates were respectively housed at the east and west sides of the inner courtyard. The building also included a potato cellar, flax shop, weaving room, school rooms and mortuary. Behind the women's quarters were the infirmary, which also contained a nursery, and laundry.[34] A 500-seat chapel was erected at the south of the workhouse in 1848. By 1870, a long block containing schools, male and female dining rooms and day rooms had been added to the south of the chapel. An administrative block lay at the centre east of the site, and casual wards and a stone shed faced onto Sidney Road (now Kenworthy Road).

Although Hackney did not feature in the *Lancet* reports into conditions in London workhouses, the journal placed the establishment in the best of its three grades of institution.[35] However, an LGB inspection in 1866 found many faults with the institution. The sick were not classified into medical and surgical, or acute and chronic cases. There were only two paid nurses. Many of the rooms

The ward blocks of Hackney workhouse towering over Homerton High Street in the early 1900s.

were narrow, overcrowded and poorly ventilated. There was a general lack of furniture and the plates used were of tin and were 'old and repulsive'.[36]

The workhouse accommodation was gradually expanded, particularly that housing the sick. Four large ward-blocks were erected at the north of the site between 1882 and 1910, and a lunatic ward at the west in 1911. A new administration block was built at the rear of the master's house in 1906.

In April 1930, the site was taken over by the LCC, becoming Hackney Hospital. The following Christmas, the hospital was hit by a scandal after the cries of a dying patient were ignored by nurses holding a dance in a nearby corridor. Several staff were dismissed and such functions were then banned from the patients' areas.[37]

From 1987, medical services were gradually transferred to the new Homerton Hospital. The old site was then redeveloped to become the John Howard Centre for Forensic Mental Health but two workhouse ward-blocks still survive.

In 1885, the union took over the former Brentwood District School on Brentwood Hill (now London Road), Brentwood (TQ587936) to house its pauper children. In 1893, the establishment's nurse, Ella Gillespie, was sentenced to five years' penal servitude after being found guilty of cruelty to those in her care.

Around 1898, the Guardians began to acquire houses on Sidney Road for use as children's homes. A large cottage homes development for 300 children was opened in 1905 at Ongar, Essex (TL553038). In 1930, the site was renamed Ongar Public Assistance School, then in 1939 became a residential school for educationally subnormal boys. After the Second World War, it housed children with special needs and was known as Great Stony School. The school closed in 1994 and the buildings were converted to residential use.

From 1898 to 1904, Hackney developed a large casual ward complex on Gainsborough Road (now Eastway), Hackney Wick (TQ367849).

HAMMERSMITH

In 1729, a workhouse was opened in Hammersmith on a site known as Shortlands, between Hammersmith Road and Great Church Lane (TQ237785). It was soon extended with the addition of two rooms 'plaistered and white-washed, to receive lying-in women and distempered persons'.[38] The workhouse suffered from severe overcrowding but appears not to have been further extended. The inmates, who numbered sixty in 1777, were employed in weaving, spinning and basket-making. In 1832, the average number of occupants was just over 100 – the men and women were said to be old and infirm, the children orphans or bastards.

In 1837, Hammersmith joined the new Kensington Poor Law Union, with the Shortlands workhouse used to house 132 boys who were employed in wood-chopping, making fruit baskets, shoemaking and tailoring.[39]

In 1845, the Kensington Poor Law Union was dissolved and Hammersmith united with Fulham to form the Fulham Poor Law Union. The Shortlands workhouse was closed in 1850 following the opening of the union's new workhouse on Fulham Palace Road.

In 1899, Fulham and Hammersmith became separate Poor Law Parishes. In 1902, Hammersmith decided to erect a new workhouse and infirmary on a 14-acre site on Du Cane Road, next to Wormwood Scrubs prison (TQ225813). When the extensive buildings were completed in 1905, the cost had risen to the then enormous sum of £261,000 and virtually bankrupted the Guardians. The grandeur of the workhouse dining hall and rumours of teapots costing 18*s* 6*d* led to the establishment being condemned by some critics as a 'Pauper's Paradise'.[40] However, the medical and other facilities were among the best to be found in Poor Law institutions at the time.

The pavilion-plan buildings were designed by Giles, Gough and Trollope. The workhouse section, at the north of the site, accommodated 428 inmates. A central administrative block contained committee rooms and staff accommodation in its three-storey northern portion, and a dining hall/chapel at the south. Two pavilions for males were at the east and two for females at the west, all linked by a corridor. The pavilions, three storeys high, each housed 100 inmates with separate sections for the infirm, aged healthy and young able-bodied. A separate block contained quarters for six aged married couples, each having a separate bed-sitting room. The workhouse interior was left unfinished by the builders with internal plastering being carried out by the first inmates. A 330-bed infirmary at the south of the site followed the layout of the workhouse. A central administrative building was linked by a corridor to male and female ward pavilions at the east and west. Each pavilion was three storeys high, with two 24-bed wards on each floor, one each side of the central corridor. A laundry, serving both the infirmary and workhouse, lay at the centre of the site. An inmates' workshop block had sections for carpenters, joiners, plumbers, smiths, etc. and a stone-breaking shed and corn mills. It also included a large room where any inmates with a prospect of setting up a home of their own again could temporarily store their furniture. Electric lighting was installed throughout the establishment.[41]

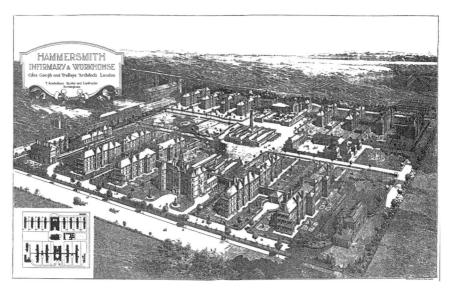

Opened in 1905, the new Hammersmith infirmary and workhouse was criticised for the extravagance of its design and fittings.

In 1916, the site was requisitioned by the War Office for use as the Military Orthopaedic Hospital. After the war, it became the Ministry of Pensions Hospital, only being returned to the Hammersmith Guardians in 1926. By then known as Hammersmith Hospital, the site was taken over by the LCC in 1930, then joined the NHS in 1948. It still serves as Hammersmith Hospital, although many of the original buildings have been replaced or much altered. Of the workhouse section, only the administrative block survives.

HAMPSTEAD

The parish of Hampstead St John opened a workhouse in 1729 in leased premises at Frognal, near the parish church. In 1731, there were twenty inmates, almost half of whom were children. Those that were able were employed in spinning mop-yarn and making it into mops, which were sold locally.[42] Vegetables were also grown in the garden.[43] In 1777, the workhouse could house eighty inmates.

In 1800, the deteriorating fabric of the workhouse led the parish to obtain a Local Act enabling it to raise money for a new building. The sum of £6,000 was amassed by the sale of debentures and a house with a large garden was purchased at New End (TQ264860). The building was enlarged and the existing residents at Frognal were transferred in July 1801. By 1813, there were 155 inmates.[44] In 1832, the 133 residents ranged in age from infancy to 87 years.

In February 1837, Hampstead became part of the Edmonton Poor Law Union. The New End building continued in use until 1842, when its inmates were transferred to the union's new workhouse at Edmonton.

In 1848, Hampstead became a separate Poor Law Parish and the old New End workhouse was brought back into use. The Guardians originally intended to enlarge the existing premises but it appears that a new building was ultimately constructed. It became known as Kendall's Hall, after the architect of the scheme, H.E. Kendall junior. The corridor-plan main block was a long, narrow, red-brick building, three storeys high and Italianate in style.

In 1869, a dispensary was built at the west of Kendall's Hall and a four-storey pavilion-plan infirmary erected at the rear, both designed by John Giles. The infirmary included early examples of 'Nightingale' wards.[45]

Growth in demand for hospital accommodation led to the erection of a further ward building in 1884–85. Designed by Charles Bell, it was constructed as a circular tower, a layout which had begun to appear on the Continent in the 1870s. It had three floors of wards, with nurses' accommodation on an attic floor, and a 12,000-gallon water tank at the top. Each ward was 50ft in diameter and had twenty-four beds arranged radially with their heads against the outer wall. A central shaft contained heating and ventilation services. A further four-storey infirmary block, designed by Keith Young, was erected at the corner of New End and Heath Street in 1896.[46] A mortuary was erected opposite the workhouse in 1890.

In 1896, two elderly inmates, Mr and Mrs 'Pigeon' Hill, left the workhouse for an hour or so, went to church and got married. They then returned and demanded a place in the workhouse's special quarters for elderly married couples. The pair, both over 60, had each been married twice before. The Guardians, who clearly felt they were being manipulated, called for an alteration in the law to limit the privilege of special quarters to those who had been married for six months previously.

During the First World War, the workhouse served as a military hospital, with its pauper inmates temporarily transferred to the Marylebone workhouse. After the war, the institution adopted an increasingly medical orientation, with its management placed under a medical superintendent. By 1924, it was known as New End Hospital. In 1930, the site was taken over by the LCC then joined the NHS in 1948. It closed in 1986 and the buildings were converted to other uses. From 1974–2011, the mortuary building was home to the New End Theatre.

An ambulance stands outside the Hampstead workhouse during its use as a First World War military hospital.

HOLBORN

The Middlesex portion of the parish of St Andrew Holborn Below the Bars (see page 53) had two parts. In 1730, one of these – the Liberty of Saffron Hill, Hatton Garden, Ely Rents & Ely Place – opened a workhouse on Little Saffron Hill (TQ312819). It consisted of several old houses plus a new brick building. Its upper section served as a dining room, and the lower part as a work-room. In October 1731, the inmates comprised forty-six men, women and children who were occupied in spinning candlewick.[47]

The other Middlesex part, which in 1723 had become the separate parish of St George the Martyr, opened a workhouse in the 1730s on Little Gray's Inn Lane (now Mount Pleasant, TQ310820).

In 1767, the whole of the Middlesex portion of St Andrew Holborn joined to create St Andrew Holborn Above the Bars with St George the Martyr. In 1776, the Little Gray's Inn Lane workhouse could house up to 400 paupers. In 1813, the joint parishes erected a new building on the site, designed by Robert Leave.[48] In 1832, the workhouse had 454 inmates. The men were employed in picking wool, hair and oakum, and in bristle-sorting, shoemaking and tailoring. The women were occupied in winding cotton, needlework and nursing.

Holborn Poor Law Union was formed in April 1836 from the joint parishes and took over the Gray's Inn workhouse, which was greatly enlarged at a cost of £9,000 to house 700 inmates.

The Local Act parish of St Sepulchre joined the union in 1845, followed by Clerkenwell and St Luke Old Street in 1869, the latter two each adding a workhouse to the union's stock. Able-bodied inmates were then housed at Clerkenwell, and the aged and infirm at Gray's Inn Lane, while the St Luke's site on City Road became the union infirmary. In 1869–70, an accommodation shortage led the union to hire the old French Hospital in Bath Street, City Road, to house up to 200 aged and infirm inmates.

In 1877–79, a large four-storey infirmary, designed by Henry Saxon Snell, was erected on Archway Road, Highgate (TQ293870). Its unusual design featured a central building where the wards had beds placed along internal partitions at right angles to the main walls. To the north and south of this block, linked by ground-floor corridors, were male and female 'Nightingale' pavilions where beds were placed in a long row along each side of the ward.[49] The site was later known as Archway Hospital, then from 1948 as Whittington Hospital, Archway Wing. From 1999–2013, the premises housed a medical research and education facility known as the Archway Campus. It is currently undergoing redevelopment.

A ward at the Holborn Union Infirmary, Highgate, in the 1890s. Its crossways layout allowed a more compact arrangement of the beds than in a 'Nightingale' ward.

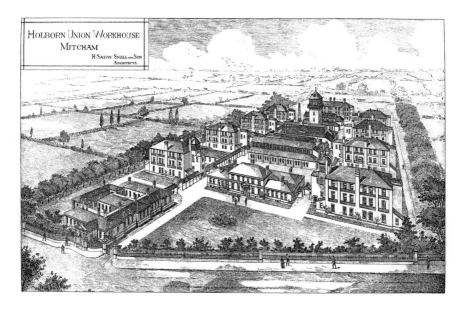

Henry Saxon Snell's pavilion-plan design for the new Holborn Union workhouse at Mitcham in 1885.

In 1870, Holborn purchased a large industrial school at Mitcham formerly run by the Southwark parish of St George the Martyr. It stood in the grounds of Eagle House, an old mansion at the west side of the High Street (now London Road, TQ278694).

In October 1885, a new pavilion-plan workhouse for 1,000 inmates was opened at Western Road, Mitcham (TQ276693), on a site adjacent to the industrial school. It was designed by Henry Saxon Snell and his son Alfred. A lodge and casual wards were situated at the main entrance. At the centre of the site, progressing from west to east, were the administrative block and boardroom, dining hall and kitchens, laundry and chapel. Ward-blocks for males were to the north and for females to the south. A covered walkway ran between all the blocks.[50] Work performed by inmates at Mitcham included corn-grinding, firewood chopping, tailoring, bricklaying, painting, plumbing, basket and mat-making. The workhouse also had its own farm to the north of the main site. The farm incorporated a gasworks from which gas was supplied to the workhouse.

During the First World War, the Mitcham workhouse was used as a military hospital, but afterwards stood empty for many years. In March 1933, following a huge explosion at a chemical works on Batsworth Road, Mitcham, the buildings were reopened to provide emergency shelter for 200 families whose houses had been damaged by the blast. The premises were later used for commercial purposes but no longer exist.

The Little Gray's Inn Lane workhouse was closed in 1894 and its inmates transferred to the St Luke's site. The premises were then rented to the St Marylebone Guardians during the rebuilding of their own workhouse. In 1902, most of the site was sold off, but a portion adjoining Little Gray's Inn Lane was kept for construction of a new casual ward to replace an existing one on Vine Street (TQ311821). In 1923, by then under MAB management, the new establishment became 'The Hostel', where genuine work-seekers could reside in more amenable conditions than usually found in casual wards.

ISLINGTON

St Mary Islington had a workhouse from 1726 in a rented house at Stroud Green. Around 1731, another workhouse was set up on Holloway Road, near Ring Cross. Both establishments were shared with Hornsey. Various other rented premises were used for the purpose, including one in 1758 on Lower Street, near the chapel. The inmates performed spinning, oakum picking and other tasks.[51] In 1777, the workhouse could house up to sixty inmates.

The parish obtained a Local Act in 1776 enabling it to administer poor relief through a board of trustees and raise money for the construction of a new workhouse. It was built the following year at the junction of Liverpool Road and Barnsbury Street (TQ314841). The three-storey brick building consisted of a central section with two wings and had a vegetable garden. It was extended in 1802, with an infirmary being included. In 1814, the 407 inmates comprised 95 men, 186 women, 67 boys, 48 girls and 11 lunatics. Male inmates picked oakum and mended local footpaths, while females were occupied in slop-work and nursing.[52]

By 1814, the parish had an 'infant poorhouse' at Ford's Green, Southgate.

Islington's Local Act status exempted it from the 1834 Act until 1867, when it was constituted as a Poor Law Parish. Up to that date, poor relief was administered by the trustees. In 1860, the Barnsbury Street workhouse could hold 477 inmates.

A *Lancet* report on the establishment in 1865 described its infirmary as a 'thoroughly bad edifice' but also praised its operation. Although the nursing was carried out by pauper inmates, they appeared to be experienced, well managed and paid up to 1s 6d a week. On the more critical side, the midwifery ward was said to be 'wretchedly cheerless', and with regard to the tramps in the casual ward, 'to bathe them is exceptional'.[53]

The Islington workhouse on St John's Road opened in 1870. Only the Guardian's roadside boardroom block now survives.

The old premises at Barnsbury Road were demolished in the 1870s and a new building containing a dispensary and relief offices was erected at the south of the site.

A new workhouse was opened in 1870 on St John's Road (now Way) in Upper Holloway. Built of yellow brick at a cost of £63,300, the design by R.H. Burden had a typical corridor-plan layout. The main building, 420ft long, had a central section containing the master's quarters and administrative offices, behind which lay a dining hall and chapel above. Male inmates were housed at the west side and females in the east. A separate infirmary with four pavilion ward-blocks lay at the rear. In 1930, the site was taken over by the LCC, becoming a PAI known as Hillside. It closed in 1972 and only the former boardroom and office block now survives.

In 1900, the union opened an 800-bed infirmary at Highgate Hill (TQ290869), a site previously occupied by the Highgate Smallpox Hospital. Designed by William Smith, the pavilion-plan layout had a central administration block connected by a long corridor to four double ward pavilions placed 100ft apart. Large bridges connecting the ward-blocks' upper floors could be used for the open-air treatment of tuberculosis patients. The laundry, mortuary and coffin store were located at the rear of the old smallpox hospital, which itself provided offices and a nurses' home.[54] In 1930, the LCC took over the site which was renamed St Mary's Hospital. Joining the NHS in 1948, it became the St Mary's wing of Whittington Hospital.

In 1853, the parish erected a children's establishment on Porter's Acre, at the east side of Hornsey Road (TQ307866). By the 1880s, it housed over 360 children.

In 1882, Islington took over the former West London Union workhouse on Cornwallis Road (see page 66).

KENSINGTON

St Mary Abbots, Kensington, had a workhouse from around 1726, perhaps on Gore Lane (now under by Jay Mews, TQ264795).[55] A Local Act in 1777 enabled money to be raised for a new workhouse at the east side of Hogmore Lane (now under Kensington Gate, TQ262794). The H-shaped building was designed by Thomas Callcott.[56] From 1818, the inmates were occupied in dressing and spinning flax.[57]

In 1832, the workhouse was very overcrowded, with 260 inmates in accommodation intended to house 160. Their work now included preparing firewood for shops and private families, making bed sackings and mats, and winding cotton for tallow chandlers.

Kensington Poor Law Union was formed in July 1837 from the parishes of Kensington, Fulham, Hammersmith, Paddington and Chelsea. The union took over four existing workhouses, with men housed at Kensington, women at Chelsea, boys at Hammersmith and girls at Fulham.

Chelsea left the union in 1841 and it was dissolved entirely in 1845. Kensington became a Poor Law Parish and adopted the name St Mary Abbots.

In 1846, the Guardians purchased a site at the east of Wright's Lane (now Marloes Road, TQ256793) on which to erect a new workhouse for 400 inmates. A competition for its design was won by Thomas Allom. His Jacobean-style red-brick building had a double-courtyard layout, with a dining hall and chapel placed at the centre between the male section at the north and female at the south. The aged and infirm were placed at the west side where they could enjoy the arcades and gardens in front of the building. A small infirmary stood at the east of the site.

In 1871, a 300-bed infirmary was erected at the west of the workhouse. Designed by Alfred Williams, the four-storey building included a new laundry and dining hall. In 1875, a chapel was erected at the north of the infirmary.

The surviving part of the former Kensington workhouse main building on Marloes Road.

In the same year, the parish achieved a notable first when Martha Merington, the first ever female Guardian, was elected to its board.

At the end of 1880, St Mary Abbots acquired the neighbouring work-house site of St Margaret & St John (see page 115). From around 1890 to 1922, the sites' combined hospital facilities operated under the name of Kensington Infirmary.

In 1893, a new administrative block was built on Marloes Road, together with a new male infirmary to its south which comprised three linked three-storey ward pavilions. The buildings were designed by Thomas W. Aldwinckle. The 1871 infirmary was then used for female inmates.

After 1922, the site was known as St Mary Abbots Hospital. The buildings suffered substantial bomb damage during the Second World War, including the demolition of the southern end of the 1847 main block, known as Stone Hall. The site has now been converted to residential use.

In 1870, the Guardians set up a labour yard and relief office at Mary Place, Notting Hill (now Avondale Park Gardens, TQ240807), where able-bodied men received out-relief in return for breaking stone. A dispensary was added in 1871 and a casual ward in 1878. In 1882, the site was converted into an able-bodied 'test' workhouse for able-bodied men from all London's unions. Inmates performed tasks such as stone-breaking, corn-grinding, and oakum-picking for fifty-five to sixty hours a week. The only hour of leisure, from 7–8 p.m., was filled with lectures from a 'Mental Instructor', at which attendance was obligatory. The diet was coarse and monotonous and smoking was forbidden. Inmates were never allowed to go out.[58] In 1904, the site became a branch workhouse for Kensington's own inmates, closing in 1913. The site is now occupied by housing.

LAMBETH

In 1726, Lambeth St Mary opened a large brick-built workhouse near Lambeth Butts (TQ308785). In 1731, its sixty inmates were employed in spinning mop yarn or knitting stockings for the inmates. The children were taught to read but not to write.[59] In 1768, new buildings were added at the west of the original house, taking its capacity in 1784 to eighty places. After further extensions in 1786 and 1805, the buildings formed three sides of a quadrangle.

In December 1835, Lambeth was constituted as a Poor Law Parish and continued using its existing workhouse on what was then known as Princes Road, now Black Prince Road. In 1866, the establishment received huge publicity after an undercover exposé of its casual ward by a journalist, James Greenwood, who gave graphic descriptions of the primitive accommodation (thirty men in a room 30ft square), the inmates, and the 'mutton broth bath' in which they were expected to bathe.[60]

Later in 1866, a *Lancet* report noted that the workhouse had an official capacity of 1,100 which, in winter, was regularly reached or even exceeded. Almost five-sixths of the inmates required medical care – a sick population equalling that of Guy's Hospital. Around seventy inmates were in the workhouse insane wards.[61]

In 1887–88, the Princes Road premises were rebuilt for use as a 'test' workhouse for 200 men and 150 women. It was solely for able-bodied inmates and had a particularly strict regime including work such as stone-breaking and oakum-picking. Each sex was segregated into three classes, according to their previous known conduct and character. Those deemed to be of bad character performed their work in isolation from one another. The building, designed by Thomas Aldwinckle, was of the plainest possible character.[62] The premises no longer exist.

In 1871–73, a new workhouse for 820 inmates was erected at Renfrew Road, Lambeth. Designed by Thomas Aldwinckle, it was one of the earliest pavilion-plan workhouses to be built in England. A central administrative block contained

The administrative block of Lambeth's Renfrew Road workhouse, latterly home to a cinema museum where Charlie Chaplin's connection to the site is documented.

the master's quarters, committee room, chapel, male and female dining rooms, kitchen, etc. Males were housed at the north of the site and females at the south. The innermost pavilions at each side housed 'able-bodied good' at their eastern end and 'able-bodied bad' at their western end. The outer ones housed the aged inmates. A corridor linked all the blocks. Some accommodation was also provided for aged married couples and a small number of children. A porter's lodge and receiving wards stood alongside the entrance on Renfrew Road.[63] A 'labour test' facility included a large stone-yard, with 150 stalls, oakum and wood picking sheds and yards, and hand corn-mills where 400 men and 200 women could gain out-relief on a daily basis.[64]

When the test workhouse opened at Princes Road in 1888, it took all the able-bodied inmates from Renfrew Road which then received only the aged and infirm.

In 1877, a new infirmary was opened on Brook Street, adjacent to the Renfrew Road site, together with casual wards on Walcott Street.

The Renfrew Road workhouse and infirmary amalgamated in 1922 as Lambeth Hospital. The site was taken over by the LCC in 1930, then joined the NHS in 1948, finally closing in 1976. By 2018, only the administration block (latterly housing a cinema museum), water tower, porter's and receiving blocks survived.

In 1898, future screen star Charles Chaplin, then aged 8, was briefly an inmate at Renfrew Road before being transferred to Lambeth's workhouse school at Elder Road, Norwood (TQ323711). Founded in 1810, the school could eventually house 576 children.[65] Most of the buildings have now been demolished.

LEWISHAM

In 1612, a house on Rushey Green was bequeathed to the Lewisham vestry for the relief of the poor.[66] In 1777, the workhouse housed up to twenty-five inmates. By 1814, the premises, nearly opposite the George Inn (TQ378742), had become run-down and overcrowded and the parish obtained a Local Act enabling it to appoint a Board of Guardians to administer poor relief. A new workhouse was erected in 1817 at the west side of Lewisham High Street (TQ378745). In 1832, the 183 inmates were aged from six months to 89 years and comprised 106 adults and 77 children.

In 1777, Plumstead had a workhouse for up to forty-five inmates. It was located on Cage Lane (now Lakedale Road), at the eastern end of Plumstead Common.

Lewisham Poor Law Union was formed in November 1836 and took over the existing Lewisham workhouse. New wards for cholera cases were added at the rear of the building.

In 1865, a *Lancet* report described the workhouse as a three-storey brick building which formed three sides of a square, enclosing male and female airing yards. At the rear were well-cultivated kitchen gardens, yards for work and laundry, accommodation for infectious cases, and a mortuary. The sick wards were generally satisfactory except for the iron bedsteads, which were only 5ft long and 2ft 5in wide. There was a total absence of water-closets in the wards and only one bath in the whole workhouse. The bath was movable and when in use, water had to be specially heated and carried to the ward where it was required. The food served to the inmates was commended for both its quality and the amount served. The nursing staff consisted only of the matron, one paid nurse, and thirteen pauper assistants, the latter all being judged by the report as unsuitable and in need of nursing themselves.[67]

Following acquisitions of land adjacent to the workhouse in 1877 and 1882, the building was extended northwards. In 1892–94, a separate infirmary building was erected at the north of the site.

The original 1817 block of the former Lewisham workhouse.

In 1868, the parishes of Charlton, Kidbrooke and Plumstead left to form part of the new Woolwich Union.

From 1904, the birth certificates for those born in the workhouse gave its address just as 390 High Street, Lewisham.

During the First World War, the site served as Lewisham Military Hospital. After the war, the institution adopted an increasingly medical orientation, with its overall management placed under a medical superintendent. In March 1920, the whole site was renamed Lewisham Hospital, now known as University Hospital, Lewisham. The 1817 block still survives.

MILE END OLD TOWN

Mile End Old Town opened a workhouse in March 1725 in a 'strong brick building near Stepney Church'. In June 1729 there were thirty-one inmates, all employed in picking oakum. They ate meat three times a week and their breakfasts and suppers were milk and bread, cheese and butter. The lower part of the building housed a charity school for twenty-one boys and ten girls.[68]

In 1803, in what was viewed as retaliation for local protests about the vestry's misuse of the poor rate, a new workhouse was opened in a house on Alderney Place, off Globe Road, Mile End (TQ356822). By 1828, 284 inmates occupied the then hopelessly overcrowded premises.[69]

In 1836, Mile End Old Town became part of Stepney Poor Law Union and the Alderney Place workhouse was used to house able-bodied men and fever patients.

In 1857, a large population increase in the area led to Mile End Old Town being constituted as a separate Poor Law Hamlet. A new workhouse was built in 1858–59 to the north of Mile End Road, next to the Jews' burial ground (TQ359825). A new road, Bancroft Road, was created to give access to the site. The building, designed by William Dobson in a plain Tudor style, housed 500 inmates. An entrance block, facing Bancroft Road, included a boardroom and offices. The T-shaped main block, three storeys high, contained the inmates' wards, dining hall and chapel. To the rear were a small infirmary and an imbeciles' block. Accommodation for up to 300 children was placed along the back of the site and included a three-storey school block, workshops, laundry, playgrounds and a separate children's infirmary. Casual wards were located near the entrance block.[70]

In 1881–83, the old infirmary and imbecile wards were replaced by a larger, pavilion-plan infirmary. It comprised a central two-storey administration block flanked by three-storey male and female ward pavilions.

In 1908, a number of the Guardians were found guilty of receiving bribes from local tradesmen and contractors. For his part in the events, former Stepney mayor, Rowland Hirst, received a £250 fine and two years in prison with hard labour.

The Tudor-style main building of the Mile End Old Town workhouse.

In 1925, Mile End Old Town joined an enlarged Stepney Union. In 1930, the workhouse premises were taken over by the LCC and became Mile End Hospital, which still operates at the site. Many of the old buildings have now been replaced.

NEWINGTON

The parish of St Mary, Newington, which included the hamlet of Walworth, opened a workhouse around 1734.[71] In 1777, the establishment, at the west side of Walworth Road (TQ324779), housed 200 inmates.

In 1814, the parish obtained a Local Act, enabling the appointment of Guardians of the Poor to administer the poor rate and rebuild or repair the workhouse which was 'insufficient for the accommodation and proper employment of the poor'.

Newington's Local Act status largely exempted it from the 1834 Act and its existing poor relief arrangements continued in operation.

In 1850, the parish erected an industrial school on Westmoreland Road (now Beaconsfield Road) in Walworth (TQ331780). When the building was completed, however, the Guardians decided to use it to house able-bodied paupers, while the children were instead placed at the North Surrey District School.[72] The new workhouse had a T-shaped main building which housed male inmates at the west side and females at the east. The dining hall and kitchens were at the centre, with a laundry to the rear on the female side, and a bakehouse and work-rooms on the male side. A separate complex of buildings to the north-west contained sick wards and lock (venereal) wards, together with a mortuary and casual wards.

In October 1869, the parish became part of the St Saviour Poor Law Union. The Westmoreland Road site then housed able-bodied women and also acted as the St Saviour Union infirmary until 1887, when a new infirmary was opened at East Dulwich.

In 1896, future screen star Charles Chaplin, then aged 7, became an inmate of the workhouse, together with his mother, Hannah, and half-brother Sydney. After three weeks, the boys were transferred to the Central London District School at Hanwell. Two months later, the children were returned to the workhouse to be met at the gate by Hannah. Desperate to see them, she had discharged the family from the workhouse. After a day spent playing in Kennington Park and visiting a coffee-shop, they returned to the workhouse to be admitted once more.

St Saviour was renamed Southwark Union in 1901. The following year, additions to the Newington workhouse included a relief office, dispensary and nurses' quarters on Boyson Road, and a block facing Westmoreland Road for infants and aged married couples. The institution then housed 1,240 inmates.[73]

In 1930, the LCC took over the site which became Newington Lodge PAI. The premises later provided short-term accommodation for homeless families and appeared in the 1966 TV play *Cathy Come Home*. The buildings were demolished around 1970.

PADDINGTON

Paddington opened a workhouse around 1736.[74] In 1777, it could house twelve inmates. The parish subsequently farmed out its paupers but a new workhouse was established in 1820 on Harrow Road. In 1832, its inmates comprised seven men, twenty-four women and nineteen children. Their only occupation was housework and needlework. Refractory paupers were farmed out with William Perry at Islington.[75]

In July 1837, despite its objections, Paddington became part of Kensington Poor Law Union and the Harrow Road workhouse was closed. Following the disbanding of the union in 1845, Paddington was constituted as a Poor Law Parish and began construction of a new workhouse, situated next to the Lock Hospital on Harrow Road (TQ252819).

The new workhouse had a T-shaped main building facing towards the Grand Junction Canal, which the site bordered. Females were housed at the west side of the building and males at the east, with the children's accommodation placed at the front. The dining hall, also used as a chapel, lay at the centre rear of the block. A separate infirmary ran parallel with the main block at the north of the site. In 1886, a 284-bed infirmary was erected between the workhouse and the Lock Hospital.

In 1914, the inmates were transferred to the Marylebone workhouse and the site was used as a military hospital which specialised in the care of limbless men.[76]

After the war, the institution adopted an increasingly medical orientation, with its overall management placed under its medical superintendent. In 1921, it adopted the name Paddington Hospital and a nurses' home was opened in the same year. Links were also developed with St Mary's Hospital, Paddington.

Paddington's parish infirmary was squeezed into a narrow strip of land alongside the workhouse.

The LCC took over the establishment in 1930. After joining the NHS in 1948, it became Paddington General Hospital in 1954, then from 1968 was the Harrow Road branch of St Mary's Hospital. It closed in 1986 and the buildings have since been demolished. Elmfield Way now occupies the site.

POPLAR

Poplar, originally a hamlet in the parish of Stepney, may have had a workhouse in the 1720s in a cottage on the High Street. In 1735, a workhouse was opened in three leased houses at the north side of the High Street. It moved in 1757 to premises on the south side of the High Street, which were extended the following year. Part of the frontage was taken over in 1771 to house a new town hall.[77] In 1777, the workhouse could house sixty inmates.

A Local Act in 1813 enabled poor relief in the hamlet to be administered by a board of trustees. In 1815, a new four-storey wing was erected at the east of the workhouse, followed in 1817 by a replacement of the buildings facing the High Street, the architect in both cases being James Walker.[78]

Bromley St Leonard's had a workhouse which in 1777 housed fifty-six inmates. By 1804, its indoor poor were being farmed.[79]

Stratford-le-Bow's workhouse held forty inmates. It was located to the north-east of St Mary's Church on Bow Road (TQ376830) in a 'mansion of some antiquity'.[80]

Poplar Poor Law Union, comprising Poplar, Bromley and Stratford-le-Bow, was formed in December 1836 and retained the existing Poplar workhouse. Subsequent additions included separate children's accommodation, a male infirm ward, and a casual ward with adjoining stone-breaking yard. The union had an infirmary on Upper North Street (TQ374811), originally used as an isolation hospital during the cholera epidemic of 1831–32 and enlarged during another outbreak in 1849.

A PLB inspection in 1866 found irremediable defects in the workhouse premises and recommended immediate closure of the infirmary site. It proposed that a new workhouse, with proper hospital facilities, be built elsewhere.[81] The Guardians, however, decided to reconstruct the High Street site, though retaining the 1817 front block. A total of eighteen new buildings were erected, the principal departments, mostly of four storeys, were linked by a corridor running across the site. There were two large ward-blocks for adults (women at the east and men at the west), with separate buildings for children, infants, lunatics and probationers. A dining hall lay at the centre of the site, with a Gothic-style chapel to its rear. The architect was John W. Morris.[82]

A men's ward block at Poplar workhouse in about 1902.

During the workhouse rebuilding, construction was also taking place of the Poplar and Stepney Sick Asylum, at Devon's Row, Bow (TQ379824). Opened in August 1871, it provided 572 beds for the sick and infirm from the two unions.

From 1871–82, the High Street site acted as a 'test' workhouse for able-bodied paupers who endured a strict regime and hard manual labour in return for a subsistence allowance for their families. Spare capacity was offered to other metropolitan unions but was increasingly used by them to get rid of undesirable or troublesome applicants, including the aged and infirm. During this period, Poplar had an arrangement with the Stepney Union to house its other classes of inmate.

In 1930, the LCC took over the workhouse site. The buildings were severely damaged during the Blitz in 1940 and the inmates transferred elsewhere. The site then became a supplies depot, finally being demolished in 1960. The Devon's Row hospital was renamed St Andrew's Hospital and was demolished in 2008.

In 1896, a casual ward was erected at St Leonard Street, Bromley (TQ380825).

In 1897, Poplar took over the former Forest Gate District School on Forest Lane, Forest Gate (TQ399852). It was used as a training school until 1907, then from 1908 until its sale in 1911, became a branch workhouse for able-bodied paupers.

In 1907, the Guardians erected training schools for 700 children on a 100-acre site at Rayleigh Road, Hutton, Essex (TQ621953). Arranged around a large central green, the facilities included cottage-homes-style accommodation, a swimming bath, gymnasium, workshops and training laundry. The site continued in use until 1982. Most of the buildings have now been demolished.

In 1904, the union set up a labour colony on a 200-acre farm near Laindon, Essex (TQ663884). Unemployed able-bodied men were admitted as workhouse inmates, while their wives and families received out-relief. The colony provided productive activities – farm work instead of stone breaking and oakum picking – and encouraged self-sufficiency. The experiment was not successful, however, with discipline being poor and little labour performed by the inmates. It closed in 1912 but the site was retained as accommodation for able-bodied male paupers.

ROTHERHITHE

The parish of St Mary, Rotherhithe, opened a workhouse in 1729 on what is now Lower Road, opposite the southern end of Neptune Street (TQ351793). Its inmates – eighteen adults and thirty-two children – were employed in picking oakum.[83]

Rotherhithe was constituted as a Poor Law Parish in February 1836 and continued using the Lower Road workhouse. The oldest part, facing to the east, was used for the able-bodied and for offices. A new block, added to the west in 1837, was occupied by the old and infirm, and by the midwifery and nursery wards. A new infirmary was erected in 1864, away from the other buildings, in what had previously been the garden.

A *Lancet* report in 1865 found much to criticise. The infirmary, though new and well equipped, had only one paid nurse. She was assisted by four pauper assistants aged from 60 to 75, none of whom was 'physically or mentally qualified for the duties of nursing'. The wards for the aged and infirm and the lying-in women had no nurses and their sanitary facilities were 'disgraceful'.[84]

In 1868, the MAB set up the Rotherhithe Sick Asylum District, which comprised the St Olave Union and the parishes of St Mary Magdalen, Bermondsey and St Mary, Rotherhithe. However, the new hospital required by the new scheme was felt to be too expensive and the district was reconstituted as an enlarged St Olave Poor Law Union (see page 121).

ST GEORGE HANOVER SQUARE

A parish workhouse for St George Hanover Square was erected in 1726 on Mount Street, Westminster (TQ285806). Designed by Thomas Phillips and Benjamin Timbrell, the building was plain in appearance, three storeys in height, and with a street frontage of around 160ft. The ground floor had a work-room at the centre, kitchen and dining rooms in one wing and charity schools for boys and girls in the other. The two upper floors had living and sleeping accommodation for up to 200 inmates.[85] Those that were able spun mop yarn or picked oakum, while the sick were nursed in an infirmary. The children were taught to read, write and say their catechism, and also received training for future employment.[86]

The workhouse was extended in 1743 and again in 1772. By 1777, it was one of the largest in the country, housing 700 inmates. In 1786–88, the building was further enlarged and additional premises were purchased on Fulham Road, Little Chelsea (TQ264777), to house children and lunatics.[87]

The parish obtained a Local Act in 1753 enabling it to appoint Governors and Directors of the Poor to administer poor relief. Its Local Act status subsequently exempted it from the 1834 Act.

In 1834, the Commissioners of Sewers were told that owing to the Little Chelsea workhouse being some considerable distance from the nearest sewer, its premises were in a dreadful state. Cholera had broken out and several paupers had died.[88]

In 1853–56, a new workhouse was erected at the Little Chelsea site. It housed female paupers, children and married couples, with male paupers remaining at Mount Street. Its new school building accommodated up to 300 children. It had a spacious schoolroom, also used as a chapel for the whole establishment, an infants' school and dormitory, a large dining room, lavatories, workshops for shoemakers and tailors, and large airing grounds equipped with gymnastic apparatus. The workhouse inmates were divided into classes, namely able-bodied, infirm, bedridden, infectious and infirmary cases, and those in suckling wards. The classes never came into contact, each having a separate staircase, with a portable bath, sink, with hot and cold water, and water closets on every floor. The married couples' department housed twelve aged couples, each having their own dormitory. Their common day room had a large open fireplace, with two armchairs and a table to each couple, and closets for their books, etc. They also had a large well-stocked garden as an airing ground.[89]

In 1870, the parish became part of the new St George's Union, which took over the Mount Street and Fulham Road sites (see page 105).

ST GEORGE IN THE EAST

In 1723, St George in the East opened a workhouse in a large warehouse on Virginia Street, near Ratcliff Highway (TQ343804). In June 1731, it had sixty inmates who were mainly employed in picking oakum. Their diet included meat four times a week.[90] The workhouse subsequently moved to the east side of Princes Street (now Raine Street and Choppins Court, TQ349804). In 1777, it housed up to 600 inmates.

On 5 November 1823, a serious fire broke out in an oakum-picking room. Over 700 inmates were evacuated but the bodies of four women were later found in the dormitories over the oakum room, suffocated by smoke. One had apparently escaped in a state of nudity, but modesty had caused her to return for her clothes.

In 1832, the workhouse contained 175 men, 244 women, 144 boys, 134 girls and 13 infants at breast. Those who were able were employed in weaving, shoemaking, tailoring, willow-plaiting, oakum picking and needlework.

In March 1836, St George in the East was constituted as a Poor Law Parish. It continued to use its existing workhouse, which was enlarged in 1838.

A report in 1866 described the buildings as being in four sections: a very old part, which included two sick wards; a relatively new part, where the men's sick wards were located; a detached new building placed, improperly, in the middle of the yard, containing female venereal wards, imbeciles and sick children; and a range called the Stone Buildings, in which the aged and infirm, the sick, and those with 'the itch' and offensive cases were placed. There were 770 inmates, of whom 30 were able-bodied (all women), 36 imbeciles, and 225 sick. The report recommended that the very old part should be demolished and rebuilt.[91] The 1875 Ordnance Survey map indicates that males were housed at the north of the site and females at the centre, with the new infirmary at the south. A males' ward, offices and kitchens lay at the east, along Silver Street (now Penang Street). At the west side of Princes Street were receiving wards, a dispensary, casual wards, workshops and woodsheds.

In 1895, a new casual ward was opened on Raymond Street, Wapping (TQ347801), to deal with a large influx of casuals to the area, which had necessitated some of them being housed in the main workhouse. The new cellular-style building had three storeys and accommodated 102 inmates.[92]

In 1925, St George in the East joined the Stepney Union and the workhouse closed. After being taken over by the LCC in 1930, the building became the St George in the East Hospital. The hospital closed in 1956 and for a short time housed refugees from the Hungarian uprising. The building was demolished in 1963.

In 1851, the parish opened an industrial school at the east side of Gipsy Lane (now Green Street), Plashet (TQ412842). It accommodated 150 boys, 120 girls and 80 infants. After closing in 1927, the building was used as a cinema until 1983.

ST GEORGE'S

The St George's Poor Law Union was formed in March 1870 from the parishes of St Margaret & St John Westminster and St George Hanover Square. The new union inherited the former's workhouse on Wright's Lane and the latter's premises on Mount Street and on Fulham Road.

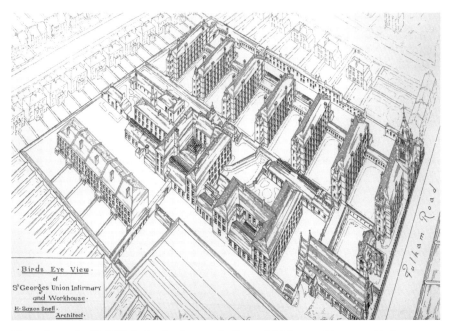

Henry Saxon Snell's 1878 design for the new St George's Union workhouse and infirmary on Fulham Road.

The Fulham Road entrance block of the St George's workhouse in about 1915.

In 1876, the union acquired extra land adjacent to the Fulham Road site, allowing the buildings to be extended and a separate infirmary erected, all designed by Henry Saxon Snell. Additions to the workhouse included new offices, receiving wards, dining hall, blocks for able-bodied inmates and married couples, and a 600-seat chapel. The infirmary consisted of seven four-storey pavilions, all linked by a ground-floor corridor. Each pavilion contained a twenty-eight bed ward on each floor.[93] The infirmary housed 808 patients in all, the largest number of any London hospital at that date.[94] In 1880, the Wright's Lane site was sold to the parish of St Mary Abbots.

In 1895, a *British Medical Journal* report on the Fulham Road site found many faults. The wards were overcrowded. The old and infirm, 60 in the male wards and 153 in the female, were looked after by just two nurses assisted by pauper assistants who, it was alleged, took advantage of those in their care. In the dormitories, cleaners were observed trying to 'eradicate the vermin by burning out the nests and eggs in the interstices of the bedsteads'. The inmates often preferred to use their chamber pots in preference to the washbasins for washing themselves. The laundry, where more than 16,000 items were washed each week, was poorly equipped.[95]

The Fulham Road site was renamed St Stephen's Hospital in 1925. It was taken over by the LCC in 1930 and joined the NHS in 1948. It continued in operation until 1989, when it was replaced by the new Chelsea and Westminster Hospital.

In 1883, when the old Mount Street workhouse site's lease ended, the land's owner, the Duke of Westminster, offered the union an alternative location at 20 Wallis's Yard (now Warwick Row, TQ290794). The site was used to erect a new casual ward and receiving house, the latter being used to examine new applicants for admission to the main workhouse. The establishment closed in 1921.

St George's was renamed the City of Westminster Union in 1913.

ST GEORGE THE MARTYR SOUTHWARK

The Southwark parish of St George the Martyr erected a workhouse in 1729 at the north side of Mint Street (TQ322799). In October 1731, there were sixty-eight inmates. Those who were able spun mop yarn, and yarn for stockings, which were knitted by the women. The children were also taught to read and to say their catechism. The establishment was run by a married couple, the husband being a wool dealer who made a good profit from the inmates' work. The spinners themselves received 1*d* in the shilling of the income, while those occupied in household work could receive 'encouragement money'.[96] In 1777, the workhouse housed up to 220 inmates.

A new building was erected on the site in 1782. It comprised three blocks arranged in a U-shaped layout. In 1832, there were about 360 inmates, mostly old men and women. Those able to work were employed in oakum picking, willow plaiting, needlework and hair-picking.

St George became a Poor Law Parish in October 1835, one of the earliest Boards of Guardians to be formed in the metropolis. Although the parish had two Local Acts relating to poor relief, neither had established a new adminis-trative body and so did not qualify it to continue as a Local Act administration.

The Mint Street workhouse continued in use. A visitor to one of the wards in 1836 described it as a small room, about 25ft by 20ft, containing seven double beds, and occupied by thirteen old and decrepit women. The inmates took their meals in the room, but due to the lack of tables and chairs, the food was eaten on the beds.[97] Additions to the buildings were made in 1844 and 1859.

In September 1865, a *Lancet* report on the workhouse portrayed the site as being surrounded with every possible nuisance, including bone-boilers, and grease and cat-gut manufactories. The building was described as a brick structure of three storeys, forming three sides of a square, while its south front

The St George the Martyr workhouse, Mint Street, Southwark.

consisted of low buildings used as offices. Other than a division of male and female wards, and the separation of the 'foul' (venereal) cases, classification of the sick inmates was lacking. Sanitary facilities in the sick wards were inadequate and neglected. A single water closet sometimes served two or three wards – in one case, thirty men used one closet in which there had been no water for more than a week. There were several patients with offensive discharges. A cancer case where no disinfectant was being used rendered the room almost unbearable to the other inmates. The sick and infirm, who numbered between 200 and 300, were attended by pauper nurses, who received up to 2s a week, meat and beer daily, and dry tea and sugar. When washing those who were incapable of doing it for themselves, the nurses' favourite utensils were chamber pots. Intemperance was also common among the nurses. The female tramp ward was a miserable room, foul and dirty, with poor light and ventilation, the floor being simply bedded with straw. There was no water closet, but a large tub was placed in the room. Women staying in the ward frequently developed typhus fever. The report concluded that the workhouse should be condemned.[98]

In 1868, the parish became part of the St Saviour Union, which took over the Mint Street site. Despite the criticisms it had received, the establishment continued in use until the 1920s, then became a council depot. A park now covers the site.

From about 1830 until 1860, the parish housed its infant poor in premises at the east side of Lewisham High Street (TQ379744). In 1856, a large industrial school was erected in the grounds of Eagle House at the west of the High Street in Upper Mitcham (TQ278694). The site was sold to the Holborn Union in 1870.

ST GILES IN THE FIELDS & ST GEORGE BLOOMSBURY

St Giles in the Fields opened a workhouse in 1675 in Browne's Gardens, near the parish church (TQ299811). The inmates, like other parish paupers, wore brass badges. When the building was demolished in 1680, perhaps due to the building of Seven Dials, several alternative properties were investigated, including one 'near Whetstone'.[99]

In 1725, a new workhouse was opened at the north side of Short's Gardens, Holborn (TQ302813), with its entrance on Vinegar Yard. Matthew Marryott was engaged to manage the establishment. An infirmary was added in 1727. In

July 1728, there were 238 inmates in twenty-three wards, containing a total of 157 beds. They were served by fourteen nurses and eight assistants.[100] The daily routine began with a rising bell at 5 a.m. Work began at 6 a.m. in summer or 8 a.m. in winter. To encourage their labour, inmates received a payment for various tasks; for example, 1*d* for knitting a pair of stockings, or 2*d* for spinning a pound of flax. Unskilled work such as helping in the kitchen or laundry could earn from 1*d* to 3*d* a week. The inmates' diet was very similar to that at Greenwich (page 77), also run by Marryott. Punishable offences included swearing, fighting, bringing strong liquor onto the premises, coming back from church late or drunk, or smoking in bed.

The premises gradually expanded to incorporate adjacent properties including several houses and an inn, resulting in a very irregular collection of buildings. In 1777, up to 520 inmates could be accommodated.

In 1731, part of St Giles separated to form the new parish of St George, Bloomsbury. The two parishes shared use of the existing workhouse. In 1776, it housed 530 inmates, who were employed in winding silk and picking oakum, while the children knitted stockings for the use of the house.

In 1832, the inmates numbered 816, who were assigned to tasks as follows. Men: one clerk, seven overlookers, eleven gatesmen, six cooks, one servant, two washing, four cleaning beds, four carpenters, three bricklayers, three plasterers, three painters, eight tailors, four shoemakers, twenty-eight picking oakum, hair, etc., twelve wood-chopping. Women: four overlookers, fifty-one nurses, three cooks, four servants, thirty washing, fifty-six needlework, forty picking oakum, hair, etc., eighteen wood-chopping. Boys: three clerks, three gatesmen, one servant, two carpenters, three tailors, eight shoemakers, thirty-four making hooks and eyes. Girls: eight nurses, nineteen at needlework.

Local Acts obtained in 1774 and 1830 allowed the parishes to be largely exempt from the 1834 Act. The old workhouse continued in use, with the addition in 1844 of a 105-bed infirmary at the north of Vinegar Lane.

A *Lancet* report in 1865 described the buildings as brick-built and consisting of detached and connected sections, three or four storeys high. There were numerous criticisms of the medical provision. The wards were cramped and the ventilation was the worst the inspectors had ever seen. The iron bedsteads were too short and too narrow, and the bedding was ragged and dirty. The one paid nurse, a 63-year-old female, was assisted by fourteen pauper helpers; two night nurses were selected from those who performed the day-nursing. The infirm wards, at the north of the site, contained 100 aged inmates and were dark and poorly ventilated, with worn-out and dirty bedding. Much of the dirt came from coal being delivered into the cellars through holes in the floors of the basement wards. On the more positive side, the inmates' food and drink were commended.[101]

In 1868, St Giles & St George were constituted as a single Poor Law Parish. A new infirmary, designed by W. and A. Beresford Pite, was erected in 1888 at the south of the workhouse site, facing Short's Gardens. The square, five-storey tower had administrative functions on the ground floor, with separate staircases for males and females leading to the upper floors. On the first and second floors were wards for imbecile inmates, including two padded rooms. The third and fourth floors accommodated itch and bad leg cases.[102]

In 1914, the parish became part of Holborn Poor Law Union and the workhouse was closed. During the First World War, the building became the Endell Street Refuge, accommodating destitute enemy aliens, then sick refugees. As Dudley House, it then housed Customs and Excise Offices. The buildings were demolished in about 1980.

Around 1878, casual wards were erected at 25–27 Macklin Street (TQ304814).

The St Giles & St George workhouse infirmary erected in 1888 on Shorts Gardens.

ST JAMES WESTMINSTER

In 1688, St James opened an establishment to house the old and infirm poor at Salter's Court (now Smith's Court, TQ295808). In 1721, it moved to New Street (now Ingestre Place, TQ294809) and continued in operation until 1748.

In 1725, the parish erected a workhouse on Poland Street (TQ293812). The spacious, brick-built premises were designed by a carpenter named John Ludby. In September 1731, there were 302 inmates, about 80 of whom were children. Those that were able worked at spinning jersey, mop yarn and flax, with the jersey and flax then being woven by any weavers among the inmates. The women and girls also knitted stockings for the inmates, while the men carded wool or assisted the cook in tending the fires and coppers. The children were taught to read and to say their catechism. There were four wards for women, two for men, one for boys and one for girls, each containing eighteen beds. At that date, the house was so full that nine beds were placed on the stair landings and other open spaces, making over 150 beds in all. There was also an infirmary ward and a lying-in ward.[103]

Its chaotic management and high inmate death rate caused the workhouse to be closed in 1742. It reopened in 1762 after a Local Act placed the administration of poor relief under a Board of Guardians elected from the local ratepayers.

In 1776, the workhouse could house 650 inmates and was one of the largest in the country. The building was 146ft long, 40ft deep, 58ft high, and

A women's dayroom at the Poland Street workhouse of St James Westminster in 1809. The inmates' activities include sewing and spinning.

consisted of thirty-two apartments. Inmates were employed in needlework, quilting, carding wool, spinning yarn, making regimentals and winding silk. The children were occupied in reading, writing, needlework, knitting, spinning, opening horse-hair, and making lace. On the workhouse payroll were a chaplain (£20 a year), a clerk (£40), a master (£30 and 5 per cent of the labour profits), matron (£21), schoolmaster (£20), schoolmistress (£10), lace mistress (£7 7s and 5 per cent of the profits), cook (£10), with porter, nurses and petty servants paid weekly at the discretion of the governors.

St James' Local Act status largely exempted it from the 1834 Act and it continued to operate as an independent administration.

In 1851, the parish bought 20 acres of Wandsworth Common west of St James's Road (now St James's Drive, TQ277732) for the erection of an industrial school. The E-shaped building was designed by Charles Lee. Most of the boys were occupied on the land to fit them for employment in the countryside or the colonies.

In 1868, St James joined St Anne's Soho to form the new Westminster Union which took over the Poland Street workhouse and the Wandsworth school. In 1871–72, the union built new offices at 49–52 Poland Street, with workhouse wards on the upper floors.

In 1884, the industrial school was extended, then providing almost 200 places. The site was sold in 1904 to the Wandsworth Union for use as a workhouse.

In 1913, the Westminster, Strand and St George's Unions merged to form the City of Westminster Union. The Poland Street workhouse was closed and on 5 September 1914 was taken over by the MAB to house wartime refugees. When the first arrivals were 200 Russian Jews, the premises was handed over to the Jewish authorities and continued in operation as the Poland Street Institute for Jews.[104]

In 1925, the buildings were reconstructed as a garage. A multi-storey car park now occupies the site.

ST LUKE OLD STREET

St Luke Old Street was created in 1733 from the Middlesex part of the parish of St Giles without Cripplegate (see page 58). The new parish retained the existing workhouse at the north side of Featherstone Street, Bunhill Fields (TQ326823), erected in 1724. In September 1731, it housed 110 old men and women, and 53 boys and girls, who were chiefly employed in picking oakum, knitting and spinning. The inmates' working day was 6 a.m. till 7 p.m. in summer and 7 a.m. till 5 p.m. in winter. Bedtime was 9 a.m. in summer and 8 p.m. in winter. Breakfast was from 9 till 9.30 a.m., dinner from 1 till 2 p.m. and supper at 7 p.m. in summer and 6 p.m. in winter. The mistress of the workhouse was required to see that the children's heads were combed every day, that they were taught to read and instructed in spinning or knitting. Any inmate refusing to work or misbehaving by fighting or making a disturbance was placed on half-rations or on bread and water for two or three days, then taken before a magistrate to be sent to the house of correction. No distilled liquors were to be brought into the house and the smoking of tobacco was also prohibited. On Wednesdays and Fridays after break-fast, the psalms for the day, a chapter in the Old and New Testaments, the Litany, and other prayers for the day, were read by the master. The same were to be read at 9 a.m. on Sundays and those who were able attended church. Any inmate found loitering in the fields or begging could be sent to Bridewell.[105]

In 1749, St Luke obtained a Local Act for 'better ordering and regulating' its poor. By 1776, the workhouse could hold 400 inmates, who were employed in spinning cotton and jersey, picking oakum and slop-work.

In 1782, following the expiry of the lease at Featherstone Street, a second Local Act enabled the parish to spend £2,000 on building a new workhouse at the junction of City Road and Shepherdess Walk, Islington (TQ323829). In 1832, the workhouse inmates comprised 174 men, 252 women, 111 boys and 56 girls. The men picked oakum, the women and girls did slop needlework, and the boys and some women wound silks, cotton or worsted. Hard workers could receive gratuities of money or provisions. The workhouse had separate wings for males and females, with the aged and impotent housed in a separate infirmary.

A surviving 1871 ward block at the St Luke's Shepherdess Walk site.

St Luke's Local Act status largely exempted it from the 1834 Act and its existing poor relief administration and workhouse continued in operation.

In 1869, St Luke joined the Holborn Union and the Shepherdess Walk premises became the union's hospital. In 1870–71, new female wards for 450 patients were erected at the north of the site. Designed by Henry Saxon Snell, the forty-bed wards had a novel layout with rows of eight beds ranged opposite one another along internal transverse partitions.

There was a major reconstruction of the Shepherdess Walk side of the premises in 1877–79. The new four-storey building, housing 930 inmates, was again designed by Henry Saxon Snell and on similar lines to the earlier female block. The central portion contained receiving wards, master's offices and residence, lying-in wards, and dormitories for the able-bodied paupers who assisted in the work of the establishment. The wings on either side housed male and female infirm inmates.[106]

In 1916, the establishment was renamed the Holborn and Finsbury Institution. It was taken over by the LCC in 1930 for the care of the chronic sick and renamed St Matthew's Hospital in 1936. The following year, it became a 627-bed general hospital, ending its association with Poor Law patients. On 8 October 1940, the old south ward-block suffered a direct hit from a high explosive bomb, which killed many patients and some members of staff.

In 1948, the hospital joined the NHS. In 1952, visitors from the King Edward's Hospital Fund for London described the establishment as 'a dump for the chronic sick ... patients still being accommodated in great 40-bedded wards'.[107] The establishment finally closed in 1986 and most of the buildings demolished. A section of the 1871 ward-block was converted to flats.

ST MARGARET & ST JOHN WESTMINSTER

St Margaret opened a workhouse in 1726 at Little Almnery, north of the present-day corner of Great Smith Street and Abbey Orchard Street (TQ299794). In September 1731, the 326 inmates included about 200 children. The old people picked oakum. Women that were able spun jersey and mop yarn, or flax for sheeting and shifts, while others knitted stockings for the inmates. The children were taught to spin, to read, and to say their catechism.[108]

In 1727, the southern part of the parish separated to form the new parish of St John the Evangelist. The two parishes operated jointly in matters such as poor relief and use of the workhouse. In 1752, they obtained a Local Act enabling the appointment of Governors and Directors of the Poor to administer poor relief.

The parishes' Local Act status largely exempted them from the 1834 Act and they continued with their existing poor relief arrangements. By the 1840s, the workhouse buildings had become very dilapidated and the Westminster Improvement Commissioners demanded their demolition as part of a scheme to create Victoria Street. When a new site in Westminster proved impossible to find, the commissioners offered to fund the erection of two new workhouses. The first, to house 650 inmates, was at the south of the St Mary Abbots workhouse on Wright's Lane (now Marloes Road), Kensington (TQ256793). The second, at the corner of what are now Petty France and Buckingham Gate (TQ294794), was to provide offices, casual wards and some accommodation for the sick. The old workhouse continued in use until its closure and demolition in 1852.

The workhouse at Kensington was designed by H.A. Hunt and was Italianate in style. The front block, facing Marloes Road, had a three-storey central portion containing an entrance archway, porter's lodge and waiting room. Two-storey wings at each side housed the children's schools and dormitories, boys at the north and girls at the south. The south-facing main building was three storeys high, housing males at the west and females at the east. The cross-wing at the west contained the chapel, while that at the east included accommodation for eight married couples. To the rear, a long, single-storey block had the dining hall at its centre, a laundry on the women's side, and tailors', shoemakers' and carpenters' workshops on the men's side. An infirmary and lying-in wards lay at the south-east of the main building. The south of the site was laid out to gardens. Unusually for its time, the institution had gas lighting and a mains water supply. Its facilities also included sixteen baths, which some of the committee thought rather excessive for 650 inmates.[109]

In 1861, the dreadful state of relations among the staff at the Kensington workhouse was revealed after the schoolmaster's wife, Mrs Bernell, claimed that the matron, Eliza Burridge, had tried to poison her. After a PLB inquiry revealed the soap-opera-like intrigues that had gone on, the matron was dismissed.

In April 1866, a *Lancet* report on conditions at the parishes' two establishments found much to criticise.[110] At Kensington, the infirmary was overcrowded, badly ventilated, and one of the wards suffered the daily noise of inmates' stone-breaking outside its windows. Some of the water closets were badly maintained. There was no regular night nurse in the infirmary and patients were locked in at night, with no fires or hot water, and no bell to summon help if needed. Despite the original intention, no casual wards were provided at the Petty France site and casuals had to walk 3 miles to Kensington, where the arrangements for housing them were 'disgraceful'. The Petty France building, it was noted, had been 'condemned as thoroughly unfit for its purposes, and is to be pulled down'.

In 1870, the parishes joined St George Hanover Square to form the St George's Union (page 105). The Kensington site was sold to St Mary Abbots in 1880.

ST MARTIN IN THE FIELDS

In 1665, St Martin in the Fields erected a workhouse in the parish churchyard. In 1672, the vestry was found guilty of the 'scandalous offence' of letting the vaults as wine cellars, possibly by the parish-owned King's Head alehouse in St Martin's Lane. The workhouse appears to have been little used, and in 1683 it was let until such time as demand justified the opening of a new establishment.[111]

Its successor was erected in 1725 at the west side of the churchyard, facing what were then Hemming's Row and Castle Street (TQ300806). In September 1731, there were 344 inmates. The elderly that were able were employed in spinning and carding. The boys spun mop yarn and the girls knitted stockings for the inmates.

The parish obtained a Local Act in 1770 enabling it to rebuild the workhouse. This took place in 1772–73, extending the building's footprint to the south along Duke's Court. In 1777, the workhouse could house up to 700 inmates, making it among the largest in the country.

In 1797, there were 473 adults and 100 children in residence, mainly employed in spinning flax, picking hair and carding wool. Breakfast each day was bread and butter with milk pottage, or sweetened and spiced water-gruel on Fridays. Dinner on Sunday was 6oz meat without bone; Monday and Wednesday, pease soup; Tuesday and Thursday, beef and greens; Friday, barley gruel with milk; and Saturday, 1lb plum pudding. Supper every day was bread and cheese or butter. Each person received a daily ration of 14oz bread and a quart of beer. Occasional treats include boiled mutton with potatoes, pease and beans with bacon, and mackerel and salmon.[112] Inmates were allowed out on Tuesdays and Thursdays by forfeiting their provisions for the day, while those staying indoors were allowed one penny in lieu of the beef. At the same date, about eighty pauper children were out at nurse in the countryside. At the age of 7 or 8, they were taken into the workhouse, taught to read, then put out as apprentices three or four years later.[113]

In 1835, St Martin's was constituted as a Poor Law Parish and continued to use the Hemming's Row workhouse.

In 1865, *The Lancet* rated the establishment as one of the very worst of its kind, and its building as hopelessly bad. The whole workhouse was described as a gloomy, prisonlike structure, forming an irregular four-sided enclosure with the infirmary occupying the south side. The sick wards were dark and badly ventilated, and the beds 'lumpy and comfortless'. The washing facilities were 'extremely deficient' and the water closets 'decidedly bad'. The tramp wards were 'abominable' – the one for males, in which up to twenty men slept, was completely underground, with just one window, closely grated, and had a 'concentrated vagrant-stink'.[114]

In 1868, St Martin's was absorbed by the Strand Poor Law Union. Its workhouse was demolished in 1871 to make way for an extension to the National Gallery.

ST MARYLEBONE

In 1730, St Marylebone rented a property to house pauper infants and their nurses. From 1736, the parish's poor were farmed at 2*s* a head per week in the former Golden Lion alehouse in Marylebone Passage (TQ292814).[115]

A new workhouse was built in 1750–52 opposite the south end of Northumberland Street (now Luxborough Street, TQ281817). It was originally run by a contractor. The first, Francis Parent, was dismissed as a result of his drunkenness, frequent absences, misappropriation of supplies, and the discovery of one of his sons in bed with a female inmate.[116]

The size of the building soon proved inadequate. It also became infested with rats from sewers under the adjacent burial ground. By 1772, 220 inmates were occupying accommodation designed for forty. Two extra storeys were added and the former Neptune public house was hired to house the sick. In 1774, the vestry proposed the construction of a large new workhouse. A local land-owner, the Duke of Portland, offered a site at the south of the recently laid-out Marylebone Road (TQ281819). The scheme required a Local Act, obtained in 1775, which also created the Directors and Guardians of the Poor. The new building, designed by one of the Guardians, Alexander Allen, accommodated up to 1,000 inmates. The two-storey premises included a main block running north–south along Northumberland Street, with separate blocks at each end running east–west. In 1776, nearly 300 inmates were transferred from the old building to their new quarters. In 1786, a chapel was added at the west of the site, to complete a quadrangle. The old workhouse was retained for a while as an infirmary, but its size and location led to periodic fever outbreaks, such as one in 1791 when the matron and apothecary died. In 1792, a new 300-bed infirmary block was built at the north-west of the new workhouse and the old building was then demolished.[117]

St Marylebone was opposed to the 1834 Act and its Local Act status enabled it to retain its existing poor relief administration.

At the end of 1846, pressure on the workhouse was at an all-time high, largely fuelled by an influx of refugees from the famine in Ireland. After

An 1866 drawing of St Marylebone workhouse by an inmate 'W.A.D.'

reaching a peak of 2,264 inmates, the workhouse population levelled off at just under 2,000.[118]

In 1856, the master, Richard Ryan, was dismissed after being found guilty of having beaten several young female inmates. His departure was celebrated in a street ballad entitled 'The Women Flogger's Lament of Marylebone Workhouse!'

In 1865, *The Lancet* described the workhouse buildings as old, badly organised and in need of replacement. The duties assigned to the medical officer were said to be impossibly heavy and he needed at least three resident medical assistants.[119] Despite these criticisms, the workhouse was rated by the journal as one of London's better institutions.

In January 1867, ice on the frozen Regent's Park Lake gave way and 200 skaters fell into the freezing water. Witnessing the event, the workhouse master, George Douglas, immediately organised the transport of survivors back to the institution for medical attention. Forty recovered bodies were also taken to the workhouse.

Following the 1867 Metropolitan Poor Act, St Marylebone became a Poor Law Parish. In the same year, a series of major building works began with temporary casual wards. Designed by Henry Saxon Snell, these were fitted with rows of narrow 'coffin' beds. In 1868, a new boardroom, offices, and female aged and infirm wards were erected on Northumberland Street. In 1878, a three-storey

The Marylebone Road frontage of the St Marylebone workhouse in 1900.

cellular casuals' block was opened at the west of the site. Accommodation for ten aged married couples was erected in 1887 overlooking the Paddington Street burial ground, by then converted to a recreation ground. A new block for 240 able-bodied females was added at the south-west of the site in 1888.[120]

Further new building in 1897–1901 comprised two five-storey blocks for aged and infirm males on Marylebone Road, a two-storey block for able-bodied men at the west of the site, and a new administrative block and chapel on Northumberland Road. The institution could then accommodate 1,921 inmates.

In 1914–15, the casual ward housed Belgian war refugees, then in 1918–21 it was used as military detention barracks. The workhouse also received paupers from Paddington, Hampstead, Hammersmith and Lewisham, whose own institutions had been taken over for military use.

After 1930, the workhouse became the St Marylebone Institution, mainly housing the elderly and infirm. During the Second World War, parts of the Marylebone Road building were used as a recreation centre for civil defence workers, then after the war became a transit centre for displaced persons from Europe. In 1949, the institution was renamed Luxborough Lodge, overseen by a 'warden' rather than a 'master'. The establishment finally closed in 1965 and was replaced by flats and accommodation for the London Polytechnic.

In 1881, a new 744-bed infirmary was opened at Rackham Street, Ladbroke Grove (TQ237819), taking the sick poor from the workhouse. It was designed by Henry Saxon Snell, who received a letter of praise from Florence Nightingale.[121] The pavilion-plan layout had a central administrative block, flanked at each side by two double ward-blocks. The site was renamed St Marylebone Hospital in 1923, then after being taken over by the LCC in 1930 became St Charles' Hospital. The buildings still house medical services.

In 1860, a separate school housing 390 children was opened on South Road, Southall (TQ126801). Its facilities included an infirmary, laundry, swimming baths and workshops.[122] In 1916, the school was taken over by the Australian Forces as a military hospital. The buildings had been demolished by 1933.

ST OLAVE

By 1729, the parish of St Olave had erected a workhouse at the corner of Parish Street and Crucifix Lane (now Druid Street, TQ334799), Southwark. The U-shaped building housed fifty adults and seventy children, who were employed in spinning mop yarn and taught to read and say their catechism.[123] In 1733, St Olave's was divided and the workhouse lay in the new parish of St John Horsleydown. By the same date, St Olave had a workhouse with 250 places but later shared the Parish Street premises, which were rebuilt in 1831.[124]

Southwark St Thomas opened a workhouse in 1734.[125] In 1777, it could house twenty-three inmates. By 1804, the indoor poor were being farmed at 5s a week.[126]

St Olave's Poor Law Union was formed in March 1836 from the parishes of St Olave, St John and St Thomas. The union took over the Parish Street workhouse.

In 1872, the main building formed three sides of a square. The west section, facing Parish Street, contained the offices, boardroom, dining hall and kitchens. Males were housed in the south wing, and females in the north wing, with exercise yards in the area in between. The sick wards continued the frontage northwards along Parish Street. The workhouse was closed in 1922, then converted to flats in 1925. St Olave's Estate now occupies the site.

The union was joined in 1869 by St Mary Magdalen Bermondsey and St Mary Rotherhithe, and acquired their reworkhouses at Tanner Street and Lower Road. All the existing casual wards were replaced by new cellular accommodation adjacent to the Lower Road workhouse.

The St Olave Union infirmary at Lower Road, Rotherhithe.

Lower Road was also adopted as the union's infirmary and a large new building was erected in 1873–76 at the west of the site. It was designed by Henry Saxon Snell and had a pavilion-plan layout. The central administrative block contained offices, kitchens, stores and staff quarters. Males at the south side and females at the north were accommodated in double ward-blocks, three storeys in height, each ward having 32 beds.[127] The establishment was later known as Bermondsey and Rotherhithe Infirmary, then after 1930 as St Olave's Hospital. After suffering considerable damage during the Second World War, the hospital joined the NHS in 1948, and finally closed in 1985. Almost all the buildings have been demolished.

In 1897–1900, the union erected a workhouse at Ladywell (TQ373745), solely for the accommodation of the aged and infirm – possibly the only purpose-built establishment of its type. The scheme, designed by Newman & Newman, comprised a central administration block and dining hall, flanked at each side by three double pavilion ward-blocks, all linked by a central corridor. Four wards were provided for the 'infirm', six for the 'healthy infirm' and two for the 'healthy aged'. Males were housed at the north of the site and females at the south. There was also a separate block for twelve married couples, plus an isolation hospital, laundry, two chapels (Anglican and Roman Catholic) and a water tower.[128] During the First World War, Ladywell served as Bermondsey Military Hospital. After 1930, the LCC took over what became Ladywell PAI,

An aerial view of the St Olave institution for the elderly at Ladywell.

later known as Ladywell Lodge old people's home. Since its closure around 1975, most of buildings have been demolished and the remainder converted to other use.

In 1903, a large cottage homes scheme was opened at Wickham Road, Shirley (TQ357658), again designed by Newman & Newman. The thirty-eight children's cottages were spread out along a lane. The LCC ran the homes from 1930 until 1965, when Lambeth Council took over, renaming the site Shirley Oaks. The homes closed in 1983 and the site has been redeveloped for residential use. Several of the original cottages survive. Cottage homes were also opened at Peckham Rye.

In 1904, St Olave's Union was renamed the Parish of Bermondsey.

ST PANCRAS

St Pancras opened a workhouse in 1731 at the west of King's Road (now St Pancras Way, TQ294838). Its first master and matron were William Bains and Mrs Roxe, and Mr Broadhead supplied it with small beer at 6s a barrel.[129]

By 1775, the workhouse moved to a property in the fork between what are now Camden High Street and Kentish Town Road (TQ289839), with frontages of over 250ft on each. The premises included workshops, yards, gardens and

An 1889 view of the St Pancras (1809) workhouse, just before its demolition.

an infirmary, and in 1777 housed up to 120 inmates.[130] The number greatly increased, however – in 1787, inmates were sleeping five or six to a bed, and there were fears of putrid fever breaking out. Prior to moving to a new site in 1809, the establishment had 224 bedsteads, of which 149 were judged fit for use if cleansed of vermin. The remainder were said to be useless.[131]

In 1804, to deal with its swelling population, St Pancras obtained a Local Act, allowing it to appoint a committee of Directors of the Poor and erect a new workhouse. A site was obtained at the east side of King's Road, just north of the parish church (TQ29683) and construction of the new premises, designed by Thomas Hardwick, began in 1806. The earth at the site proved ideal for making bricks for the building and almost a million were produced. The new workhouse opened in 1809 and initially housed 500 inmates. In 1812, an infirmary was added to accommodate the 160 inmates who had until then remained at the old premises.[132]

St Pancras' Local Act status largely exempted it from the 1834 Act, until it was compelled to form a Board of Guardians in 1867.

In 1871, the workhouse entrance was on King's Road at the south-west of the site, with receiving wards a little way inside. The main building of 1809 faced south-west. At its centre were the master and matron's quarters, with a chapel to the left, and female inmates housed at either side. Male wards and those for imbeciles and lunatics ran along the south-east of the site. Casual wards and a stone-breaking yard were at the north-east, with a separate entrance from Cambridge Street. An infirmary lay at the north of the site, with a kitchen and nursery separating it from women's oakum-picking rooms at the west. At the centre of the site, surrounded by gardens, were the kitchen, bakehouse and laundry.

In 1856, a PLB investigation found that the workhouse was severely over-crowded, with patients in the infirmary having to be placed on the floor. Ventilation was deficient, with fetid air from privies, drains, urinals and foul patients permeating many of the wards and causing sickness, headaches and dysentery among the inmates. A lying-in room, also used as a sleeping room by night nurses, had a smell that was 'enough to knock you down'. In the women's receiving wards, more than eighty women and children slept in two rooms which provided a mere 164 cubic feet of space per adult. Worst of all were the underground 'pens' where up to 900 out-relief applicants crowded each day, sometimes waiting until 7 p.m. without food. The poor ventilation and smell caused women to faint and windows to be broken to obtain fresh air.[133]

In 1865, a report in *The Lancet* found things little improved. The infirm wards, nursery and lying-in wards were judged as unfit for the reception of sick persons; the space allocation for each inmate was inadequate; the nursing and medical staff needed to be augmented; and many of the beds were only 5ft 8in long. Overall, though, the medical facilities were rated as capable of development into a good pauper hospital.[134]

In 1870, a new infirmary was opened on Dartmouth Park Hill, Highgate (TQ288869), one of the first in London to be built on a separate site from its parent workhouse. Almost as soon as it was completed, however, it was sold to the new Central London Sick Asylum District, which St Pancras had recently joined. Designed by John Giles & Biven, the pavilion-plan layout had a central complex containing offices, kitchen, laundry and other services. This was linked by a corridor to five large 'Nightingale' ward-blocks, two for males and three for females. Florence Nightingale commended the establishment as being 'far the best of any workhouse infirmary we have'.[135]

When St Pancras left the district in 1883, it bought back the Highgate site which became known as its North Infirmary. From 1901–03, First World War heroine Edith Cavell held the post of night superintendent at Highgate, where she was the only trained nurse on duty in charge of 500 beds. In 1948, the infirmary became the Highgate wing of Whittington Hospital. In 2003, it was redeveloped as Highgate Mental Health Centre, retaining many of the old buildings.

A view of the St Pancras Cook's Terrace infirmary in the early 1900s.

At the workhouse site, large new dining halls were erected in 1876. The Guardians then began to grapple with the urgent need for extra accommodation. The architect H.H. Bridgman drew up plans for a complete redevelopment of the site. However, a more piecemeal scheme took place, beginning with a large new block to house chronic, infirm and bedridden patients. The five-storey building, which became known as the South Infirmary, was erected on an adjoining strip of land on Pancras Road, known as Cook's Terrace. It was completed in 1885 and accommodated 400 inmates, making St Pancras London's only Board of Guardians with two large purpose-built infirmaries. The 1809 workhouse was then demolished and replaced by new buildings designed by A & C Harston. Male and female admission blocks were added either side of the King's Road entrance and a new five-storey administration block was built behind the male admission block. A row of four large pavilion blocks was erected in 1890–95, the one nearest the entrance serving as a nurses' home. In 1899, separate chapels for Anglican and Roman Catholic inmates were added at the rear of the female admission block.[136] From around 1922, the workhouse site was known as St Pancras Hospital, a name it still bears. A number of the old buildings are still in use.

In 1870, the Guardians opened a residential school for 700 children on College Road, Leavesden, near Watford (TL101014). It later became Abbots Langley Hospital, which closed in the early 1990s. Only the former entrance lodge survives.

In 1877, the casual ward moved to 21 Leighton Road, then in 1897 to 41 Holmes Road, Kentish Town. The latter building is now used as a hostel. In 1904, a children's receiving home, known as St Margaret's, was opened on the Leighton Road site. It later became St Margaret's Hospital and St Margaret's Residential Nursery.

From around 1887 to 1915, St Pancras accommodated aged and infirm males in a branch workhouse at Streatham Hill (TQ305732), known as St Anne's Home.

ST SAVIOUR

The Southwark parish of St Saviour erected a workhouse in 1728 on Maid Lane (now Sumner Street and Park Street). In 1731, the inmates comprised seventy adults and fifty children, who were employed in carding and spinning wool for mop yarn, worsted and knitting.[137]

In 1777, a spacious new building was erected on Pepper Street (TQ321798). It housed up to 530 inmates, whose employment included winding silk, carding wool and coarse needlework.[138] The London Fire Brigade later occupied the site.

Around 1814, the parish opened a new workhouse at the corner of New Kent Road and Newington Road (TQ320790). The building, which was constructed entirely of wood, burned to the ground in August 1817 after being set on fire by the flue of an adjoining gingerbread baker's. It was subsequently rebuilt on the same site. In 1832, there were 200 inmates, with those under 40 said to be 'labouring under imbecility of mind and various bodily afflictions' and those above that age 'subject to debility and infirmities brought on by old age'.

In 1777, the parish of Christ Church had a workhouse housing up to 150 inmates. By the 1790s, the workhouse was located at the west side of Marlborough Street, where Southwark College now stands (TQ315799). In 1834, a new workhouse designed by George Allen was erected on the site.

The St Saviour Poor Law Union was created in February 1836 from the parishes of St Saviour and Christ Church. The union took over the Marlborough Street workhouse, which was then altered and enlarged. The range at the east, facing onto Marlborough Street, included a workroom, dining hall and kitchens. At the north side were the laundry and nursery, while along the west side facing towards Short Street were male wards and a storeroom. A block at the east side of Marlborough Street contained an infirmary, dispensary, boardroom and offices.

In 1869, the parishes of St George the Martyr and St Mary Newington joined the union, which was renamed Southwark in 1901. The enlarged union took over the St George's workhouse on Mint Street and Newington's workhouse on Westmoreland Road. Marlborough Street (renamed Gray Street in 1912) was then used for the infirm, Mint Street for able-bodied and healthy males, and Westmoreland Road for able-bodied females. The Westmoreland Road infirmary was enlarged to serve the whole union. Mint Street closed in the 1920s, while Gray Street and Westmoreland Road continued in use from 1930 as LCC PAIs.

In 1887, the union opened a new infirmary on East Dulwich Grove, Dulwich (TQ334751). The buildings, designed by Henry Jarvis, had a pavilion-plan layout, with a central two-storey administrative block flanked at each side by a pair of three-storey double ward-blocks, oriented roughly north–south to make the best use of the sunlight. There were twelve wards for men and twelve for women. Bathrooms and water closets were placed in sanitary towers at the far end of each ward, with a balcony placed in between them, onto which several beds could be wheeled. The ward-blocks and administrative block were connected by a three-storey corridor, with the upper two storeys left open to the fresh air. There was also an underground tramway on which trolleys transported coal. A condition of the site's purchase was that the buildings' exteriors should produce 'a pleasing effect'. As a result, they had rather more

A men's yard at the St Saviour's Marlborough Street workhouse, early 1900s.

architectural character than was usual in such institutions. The receiving wards, placed near the entrance, included two padded rooms. A telephone system was installed in the building.[139]

During the First World War, the infirmary was used as a military hospital. From 1921, it was known as Southwark Hospital, then under LCC control from 1930 became Dulwich Hospital. Dulwich Community Hospital still operates at the site.

In the 1890s, the union built a casual ward at 96 Great Guildford Street, Southwark, now used as a hostel.

ST SEPULCHRE

The Middlesex portion of the parish of St Sepulchre (see page 61) opened a workhouse in 1728 at the north end of Sharp's Alley, off Cow Cross Street (TQ315817). In October 1731, it contained about fifty inmates who were mostly weak and infirm, their chief employment being to teach the children to read, and to keep the house clean.[140]

The parish obtained a Local Act in 1772 for the Better Relief and Employment of the Poor. In 1776, the able-bodied workhouse inmates were employed in winding silk, as were the children, who also stripped quills.

In 1832, the Sharp's Alley workhouse was home to twenty-eight men, twenty boys, thirty-eight women and twelve girls. They ranged from 5 to 90 years of age. Males were employed in oakum picking and females in shirt and slop making.

St Sepulchre Middlesex operated as a Local Act parish until 1845, when it joined the Holborn Union.

SHOREDITCH

In 1726, St Leonard's Shoreditch opened a workhouse in some old houses at Hoxton. In 1731, the eighty-four inmates were employed in spinning mop-yarn.[141]

In 1774, Shoreditch obtained a Local Act for 'the better relief and employment of the poor'. The Act created the Trustees of the Poor and allowed money to be raised for a new workhouse, which was erected on a site known as the 'Land of Promise' on Kingsland Road, Hoxton (TQ334834). The three-storey building, which included an infirmary and apothecary, opened in 1777.

In 1813, James Parkinson was appointed parish surgeon and man-midwife. His improvements included a separate fever block in the workhouse, the first in London, for the segregation of infectious patients. In 1817, his 'Essay on the Shaking Palsy' described the condition now known as Parkinson's Disease.

Its Local Act status exempted the parish from the 1834 Act and the Trustees of the Poor continued in operation.

In 1847, a Parliamentary committee criticised conditions in the workhouse. It was found to be overcrowded, with 1,000 inmates in accommodation designed for 800, and 150 chronically ill inmates housed in poorly ventilated wards close to healthy inmates. Concerns were also expressed about the quality of the water supply. In 1849, the trustees responded with a major modernisation of the buildings, with a new accommodation block, kitchen and bakehouse, and an infirmary and fever hospital housed in a separate wing on Hoxton Street.

A further Local Act in 1858 replaced the trustees with a new body, the Guardians of the Poor, elected by ratepayers. In 1861, the Guardians agreed to comply with a PLB order to erect a new workhouse on Kingsland Road, housing 1,200 inmates. The new buildings, designed by a Mr Lee, were completed in 1866. The main block, facing Kingsland Road, contained offices and accommodation for female inmates. To its rear were the dining hall, which also

The Kingsland Road frontage of the Shoreditch workhouse, now St Leonard's Hospital.

served as a chapel, and dayrooms. Males were housed in a cross-wing at the west end of the building.[142]

In 1865, during the rebuilding work, a *Lancet* report found much to complain about. Although the new buildings appeared well constructed, and with good sanitary facilities, their design was viewed as outdated. The wards had an air of 'extreme cheerlessness and desolation', with no decoration, flowers or books. The lunatics and imbeciles were 'moping about in herds', lacking any occupation, exercise or fresh air. Bed linen in the lying-in wards was often filthy with crusted blood and discharges. The male pauper nurses were rough, ignorant and uncouth, and there were no night nurses.[143]

In 1867, the Guardians were abolished and reconstituted under the New Poor Law. In 1872, a new 150-bed infirmary and dispensary were opened at the north-west corner of the site. The building was four storeys high and had two 'Nightingale' wards on each of its upper floors.[144] At the same time, a matron was appointed for the first time. In 1903–06, First World War heroine Edith Cavell served as assistant matron at the infirmary.

From 1920, the site was solely used as a hospital, known as St Leonard's. It operated as a general hospital until 1984, when the in-patient facilities were closed. It then developed as a centre for coordinating community health services.

In 1848, Shoreditch opened an 'infant poorhouse' at Baker Street, Enfield (TQ328973). In 1851, the PLB held a lengthy inquiry into complaints that boys at Enfield had been brutally flogged by the master, Joshua Briggs. They concluded, however, that there was no foundation to the charges.[145]

In 1854, a residential school for 400 children was erected on Brentwood Hill, Brentwood (TQ587936). In 1877, the Shoreditch and Hackney Unions formed the Brentwood School District, which bought the premises. The district was dissolved in 1885 and the site was taken over by Hackney, later becoming St Faith's Hospital.

From 1885 to 1889 Shoreditch housed children at the Harold Court School on Church Road, Harold Wood (TQ559911), now converted to flats.

In 1889, Shoreditch opened a large cottage homes site on Hornchurch Road, Hornchurch (TQ529872). The scheme was laid out as a village street and included eleven two-storey cottages, each housing thirty boys or girls, schools, workshops, needle-room, swimming bath, band room and an infirmary.[146]

From 1899–1909, a property known as The Mansion, on Alexandra Park Road, Wood Green (TQ298904), was used as additional workhouse accommodation. In 1907, the purchase of the former Alexandra Orphanage on Hazellville Road, Hornsey (TQ298875), provided new quarters for 250 elderly inmates.

STEPNEY

The ancient parish of Stepney had a number of districts, such as Bethnal Green and Poplar, that went on to become independent parishes. Those forming their own administration following the 1834 Act are described separately. Others – Limehouse, Ratcliff, Shadwell and Wapping – are dealt with here.

St Anne, Limehouse opened a workhouse in 1724 and in June of the following year had thirty inmates. Most were unfit for labour, but about a dozen were employed in picking oakum. Meat was served four times a week, with 'such roots as are in season'. The children attended a local school until the age of 8, then were apprenticed until they were 24.[147] In 1746, the workhouse was located on Risbie's Rope Walk, Narrow Street (TQ364808).[148] A Local Act for rebuilding the workhouse was obtained in 1814 but was not put into effect until 1828, when new premises were erected at the west side of Church Lane (TQ347801). In 1832, the inmates comprised twenty-seven men, seventy-two women, twenty-one boys and twenty-one girls. Adults who were able were occupied in picking oakum.

Ratcliff opened a workhouse in 1723 on London Street (near what is now Barnes Street), which became known as the Town House. In 1725, the thirty inmates, mostly women, received a weekly shilling pension plus whatever else they could earn, either by spinning or winding silk on the premises, or by going outside for work such as preparing or selling fish.[149] By the 1790s, the workhouse was at Collet Place, at the corner of White Horse Street and Salmon Lane (TQ360813).[150]

St Paul, Shadwell, set up a workhouse in 1726. It housed about 100 paupers who were employed in picking oakum.[151] In 1777, the building could house 350 inmates. By the 1790s, it was located on Union Street, Shadwell, to the north of what is now Solander Gardens (TQ350808).[152]

Wapping's workhouse opened in 1723 in a large warehouse on Virginia Street (TQ343806). In 1731, the sixty inmates were occupied in picking oakum. In 1777, the establishment housed 260 inmates. A Local Act in 1817 enabled money to be raised for the building of a new workhouse. The scheme cost more than anticipated and a second Act in 1819 allowed further funds to be raised. The new workhouse was on Green Bank, Wapping, just east of Wapping Church (TQ347801).[153]

Stepney Poor Law Union was created in December 1836, its members being Mile End Old Town, Limehouse, Ratcliff, Shadwell and Wapping. The Guardians decided to close the Shadwell workhouse, due to its confined situation. The four other existing workhouses were retained by the union, with able-bodied men and fever patients at Mile End Old Town, able-bodied women at Wapping, the aged infirm at Ratcliffe, and the children at Limehouse. Mile End Old Town became a separate Poor Law Hamlet in 1857 (see page 96).

In January 1860, a magistrate commented that 'a most disgraceful and painful state of things' existed at Wapping workhouse.[154] Shortly afterwards, Charles Dickens paid an incognito visit there and, despite witnessing some grim scenes, found it to be well and kindly run.[155]

The Limehouse premises housed up to 400 children. As well as school instruction, the boys were taught shoemaking, tailoring, carpentering and spinning, and the girls learned laundry, housework, sewing and knitting. A full-sized ship's masts and rigging were erected in the grounds with a seaman employed to drill and train the boys, who were also taught to swim. All the children were taught singing, with a school choir attending choral festivals at the Crystal Palace. A boys' band was also established.[156] Limehouse was also the subject of a report by Charles Dickens, which was generally complimentary.[157] The establishment closed in 1873, when Stepney joined the South Metropolitan School District and then sent its children to the District School at Brighton Road, Sutton (TQ255626).

The main building of the Stepney Union workhouse on St Leonard's Street, opened in 1863.

In 1863, the union opened a new workhouse for 800 inmates at the west side of St Leonard's Street, Bromley-by-Bow (TQ379826). Designed by Henry Jarvis, the three-storey main building had a T-shaped layout with its main facade facing south. At the centre were administrative offices, master's quarters, dining hall and chapel, with inmates housed at each side. A separate infirmary stood at the west. Soon after the opening, additional works took place to prevent inmates climbing over the workhouse walls and escaping across the railway lines to the south.[158]

With the opening of the Bromley premises, the Wapping workhouse closed in 1863. The Ratcliff workhouse ceased receiving inmates in 1872 but remained home to the union's offices and casual wards. In 1893, a shortage of accommodation led to its being reopened to house healthy old men and women. Around 1907, the casual wards were closed and a children's receiving home established at the site. New casual wards at Eastfield Street, Limehouse (TQ364815), were opened in 1902.

In 1868, the union became a partner in the new Poplar and Stepney Sick Asylum District which erected a large hospital at Devon's Row, Bow (TQ379824). Opened in 1871, it provided 572 beds for the sick and infirm of the two unions.

In 1901, the Guardians erected cottage homes for 200 children at Stifford in Essex (TQ597800). Designed by Frank Baggallay, the homes were arranged in a south-facing arc. In 1935, the site became Ardale Approved School. Most of the buildings have now been demolished.

In 1921, the union became the Parish of Limehouse. In 1925, it was joined by Mile End Old Town, St George in the East and Whitechapel to form a new Stepney Union, renamed the Parish of Stepney in 1927.

The Bromley workhouse, known as Bromley House from the early 1900s, was mothballed from 1923 to 1928, then was taken over by the LCC in 1930 for use as a PAI. It suffered bomb damage during the Second World War and was afterwards used to house homeless families. The institution was closed in 1966 then demolished to make way for an old people's home.

STRAND

From 1697, St Anne Soho had a workhouse in twelve small houses in Symbell's Alley. In 1711, the establishment moved to small premises now the site of 103a Oxford Street. In 1766, it was briefly at Chapel Street (now Great Chapel Street), moving the year after to Hog Lane (now under Charing Cross Road). A new workhouse, designed by James Paine, was opened in 1771 on Rose Street (now 14 Manette Street, TQ298812).[159] In 1776, it housed eighty inmates who were occupied in oakum picking. Some of the parish's pauper children were in the Foundling Hospital.

St Mary le Strand had a workhouse by 1746 at Denham's Yard, Little Drury Lane (TQ307809).[160] It then used a mixture of its own premises and those operated by contractors. Between about 1762 and 1768 it employed work-houses at New Street, off Shoe Lane, and at Shacklewells, Hackney. From around 1777 until 1801, it used an establishment at Garratt Lane, Tooting. Premises at Swan Yard and then George Yard (both in close proximity to Denham's Yard) were in use between 1789 and 1801. In 1801–02, paupers were farmed at the Great White House, Hoxton High Street, and Robertson and Simpson's house, Hoxton. Finally, in 1811, the parish erected a workhouse south of what is now Leo Street, New Cross (TQ350773).[161]

Between about 1790 and 1801, the Precinct of the Savoy also housed pau-pers at the Great White House, Hoxton.[162]

St Clement Danes obtained Local Acts in 1764 and 1770, allowing it to appoint a committee to raise funds for a workhouse and to manage its opera-tion. The building was opened in 1773 at the corner of Portugal Street and Carey Street (TQ308812). In 1776, it could accommodate 300 inmates. Those who were able were occupied in slop-work and carding wool, and the 'infant poor' in spinning.

The Liberty of the Rolls had a workhouse from around 1737 on Elm Street, Gray's Inn Road (TQ309821). A later one was located in Bird's Buildings, Lower Street (now Essex Road), Islington, at the east of Islington Green (TQ316835).[163] In 1777, the establishment housed up to fifty inmates.

St Paul Covent Garden had a workhouse from 1702 until the 1720s on Hart Street, now Floral Street, followed by one nearby at the corner of Hart Street and Bow Street, now the site of the Royal Opera House. From 1734 to about 1778, the workhouse was at the north side of Denmark Court (now part of Exeter Street), at the rear of 14 Tavistock Street (TQ304808). After the parish obtained a Local Act in 1775, a new workhouse was erected on Cleveland Street, with a parish burial ground alongside (TQ292818). For over five years in total, Charles Dickens lived at 10 Norfolk Street, now 22 Cleveland Street, just a few doors away from the establishment, which is now thought to be the model for the workhouse portrayed in *Oliver Twist*.[164] In 1832, there were over 200 inmates. Able-bodied males were occupied in carpet-beating, hair-picking and wool-carding, and females in needlework and charing.

The Strand Poor Law Union was formed in March 1836, its members including St Mary le Strand, the Precinct of the Savoy, St Paul Covent Garden, St Clement Danes and St Anne Soho. The union took over the Cleveland Street workhouse and extended the buildings. The U-shaped main block, four storeys high, housed females at the north and males at the south. The ground-floor rooms were largely used as infirm wards. There was a chapel at the rear of the men's wing. A wash-house and laundry stood at the northern corner of the site, with workshops along the southern perimeter.

In 1853, Louisa Twining visited an elderly acquaintance in the workhouse. Her discovery of the neglect experienced by the inmates led her to set up what became the Workhouse Visiting Society.[165]

From 1856, the union's medical officer was Dr Joseph Rogers, who later described the unpleasant conditions he had met at the workhouse. The laundry was located in a cellar beneath the dining hall and filled the building with unpleasant-smelling steam. Carpet-beating was continually performed by able-bodied inmates just outside the male wards, with much resulting noise and dust. There were no paid nurses and nursing was performed by elderly female inmates who were often drunk. Excavations for a new laundry at the rear of the site revealed large numbers of skeletons under the old burial ground, which had been closed in 1853. Digging had to continue for 20ft before solid ground was reached.[166]

In 1865, a *Lancet* report revealed that despite having nearly 200 sick inmates and 260 infirm or insane, the workhouse employed no paid nurses. Instead, there were twenty-two pauper nurses, most of whom were judged unfit for the work. The patients' beds were thin, lumpy and wretched, and there were no lavatories or bathrooms attached to the wards. Overall, the buildings were described as 'atrociously bad as a residence for sick persons' and the Guardians as having neglected some of the most basic sanitary precautions.[167]

From 1873–1913, the Cleveland Street premises were used as an infirmary by the Central London Sick Asylum District. The MAB used the site as a children's infirmary from 1916–22, when it was acquired by the Middlesex Hospital, subsequently housing its out-patients' department until 2006. The original U-shaped block is now a listed building.

The disposal of the Cleveland Street site followed the opening in 1870 of the Strand's new workhouse at Tanner's End (now Silver Street), Edmonton (TQ33492), which housed over 1,000 inmates. The three-storey main building comprised two long, parallel blocks linked by short cross ranges, the central one housing the chapel which separated the male and female sides.

A 1920s view of the former Strand Union workhouse on Cleveland Street, and the probable model for the establishment portrayed in *Oliver Twist*.

In 1890, the union built casual and receiving wards at Bear Yard, Sheffield Street (TQ307812). The buildings were demolished in about 1900 as part of an improvement scheme. In 1903, a replacement building was erected facing onto Sheffield Street. After the Strand Union joined the new City of Westminster Union in 1913, the Sheffield Street Hospital was sold to the MAB. During the First World War it was used as a hospital for refugees, then, in 1920, became a hospital for women and girls suffering from venereal diseases. After the LCC took over the site in 1930, it became the Sheffield Street Hospital then joined the NHS in 1948 as St Philip's Hospital. The building was demolished in 2011.

The Edmonton workhouse was also sold to the MAB in 1913. Their plans to use the building as an asylum for 'imbeciles' were halted by the First World War when it became the Edmonton Refuge, housing 2,000 Belgian refugees. In 1925, the site was sold for use as a silk stocking factory. The buildings no longer exist.

In 1849, the union opened a residential school at Millfield House, an old mansion on Wye Hall Road (now Silver Street), Edmonton (TQ329926). The premises eventually housed almost 400 children. Two infirmary blocks were added, one specialising in the treatment of ophthalmia, a serious eye condition common in pauper children. The school's facilities included a swimming bath which converted into a girls' playroom during the winter. Like other Strand establishments, Millfield House was sold to the MAB in 1913. In 1914–16, the site housed Belgian refugees, then became a colony for up to 300 male 'sane epileptics'. It was taken over by the LCC in 1930, and around 1936 renamed St David's Hospital, finally closing in 1971. In 1979, the premises reopened as an arts centre.[168]

WANDSWORTH & CLAPHAM

Wandsworth built a workhouse in 1730 on East Hill, on land leased from the local lord of the manor, Earl Spencer. In 1777, it could house 100 inmates.

Clapham had a poorhouse at the junction of Broomhill (now Clapham Road) and Bedford Road (TQ300756). In 1745, the premises were converted to workhouse use.[169] In 1832, the eighty-eight inmates ranged in age from infancy to 86 years. The men knotted yarn, carded flock and picked hair, while the women did slop-work.

Battersea's first workhouse was opened in 1733. The rented building included a parlour, master's room, a hall with tables and benches, an infirmary, and a well-equipped wash-house.[170] In 1777, the premises housed up to seventy inmates. Around 1791, the workhouse moved to a larger property in Battersea Square (TQ268766). There were 100 inmates in 1832, none of them fit for labour. They were employed in household work, with the children occupied in needlework, knitting stockings, reading and writing.

In 1777, Streatham's workhouse housed up to thirty inmates. After obtaining a Local Act in 1790, the parish built new premises on Tooting Bec Common, at the junction of what are now Elmbourne Road and Dr Johnson Avenue (TQ287723). In 1832, the were forty-nine adult inmates and thirty-six children.

Putney had a workhouse from 1726, perhaps located at the end of what is now Weimar Street (TQ240755). It had a well-stocked garden and was probably self-sufficient in vegetables. The inmates were occupied in spinning wool and picking oakum.[171] The establishment accommodated seventy inmates in 1777. In 1832, the residents numbered sixty-one, of whom twenty-one were under 12 years of age. No employment was provided as able-bodied men were not admitted.

In 1768, a building to house Tooting Graveney's paupers was erected by Lord of the Manor, Morgan Rice, on Tooting Graveney Common. The parish built a new workhouse in 1784 at the junction of Church Lane and Rectory Lane (TQ284713). Paupers from Beddington and Sutton were also received at the establishment. In 1822, following the birth of three illegitimate children at the workhouse, its officers were recommended 'to procure a party-coloured gown for them to wear as punishment for their offence, as was formerly the custom in this parish'.[172]

Wandsworth & Clapham Poor Law Union was formed in March 1836 from the parishes of Battersea, Clapham, Putney, Streatham, Tooting Graveney and Wandsworth. The Guardians leased another site from Earl Spencer on the north side of East Hill (now St John's Hill, TQ265751) where a new workhouse was erected. The cruciform design, by George Ledwell Taylor, had an entrance block at the front, behind which the inmates' accommodation wings radiated from a central hub. A detached infirmary was erected behind the main building.[173]

A visitor in 1841 likened the workhouse's appearance to that of a gentleman's residence rather than a receptacle for paupers. Elderly men were employed in picking oakum, while the able-bodied pumped water to a cistern at the top of the building. The cellar contained barrels of ale and porter which were served to old or infirm paupers on medical orders, or to those performing heavy labour.[174]

In 1870, a much larger infirmary was erected at the north of the workhouse, on ground previously occupied by gardens. It comprised four three-storey ward pavilions linked to a central four-storey administration block.

After a new workhouse was opened in 1886, St John's became the union infirmary and substantial alterations were made to the buildings. Its staff

The entrance of the Wandsworth & Clapham Union infirmary (previously workhouse) on St John's Hill.

included sixty-three female and four male nurses A celebrated inmate of St John's was a Mrs Blower who in 1896, at the age of 107, was said to be the oldest workhouse inmate in the country. Still active and cheerful, she regularly ran the length of the ward.[175] The site was known as St John's Hospital from around 1921. It was taken over by the LCC in 1930, and after 1948 continued as an NHS geriatric hospital until its closure in 1985. Surviving parts include the 1870 infirmary.

The new workhouse was at Swaffield Road, off Garratt Lane (TQ260737), in what was then open countryside. Designed by Thomas Aldwinckle, it had a central administration block containing dining rooms, kitchens and a large chapel on the upper floor. A three-storey ward pavilion was placed at each side, for males on the left and females at the right. Separate areas housed inmates of good and bad character. On the women's side, there were also separate nursery and children's blocks. The men's side included a stone-breaking yard. A large casual ward lay at the left of the entrance driveway. At its rear was an unusual semi-circular array of thirty sleeping and stone-breaking cells.[176] The site was taken over by the LCC in 1930 and in 1948 was renamed Brockle Bank.[177] In 1946, the casual ward became the Wandsworth Hostel for single persons needing temporary lodgings. Brockle Bank closed in 1972 and the buildings were demolished.

The architect's design for the Wandsworth & Clapham Union workhouse, Garratt Lane, opened in 1886.

In 1897, extra accommodation was provided for about 600 'deserving' old and infirm inmates at Church Lane, Tooting (TQ281711). The buildings, previously occupied by St Joseph's College, included Hill House, the former Tooting Graveney workhouse, which then became a nurses' home. In 1902, cottage-style accommodation for twenty-two aged married couples was added. During the First World War, the site served as Church Lane Military Hospital. In 1930, the LCC took over the establishment which, renamed St Benedict's Hospital, provided care for the chronic sick. The hospital closed in 1981 and housing now occupies the site.

In 1903, a large 'Intermediate Schools' building, designed by Landsell and Harrison, was erected on Swaffield Road opposite the workhouse entrance.

In 1904, the union was renamed the Wandsworth Union. In the same year, the Guardians bought the St James' Road Industrial School, Wandsworth (TQ277732), from the Westminster Union for use as a branch workhouse. In 1910, a new pavilion-plan infirmary was erected at the site. In 1930, the infirmary was taken over by the LCC and became St James' General Hospital. The ward pavilions were extended, and the old workhouse blocks replaced by a new central complex.[178] The hospital closed in 1988 and the buildings were demolished around 1992. The site has now been redeveloped for housing.

WHITECHAPEL

Whitechapel opened a workhouse in Ayliffe Street (now Buckle Street) in 1724. It subsequently acted as a lodging house whose residents went out to work during the day. In May 1729, there were sixty inmates and a resident housekeeper.[179]

Construction of a new workhouse began in 1768 at the north side of Whitechapel Road, just east of what is now Davenant Street (TQ344817). In 1776, the building was described as brick-built, 165ft long, 126ft deep, and having thirty rooms. It could house 600 inmates. In 1832, the inmates numbered 498, of whom 158 were under 15. Those able to work were employed in needlework, oakum picking, pin-heading, as shoemakers, tailors, horn-polishers, feather-strippers, scavengers and in domestic work. Married couples could sleep together.

The parish of Christ Church, Spitalfields, opened a workhouse in 1728 in a large rented house at the west side of Bell Lane (TQ335815). In September 1731, there were eighty-four inmates, including thirty children. They were employed in winding Bengal raw silk, their annual earnings amounting to £70. They were so fully occupied that they had given up their previous tasks of picking oakum and spinning wool.[180]

Christ Church closed its workhouse in 1743 but ten years later obtained a Local Act enabling it to appoint trustees to raise money for new premises. The following year, a lease was taken on a property at the north-east corner of Turnagain Lane (now Vallance Road) and Thomas Street (now Lomas Street, TQ344820).[181] After the building was enlarged in 1776, up to 300 inmates could be housed in its thirty-four rooms and were occupied in silk manufacture. In 1832, there were 356 inmates, three-quarters of whom had been employed in the silk trade. The adults were occupied in winding silk and in needlework.

St Botolph without Aldgate erected a workhouse in 1735 on Nightingale Lane, East Smithfield. In 1776, up to 200 inmates were employed in making wig cauls, winding silk, making slops, picking oakum, and spinning worsted and flax. The building was demolished in 1828 for construction of St Katherine's Dock.

In 1780, Mile End New Town obtained a Local Act to appoint trustees and open a workhouse. In 1783, it leased a pair of houses for the purpose at the north side of Spicer Street (now Buxton Street) opposite the end of Hunt Street (TQ340821). In 1832, most of the ninety-eight inmates had formerly been engaged in silk manufacture.

Norton Folgate had a workhouse by the 1740s, probably near the almshouses at the north end of Blossom Street (TQ334821). Rising numbers of paupers led to a Local Act in 1810 to fund enlargement of the premises. However, the sum specified in the Act proved inadequate and the building was instead leased out. The indoor poor were then farmed out at Mr Sutton's in Islington.[182]

Whitechapel Poor Law Union was formed in February 1837, its members including Whitechapel, Christ Church, Mile End New Town, Norton Folgate, and St Botolph without Aldgate. The Guardians retained the Whitechapel Road workhouse for female paupers and Charles Street for males.

Conditions at Whitechapel Road left much to be desired. A physician visiting the premises in 1838 found that 89 out of 104 girls in residence had recently been attacked with fever. They all slept in one room, with at least four girls in each bed. The privies were in a filthy state and there were no baths in the establishment.[183]

In 1856–60, a complete reconstruction of the Charles Street workhouse took place. Like its predecessor, the new building, designed by Thomas Barry, had two long, parallel blocks. The one facing onto Charles Street was four storeys high plus attics. It had the main entrance at its centre, wards for females at the north and for males at the south. The rear block was five storeys high plus attics. A dining hall and chapel lay at its centre, and male and female sick wards placed at each side. The two blocks were linked at the centre by a short two-storey range. When the rebuilding was completed in 1860, the Whitechapel Road workhouse was closed.

A view of the Whitechapel Union infirmary (originally workhouse) on Charles Street about 1902.

In 1868, new casual wards were opened at the south side of Thomas Street (TQ345819), with accommodation for fifty-two male and thirty-three female vagrants.

In 1872, Whitechapel erected a new workhouse on South Grove (now Southern Grove, TQ367825). The Charles Street site then became the union infirmary. From 1924, it was known as St Peter's Hospital, then was taken over by the LCC in 1930 and used as a general hospital. Due to extensive damage during the Second World War, St Peter's did not join the NHS. The buildings were demolished in the 1960s.

The South Grove workhouse was designed by Richard Robert Long and housed over 800 inmates. The entrance range had a central archway with receiving wards to each side. To the rear, a three-storey administration building was flanked by three-storey ward-blocks, women's at the north and men's at the south. On their upper floors, the latter were connected to the central block by escape bridges. The healthy aged were placed on the ground floor and the infirm on the upper. The workhouse was the subject of comment when, after its completion, the union apparently had no immediate need for

The main building of the former Whitechapel Union workhouse on Southern Grove (formerly South Grove).

its facilities. In 1873, it acted as a temporary infirmary and school for around 400 children removed from the North Surrey District School where the eye condition ophthalmia was a recurrent problem. The 'Bow School Infirmary' was in operation for about a year, with South Grove finally assuming its work-house role in 1876.

South Grove Institution, as it became known, was taken over by the LCC in 1930. Housing the elderly and infirm, it was later renamed Southern Grove House then Southern Grove Lodge. The administration block still stands.

In 1852–54, the union erected an industrial school for 800 children on a site known as Jackass Field at the north side of Forest Lane in Forest Gate (TQ399852). In 1869, the school was sold to the Forest Gate School District.

In 1899, the union erected children's homes at Grays in Essex. A headquar-ters home was located on Whitehall Lane (TQ622783) with a number of children's houses at various locations around the village.

In 1925, the Whitechapel Union was absorbed by the Stepney Union which was renamed the Parish of Stepney in 1927.

WOOLWICH

Woolwich Poor Law Union was formed in March 1868. Prior to that date, the parish of Woolwich had been a member of the Greenwich Union (see page 78), while the other three new members – Charlton next Woolwich, Kidbrooke and Plumstead – had previously formed part of the Lewisham Union (see page 95).

A site for a workhouse was purchased at the south side of Plumstead High Street, at the east of what is now Tewson Road, Plumstead (TQ454784), and on 2 April 1870 the Revd Francis Cameron laid the foundation stone for the building. It carried the inscription 'The poor ye have always with you.'

Just inside the gates at the north-west of the site were a porter's lodge, receiving and probationary wards. Casual wards, at the north-east, had their own entrance from Hull Place. The T-shaped main building had a central entrance hall, off which were a boardroom and offices, and a flight of steps leading to a landing and a 400-seat dining hall. Corridors to the right and left from the landing led to the wards for able-bodied males and females. Above the dining hall was the chapel, which contained an ecclesiastical armchair, elaborately carved in oak by a 66-year-old inmate of the institution. At the rear of the main building, on the women's side, was a laundry containing thirty-two tubs and other equipment. At the back of the men's yard were painters', carpenters', woodcutters' and smiths' shops. A bakehouse produced all the inmates' bread in 6oz loaves, plus 4lb loaves for the union's outdoor poor. A pavilion-plan infirmary lay at the south of the site. The architects for the scheme were Henry Church and William Rickwood.[184] The first inmates were transferred to the new premises on 19 January 1874.

From 1904, the birth certificates of those born in the workhouse recorded its location as 79b Tewson Road, Woolwich.

Around 1928, the infirmary became known as the Plumstead and District Hospital. In 1930, the LCC took over the site, renaming the hospital St Nicholas Hospital. The former workhouse section became a PAI, housing 576 men. In the Second World War, the site suffered serious bomb damage. In 1948, St Nicholas Hospital joined the NHS, while the workhouse building provided temporary accommodation for homeless families. The casual ward operated for a number of years as the Plumstead Reception Centre. The entire site closed in 1986 and all the buildings were demolished in 1992.

In 1899, the union erected the Goldie Leigh children's cottage homes site on Lodge Lane, Bostall Heath (TQ471776). In 1914, the premises were rented by the MAB as a hospital for the treatment of ringworm – an infectious disease

The Woolwich Union workhouse in the late 1920s, prior to its conversion to a Public Assistance Institution.

The former Woolwich Union workhouse in the 1930s after the removal of partition walls and redundant outbuildings.

of the scalp, common among pauper children. In 1930, the site was taken over by the LCC. In 1961, it was adapted for children classed as mentally subnormal and continued to provide hostel accommodation for children with disabilities until 1988. As Goldie Leigh Hospital, the site now provides a range of out-patient services. A receiving home at 43–47 Parkdale Road, Plumstead (TQ452782), dealt with children prior to their being transferred to the Goldie Leigh homes.

In 1901, a 'home of rest' for the deserving aged female poor was opened at Furze Lodge, 138 Shrewsbury (now Plum) Lane, Shooter's Hill (TQ440773). Forty-two inmates were housed in its spacious apartments.

4

BERKSHIRE

ABINGDON

In 1631, the Mayor of Abingdon reported that 'wee haue erected wthn our borough a workehouse to sett poore people to worke'.[1] Five years later, the borough purchased a house in the abbey for use as a workhouse. In 1724, the St Helen's vestry spent £200 on workhouse premises at the west side of Ottwell Lane (SU497971).[2] In 1777, the establishment could house 120 inmates. In 1802–03, the forty residents were farmed by William Middleston, who received £700 a year plus the inmates' earnings from spinning, weaving and hemp-dressing.[3] The workhouse had its own bakehouse and brewhouse. In 1827, the parish began plans for a new workhouse and a plot of land was purchased at Boxwell Piece on Oxford Road (SU500977). Detailed plans were drawn up, but the scheme appears to have stalled.

By 1777, Abingdon's other parish, St Nicholas, had a small workhouse housing up to twelve inmates.

Abingdon Poor Law Union was formed on 1 January 1835, the first new union to be created under the 1834 Act. With the Boxwell Piece site still available, the union was able to quickly begin construction of a new workhouse. The building, to house 500 inmates, was designed by Sampson Kempthorne and used his model hexagonal layout, though had four storeys rather than the usual three. It included a basic central heating system, and during its first year of operation, hot water heating apparatus and gas lighting were also installed.

On the evening of 21 November 1835, not long after the establishment began operation, a shot was fired through the sitting-room window of the master, Richard Ellis. The perpetrator appears not to have been apprehended but the deed was presumably intended as a protest against the New Poor Law regime.

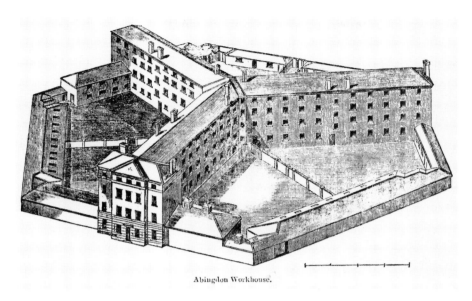

Abingdon Workhouse.

Sampson Kempthorne adopted his own model hexagonal design for the Abingdon Union workhouse, the first of its type to be constructed.

Ten acres of land at the rear of the workhouse were used for growing veg-etables – swedes, mangold wurzels, parsnips, carrots, potatoes, peas and barley. In addition, a dozen pigs were kept in a piggery. In 1849, Richard Ellis wrote to the PLC describing the cultivation scheme he had developed, whereby the crops were fertilised not only by manure from the pigs but also by liquid drained from the inmates' privies. He also reserved working in the garden as a privilege for well-behaved inmates.[4]

Life for the inmates improved considerably over the years. By the late 1920s, some were even taken on a weekly outing to a local cinema.[5]

In 1930, Berkshire County Council took over the establishment but it closed the following year. The building was demolished in 1932 and housing built on the site.

BRADFIELD

Tilehurst erected a workhouse in 1767 between what are now Lansdowne Road and Grafton Road (SU665731). In 1777 it could house up to 100 inmates. In the same year, Aldermaston's workhouse provided thirty-five places.

Bradfield Poor Law Union was formed in March 1835 and erected a new workhouse at the south-east of Bradfield on what is now Union Road

The entrance block of Bradfield Union workhouse, later Wayland Hospital.

(SU606716). The architect was Sampson Kempthorne and, as at Abingdon, used his model hexagonal plan though reduced in size to house only 250 inmates. An infirmary was added at the north-east of the site later in the nineteenth century.

After 1904, for birth registration purposes, the establishment adopted the name 'Central House'.

In 1930, the site was taken over by Berkshire County Council and became a PAI known as Wayland House. In 1948, it joined the NHS as Wayland Hospital.

In 1996, all the buildings apart from the entrance block were demolished to make way for the Wayland housing development.

COOKHAM (MAIDENHEAD)

In 1777, Cookham had a workhouse for up to ninety inmates. Originally a mansion house owned by Robert Lutman, it was located on the east side of what is now North Town Road (SU889821). A building known as Latimore House later occupied the site.[6]

Bray also had a workhouse by 1777. It occupied Chauntry House, at the south-west of the parish church (SU901796). In 1832, the inmates comprised twelve women and girls, thirteen men and fourteen boys.

The front block of the Cookham Union workhouse.

Hurley's workhouse occupied a building on the High Street known as Church House, now a private house (SU826838).[7] In 1832, it had fourteen inmates, including four aged under 16 years.

White Waltham had a workhouse by the 1790s. In 1832, its twenty-three residents included an 86-year-old.

Cookham Poor Law Union was created in July 1835 and erected a workhouse on St Mark's Road, Maidenhead (SU872814). The building, for up to 200 inmates, was designed by Messrs Cooper & Son of Henley and based on the PLC's model 'square' design. The entrance block was a long two-storey range facing east. To its rear, four accommodation wings radiated from a central hub, creating separate yards for the different classes of inmate.

In 1873, a Gothic-style church dedicated to St Mark was built at the east of the main workhouse building. In the mid-1890s, a new boardroom was erected at the left of the site entrance, with a porter's lodge and receiving wards to the right.

In 1930, the site became a PAI run by Berkshire County Council. It joined the NHS as St Mark's Hospital. The former workhouse buildings are now used for administrative purposes.

From the early 1900s, the union operated a number of children's scattered homes in the area.

EASTHAMPSTEAD

In 1777, Winkfield had a workhouse accommodating up to forty inmates. In 1832, the dozen or so residents comprised old men and women, and a few orphan children.

Binfield had a workhouse once on what is now Red Rose (SU 843712). In 1832, it was said to be a 'poor house under the care of a Master and Matron' and occupied by fourteen adults, ten of whom were over 70, three boys and a young child.

What later became the Easthampstead Union workhouse incorporated a group of almshouses dating from 1826 on Crowthorne Road at the south of St Mary Magdalen and St Michael's church in Easthampstead (SU864675). It is said that the clocktower on top of the houses was paid for by a local dignitary. He had originally planned to make the donation to the church of St Mary Magdalene and St Michael which stands opposite, but apparently changed his mind after the local clergy refused to trim an overhanging tree in the churchyard which regularly knocked off his hat.

Easthampstead Poor Law Union was formed in July 1835. A workhouse was established at the almshouse site, with a three-storey block added at the rear of the main row of houses. Later additions included an infirmary in 1869, and a boardroom block in 1901, both at the north-east of the workhouse.

An early 1900s rear view of the Easthampstead Union workhouse. The cupola stands over the original almshouse section of the buildings.

In 1928, longstanding inmate James Wilder, 61, made a series of charges against the workhouse officials. He asserted that while he was in the infirmary, he had had to wear the same underclothing for six weeks without a change, that there was a shortage of soap, that no night nurse had been on duty since Christmas, and that the master had not carried out the regulations. A subsequent inquiry found that the charges were without foundation. As a result of his actions, Wilder was placed on bread and water for a week, received no tobacco allowance for six months, and could take no leave for twelve months.

In 1930, the workhouse was taken over by Berkshire County Council and became a PAI. It joined the NHS in 1948 as Church Hill Hospital. The old almshouses and adjacent buildings have been refurbished and redeveloped as private residential accommodation.

By the early 1900s, the union had a children's cottage home at Wokingham Road, Bracknell. Around 1925, it moved to 76 Binfield Road, Bracknell.

FARINGDON

Faringdon had a workhouse from around 1725. Around 1801, the parish adopted Gilbert's Act and erected a new workhouse on what is now Ferndale Street (formerly Union Street, SU291955). By 1832, a contractor was paid an annual fee of £2,200 to operate the establishment and provide each inmate with 'good meat dinners three days at the least in each week' and 'mutton or such other diet as may be suitable' for any that were sick. A regime of hard labour and strict discipline prevailed.

Buckland opened a workhouse around 1739.[8]

Faringdon Poor Law Union was formed on 2 February 1835, one of the first unions to be declared following the 1834 Act. It took over the existing Faringdon workhouse and spent around £900 on adapting the premises. Assistant Poor Law Commissioner Edward Gulson gave a glowing report of the institution, praising its order and regularity, and rigidly enforced classification of the inmates, and the separation of the sexes. Able-bodied paupers were employed in digging stone out of a pit, which was situated on a piece of land attached to the workhouse.

A new workhouse was built in 1846 to a design by S.O. Foden. The main building, three storeys in height, had an unusual U-shaped layout. The area within the 'U' was divided into four walled exercise yards. A single-storey entrance block faced onto Union Street at the north of the site, with a chapel located at the west side. A workhouse school was placed at the far south of the site.

An aerial view of the U-shaped Faringdon Union workhouse.

After 1930, the former workhouse building was converted into flats which continued in use until the late 1960s. The site was subsequently redeveloped to provide accommodation for the elderly, known as Brackendale.

HUNGERFORD (AND RAMSBURY)

Hungerford had a workhouse from around 1727. Its operation was overseen by a committee of fourteen governors, two of them being responsible for each day of the week.[9] It occupied premises at 21 Bridge Street (now the John O'Gaunt Inn SU339687). In 1783, the establishment moved to a property now known as Charnham Close at 26 Charnham Street (SU338689).[10] In 1830, it could house thirty inmates.

In 1777, workhouses were also in operation at Shalbourne (for up to sixteen inmates), Great Bedwyn (thirty), Ramsbury (seventy) and Tidcombe (twelve).

In 1786, Great Bedwyn was housing its paupers at Wilton, perhaps in the property latterly known as Church Cottages (SU267615).[11] In 1795, there were eleven beds and eight spinning wheels in the house. Rules in 1797 forbade inmates to leave without permission, receive visitors, or collect firewood. The inmates numbered nineteen in 1802–03 and twelve in 1812–13. Tidcombe's workhouse was located at Fosbury and probably closed in 1783.[12]

Ramsbury's workhouse was originally near the site of 79 High Street (SU271714).[13] It was later next to the Blind House, near 34 High Street (SU273715). In 1832, its inmates were ten males aged 6 to 80 years, and eight females aged between 20 and 80 years.

In 1792, Little Bedwyn had a workhouse at Fore Bridge (SU295665).[14]

Under a Local Act of 1800, Aldbourne set up a workhouse at the junction of Oxford Street and South Street (SU265756) but it burned down around 1819.

Chilton Foliat acquired a workhouse or poorhouse around 1804 and employed a resident governor who was also a salaried assistant overseer for the parish.

Lambourn's workhouse, now converted to two cottages, stood on Baydon Road (SU322787). In 1832, it had twenty-two inmates aged from 5 months to 88 years. In the same year, Kintbury had a workhouse housing an average of twenty inmates, chiefly the infirm or orphans.

Hungerford Poor Law Union, which included a number of Wiltshire parishes, was formed in May 1835. Initially, the union retained the existing workhouses at Lambourn and Hungerford. However, it was subsequently

The master and matron of the Hungerford Union workhouse (on first and second steps), with the porter and superintendent nurse in front of the workhouse entrance doors.

decided to improve the Lambourn premises so as to house all the union's indoor poor. The existing Hungerford inmates were transferred to Lambourn in March 1836, although the Guardians continued to meet at Hungerford.

A new workhouse, designed by S.O. Foden, was erected in 1847–48 at the south side of Park Street, Hungerford (SU339683). At the front was a three-storey corridor-plan main block, with females housed at the west and males at the east. To the rear were a single-storey central range, which included a laundry on the female side, and a two-storey infirmary. An isolation block was added further to the south later in the century. A separate chapel, at the north-east of the site, was largely funded by one of the Guardians, the Revd J.L. Popham. Early plans to connect the site to a mains gas supply were dropped when it was found that candles would be much cheaper.[15]

In 1896, the union was renamed the Hungerford and Ramsbury Union.

In 1930, the site became a PAI under the control of Berkshire County Council, then joined the NHS in 1948 as Hungerford Hospital. In 1992–93 Bosnian refugees from Vukovar were housed at the premises. In the late 1990s, the buildings were demolished except for the chapel.

NEWBURY

In 1624, Newbury received a bequest of £4,800 from London draper John Kendrick, to be used to provide 'a strong house of bricke fit and commodious for setting of the poore on worke therein'. A site was purchased where Wharf Street now runs, at the south side of the River Kennet (SU472671). The new building comprised three ranges at the north, east and south of a central courtyard. The west side was formed by the existing old houses on the site. The east side included an entrance archway and contained a dye-house at its northern end, near to the river from which water was piped. The dye-house had two furnaces and two woad vats, the waste from which was taken back to the river. The workhouse had its own weaving shop fitted with four broad looms and one narrow loom. At that date, however, it was not a residential establishment, but rather a place of employment for out-of-work textile workers. That appears to have changed by the 1670s and by 1706 part of the building had been converted to a Blue Coat School for boys. In 1730, it could accommodate 'near 100 persons, young and old'. The surviving south range now houses a museum.

By 1777, Newbury had a workhouse at St Mary Hill, what is now the south end of Cheap Street (SU472668), where 120 paupers could be accommodated.

The south-west yard of Newbury Union workhouse, showing the west range (left), central hub, south range (centre) and mortuary (right).

Thatcham's workhouse, at the south end of the present-day Broadway (SU517672), could house forty inmates in 1777. In 1832, they numbered twenty-three, ranging in age from infants to 70 and upwards.

Chieveley's establishment in 1777 could hold twelve inmates, while the fifteen residents of the Speen workhouse in 1832 included four 'idiots'.

Newbury Poor Law Union was formed in April 1835. It erected a workhouse to the south of Newbury on a site that became 214 Newtown Road (SU473655). The building, for up to 350 inmates, was designed by Sampson Kempthorne and based on his model cruciform plan. The two-storey entrance range, at the north of the site, was linked to a central hub from which three other ranges radiated to the east, west and south. The original infirmary was placed at the south of complex. A new and larger infirmary was later added further to the south.

In 1930, the site became a PAI run by Berkshire County Council. It joined the NHS as Sandleford Hospital, which closed in 2004. The workhouse buildings have now all been demolished.

READING

In 1624, Reading, like Newbury, received a large bequest from London draper John Kendrick for the construction or purchase of premises in which to provide work for poor clothiers. In 1626, the town corporation paid William Kendrick (John's brother) £1,900 for his house and workshops at the south side of Minster Street (SU715733). By 1628, the site had been redeveloped to create an impressive building which became known as The Oracle – the name possibly deriving from 'orchal', a violet dye obtained from lichen. It consisted of rows of workshops around a central courtyard, entered by an ornate Dutch-gabled stone gateway. A small amount of accommodation was provided for several employees, but the establishment was otherwise non-residential. For its first two years, the operation ran at a profit but this soon began to change. In 1639, the workhouse was reorganised to provide training and employment for fatherless children. The building was demolished in 1850.

In the mid-1770s, the parish of St Mary's, Reading, opened a workhouse on Pinkney's Lane (SU710729). In 1797, the establishment usually had around ninety inmates, who slept in beds of flock and feathers. They were employed in spinning hemp and weaving sail cloth, and some were sent out to work for the farmers.

The parish of St Giles' had a workhouse in an old building on Horn Street (now the northern part of Southampton Street, SU716728), which in 1777 could accommodate 100 inmates. St Laurence's workhouse occupied a group of old cottages on Thorn Street (SU711734), where 150 inmates could be housed.[16]

Reading Poor Law Union was formed in August 1835 and took over two of the existing workhouses. St Mary's, housing up to 160 inmates, was used for the aged, the infirm, the sick, mothers and children. St Laurence's, with 190 places, was used for able-bodied paupers and vagrants. In 1846, the PLC expressed concern about sanitary conditions at St Laurence's and suggested the building be replaced. This suggestion was dismissed by the Guardians, although separate accommodation for vagrants was opened in an old granary at the entrance to King's Meadows in The Forbury.

Eventually, in 1865, a site was bought for a new workhouse on the north side of Oxford Road, near Battle Farm (SU728731). The building, designed by Mr Woodman, was based on the layout of the East Grinstead workhouse, with a receiving block, T-shaped main building, infirmary and a fever block ranged behind one another. The establishment opened its doors in August 1867.

A new infirmary was added at the west of the workhouse in 1892 and the old infirmary became a female residential block, with the old workhouse then being used entirely for males. Accommodation was also added for vagrants who, until that date, had continued to be housed at the Forbury.

In 1894, the *British Medical Journal* (BMJ) gave the establishment a glowing report. Unlike many other workhouses reviewed by the BMJ, Reading had a modern infirmary and a well-resourced nursing staff. Pauper assistance was confined to activities such as cleaning and bed-making.

An 1802 view of the entrance to
Reading's 'Oracle' workhouse.

Military personnel stand at the
entrance to Reading Union
workhouse during its use as a
First World War military hospital.

In 1909–11 an additional infirmary block was added at the north of the site for up to 150 aged, infirm and convalescent patients. A new boardroom, administrative block and master's house were also added.

In March 1915, the workhouse was requisitioned for use as a military hospital. The inmates were transferred to other workhouses and the infirmary patients moved into the nearby Grovelands School. The site was handed back to the Guardians in 1920 and the following year was renamed Battle Infirmary.

In 1930, the premises were taken over by Reading Council and renamed Battle Hospital. The hospital finally closed in 2005 and the buildings have since been demolished except for the gatehouse and boardroom.

In 1849, Reading and the neighbouring Wokingham Union formed the Reading & Wokingham School District (see page 166). In 1900, Reading switched to using scattered homes, the first two being at 17–19 King's Road, Reading.

WALLINGFORD

Dorchester had a workhouse from around 1742. It was at the south-west of the village, on the edge of the present allotments, formerly Hempcroft. In 1764, the contractor John Wallis received 30s a week and was required to maintain all the poor in a decent fashion, except for smallpox cases, those with broken bones, or bastards. He also had to buy three beds and bedding, seven bedheads and three spinning wheels. The parish paid for hemp seed which was probably intended for the paupers to harvest and spin. In 1777, the workhouse could house up to twenty inmates.

In 1777, St Mary the More, Wallingford, had a workhouse for up to fifty inmates. In 1807, St Mary and two of the town's other parishes, St Leonard and St Peter, were united under Gilbert's Act. The union built a workhouse for 282 inmates on the Wantage Road (SU600898), about half a mile west of the town centre.

In 1835, Assistant Poor Law Commissioner Richard Hall visited Wallingford to oversee the creation of a new Poor Law Union in the area. He was clearly not impressed by what he found:

> The workhouse was divided into apartments, each furnished and tenanted by a family, by whom it was evidently regarded as their freehold; one woman had resided there for eleven years, and brought up a family of nine children; a shoemaker who had been an inmate seven years, told me that he earned his

own living, and indignantly asserted, that he was entirely independent of the parish; in some rooms were young people just beginning life, having been lately married; in others three or four unmarried mothers, or those who were on the point of becoming so; in some were the sick, or those whose age and infirmities showed that they were on the verge of dissolution; 47 children were variously deposited throughout the building. There was not the slightest attempt at classification; old and young, male and female, sick and sound, were left to mingle at will.[17]

Wallingford Poor Law Union was formed in June 1835 and took over the Gilbert Union workhouse and extended it to accommodate up to 382 inmates. The architect for the new buildings was John Plowman of Oxford.

A fever block was added at the north of the site in 1871. A new infirmary, designed by Charles Smith & Son, was opened at the east of the workhouse in 1898.

In 1930, the site became a PAI under the control of Berkshire County Council. It joined the NHS in 1948 as St Mary's Hospital. In 1966, the former casual block was converted into an orthopaedic clinic. After the hospital closed in 1982, the site was sold for housing redevelopment. It was originally intended to preserve the dining hall block, a red-brick building with a slate roof crowned by a ridge lantern. Although its poor state eventually resulted in its demolition, the site is now occupied by a church building which echoes the style of its predecessor.

In 1900, the union opened a group of three cottage homes, just to the north of the workhouse (SU598900), with accommodation for forty-five children. The buildings are now used by local social services.

WANTAGE

West Hanney had a workhouse around 1739, and Wantage from around 1741.[18] In 1777, the Wantage establishment, located in Grove Street, could house seventy-five inmates. At the same date, a workhouse in Hampstead Norreys accommodated up to ten paupers.

Wantage Poor Law Union was formed in April 1835 and erected a workhouse on Manor Road, 1½ miles to the south of Wantage (SU397855). The architect was Sampson Kempthorne, whose cruciform design provided for 230 inmates.

In 1850, a chapel dedicated to St Michael was erected north of the main workhouse to a design by Mr Butterfield. The original architect for the

A rear view of the Wantage Union workhouse in the early 1900s.

scheme was George Gilbert Scott but his proposal was more expensive than the Guardians wanted. The chapel was around 80ft in length and could accommodate all the workhouse inmates. The building was demolished in the 1940s after becoming unsafe.

In 1869, a new infirmary was erected at the rear of the workhouse, designed by local architect J.P Spencer. It included ordinary and special sick-wards, day-rooms, a lying-in ward, lavatories and bathrooms.

In 1930, the site became a PAI under the control of Berkshire County Council. It joined the NHS in 1948 as the Downs Hospital. After the hospital's closure, most of the old buildings were demolished although some ground-floor sections were converted into single-storey stable buildings.

By 1911, the union operated a home for pauper children on Manor Road, Wantage, where around sixteen children could be accommodated.

WINDSOR

New Windsor erected a workhouse in 1731 at the corner of Sheet Street and Keppel Street (SU982763) – the site of the town's former pest-house and now covered by the Victoria Barracks. The extensive building included a work-room, dining room, pantry, wet larder, kitchen, master's room, brew-house and wash-house, and had a large garden at the back.[19] In September 1795, there were ninety-six inmates, mostly old people and children. Two inmates slept in each of the beds, which were feather-filled. The children were instructed in reading until they were 7 years old, then went out to a free school, where they were clothed and educated till the age of 14. The boys were then apprenticed till they were 21. Some inmates were occupied in making linen and stockings for the use of the house. For other work, such as picking hair and wool, they were allowed 2*d* in every shilling they earned for the house. Breakfast, every day, was bread and broth. Dinner on Sunday was mutton and vegetables; on Monday, Wednesday and Friday, cold meat; on Tuesday and Thursday, beef and vegetables; on Saturday, bread and cheese. Supper, every day, was bread and cheese for adults, and bread and butter for children. At dinner and supper, a pint of small beer was allowed to each adult, with a smaller amount for children. Women who could procure tea and sugar for themselves had bread and butter at breakfast, instead of broth.[20]

Datchet had a poorhouse, later a workhouse, at what is now Old Bridge House on the corner of the High Street and Southlea Road (SU985768). A later workhouse stood at the southern tip of Holmlea Road, now part of Cobb Close (SU995765). One of the inmates' occupations was cutting teasels, used to comb the surface of woollen cloth. They also grew vegetables, fertilised by manure from the workhouse.[21]

In 1777, Egham had a workhouse housing up to thirty-six inmates. Sunninghill erected a workhouse for twenty-five inmates in 1799 near what is now School Road. Clewer's workhouse was a substantial brick-built and tiled building, located near St Leonard's Hill, Clewer Green.[22]

Windsor Poor Law Union was formed in September 1835, the last Berkshire union to begin operation. A delay was caused by Tory parishes around Windsor objecting to being united with New Windsor, which was noted for its radical leanings. The dispute was resolved by adding the Surrey parishes of Egham and Thorpe to the union.

Initially, the union retained four existing workhouses. Aged inmates were housed at Windsor and Egham, the able-bodied at Clewer, and children at Sunninghill. Plans for a new building, on Crimp Hill, Old Windsor (SU977737), were delayed by a legal dispute about the demolition of old cottages on the site, with construction eventually beginning in 1839. Designed by Scott and Moffatt, it comprised a long main block running north–south, with two pairs of cross-wings creating a double-cruciform layout. Females were housed at the north and males at the south. A separate fifty-bed infirmary stood at the rear. The battlemented Elizabethan-style building was somewhat in contrast to the more severe earlier designs encouraged by the PLC.

The entrance to Windsor Union workhouse. Its design was modified during construction so that the roof would not to be visible from Windsor Castle.

Shortly after its opening, Prince Albert paid an unannounced visit to the workhouse and was said to have been highly delighted at what he saw. Queen Victoria herself visited the workhouse in March 1864. In a tour lasting ninety minutes, she visited all the wards, the chapel, and finally the boardroom where she signed the visitors' book.[23]

In 1867, a *Lancet* report gave the workhouse a broadly positive appraisal. Criticisms included the absence of indoor toilets – at night, a large tub was placed on each landing, then carried down the stairs and emptied each morning.[24]

In 1898, a new infirmary block was added at the north of the site. A casual ward with separate sleeping and stone-breaking cells was erected at the south-west. Accommodation for lunatics was added in 1900.

After Berkshire County Council took over the site in 1930, it became a PAI known as Crimp Hill House. It later became the Old Windsor Unit of the King Edward VII Hospital. The hospital closed in 1991 and the building is now in residential use.

WOKINGHAM

Wokingham had a workhouse by the 1760s, located at what is now 22 Denmark Street (SU811684). An inventory in 1769 included tableware for up to eighteen inmates, but only five beds in the establishment.[25] In 1777, the Wokingham Town workhouse was said to be able to house up to fifty inmates.

In the same year, workhouses were in operation at Shinfield (for up to fort-two inmates), Wargrave (fifty), and Woodley and Sandford (fifty).

Wargrave's workhouse was on Victoria Road, Wargrave (SU790786). In 1832, it had twenty-seven inmates, of whom twelve were under the age of 20.

The Shinfield workhouse was at Great Lea Common. The Woodley and Sandford premises were at Cobblers' City, near the present-day junction of Headley Road East and Tipping Lane (SU773736).

Wokingham Poor Law Union was formed in August 1835 and initially made use of the former Wargrave parish workhouse which was upgraded for the purpose. In 1846, however, the premises were said to be too cramped to allow proper segregation of the different classes of inmate, the rooms were damp and badly ventilated, and there was a lack of infirmary and fever wards.

A new workhouse for 250 inmates was built in 1849–50 at a site on the northern side of Barkham Road, Wokingham (SU803685). A competition held to design the building was won by Mr Richard Billing of Reading. His scheme proposed a three-storey T-shaped main block, which housed the aged

The entrance to the Wokingham Union workhouse in the early 1900s.

at the front and the able-bodied at the back. A separate infirmary block to the rear also contained the vagrants' and receiving wards. Women were housed in the eastern half of the site which also included the institution's laundry. Men were placed in the western portion, which was separated from the women's side by the dining hall. A small building housing the Guardians' new board-room was erected at the front of the site in 1898.

In 1930, the site became a PAI under the control of Berkshire County Council. In 1948, it joined the NHS as Wokingham (now Community) Hospital.

In 1849, Wokingham and Reading joined to form the Reading & Wokingham School District, opening a school in the old workhouse premises at Wargrave. The establishment generally had about 150 inmates. Some of the boys were taught tailoring and shoemaking but their main occupation was the cultivation of about 10 acres of land and tending some cows and pigs. The girls carried out all the household duties in preparation for domestic service. The school closed in the early 1900s and the two unions moved to the use of cottage or scattered homes, Wokingham having an establishment on Oxford Road, Wokingham.

5

KENT

BLEAN

A property in Herne Bay was used as a workhouse from at least the 1730s. In 1777, it had thirty inmates. In 1791, the Vicar of Herne and a group of parishioners paid £20 for a small piece of land on the Canterbury Road. A workhouse was built at a cost of £772 and places made available, for a fee, to neighbouring parishes.[1]

In 1777, parish workhouses were in operation at Chislett, St Dunstan, Seasalter, Staplegate, Sturry and Whitstable.

A Gilbert Union, eventually having seventeen members, was formed in 1807 with its workhouse located in the precincts of the Archbishop's Palace, Canterbury. In 1833, it was reported that the combined ages of twenty of the inmates was 1,460, an average of 73 years.[2]

A Gilbert Union based at Whitstable was formed in 1821, its other members being Chislett and Sturry.[3]

Blean Poor Law Union was formed in May 1835 and erected a workhouse for 460 inmates on Canterbury Road, Herne Common (TR176652). It was designed by William Edmunds and based on Sir Francis Head's model court-yard plan. To keep costs down, no outside drains were provided – something that led to problems when water attacked the building's foundations. Within a week of the workhouse opening in January 1836, the jerry-built wall separating the men from the women blew down in a storm.[4] It took more than walls, however, to keep the sexes apart – in 1864, John Harnett and Ellen Piddock, inmates of adjacent wards, received a week's hard labour for gaining night-time access to each other via the building's ceiling ventilators.[5]

The entrance range (left) and west side of the former Blean Union workhouse at Herne
Common.

In 1918, the military took over part of the workhouse to house convalescent servicemen.

The site was taken over by Kent County Council in 1930 as a home
for women with epilepsy or severe learning difficulties. By 1939, it was
almost self-supporting in vegetables and fruit, and pigs and rabbits were kept,
the rabbit skins being sold for glove-making. After 1948, the establishment
joined the NHS as Herne Hospital, providing care for the chronic sick. After
its closure around 1986, the buildings were redeveloped for residential use.

BRIDGE

From 1772 until 1793, the parishioners of Chartham took turns in running its
workhouse for a month at a time.[6] For at least part of its history, the establishment occupied Bedford House, a former inn on The Green (TR202577).

In 1777, workhouses were in use at Bridge (for thirty-six inmates),
Canterbury Holy Cross Westgate Without (thirty), Harbledown (ten),
Nackington (twelve) and Thanington (twelve).

The Waltham (or Petham) Gilbert Union was formed in 1800 and eventually
had thirteen members. It erected a workhouse north of Handville (or Anvil)
Green, Waltham (TR113498).[7] It closed in 1828 and the building became a
chapel, beer shop and bakery. Now known as Waltham Court, the property has
latterly been used as a hotel, restaurant and private residence.

A Gilbert Union based at Harbledown was formed by 1806. In 1832, its workhouse at Rough Common, to the north of Harbledown, had forty inmates.

Littlebourne had a workhouse, now the Old Oast, at 72 The Hill (TR202577). A house on The Street, Wickhambreaux (TR222588), is known as the Old Workhouse.

An existing workhouse at Barham was demolished in 1821 and relocated to Blackingbottle Cottages, at the rear of the Duke of Cumberland pub on The Street (TR207501).[8] In 1832, the inmates comprised eleven adults, a girl with child, and thirteen children under 14 years of age.

Ickham's workhouse was on The Street and is now Ickham Lodge (TR222579).

The Bridge Poor Law Union was formed in May 1835. In February 1836, it opened its newly built workhouse on what became known as Union Road, at the west side of Bridge village (TR179544). Designed by George Lancefield of Canterbury, it followed Sir Francis Head's model courtyard plan and could house up to 350 inmates. The building was extended at its west side around 1870 to add a coach house, dead house and new vagrant wards.

After 1930, the workhouse became a PAI run by Kent County Council, mainly accommodating the elderly. In the 1970s, the buildings were still in use as The Close old people's home but were converted to residential use around 1982.

Some of the original steps, balcony and part of the courtyard's inner dividing wall at the former Bridge Union workhouse, now converted to residential use.

BROMLEY

The original Hayes workhouse caught fire in 1723. It later occupied premises on West Common Road, now known as Redgate Cottage (TQ404655). Inmates had to be in bed within an hour of supper, which was at 5 p.m. from November to February, 7 p.m. from May to August, and 6 p.m. at other times. Anyone earning wages could keep one third, the rest being taken for general workhouse expenses.[9]

Bromley erected a workhouse in 1731. It was located at the west of London Road, almost opposite what is now Farwig Lane (TQ399695), and could house eighty inmates. In March 1744, Thomas Richards was appointed workhouse master. He was paid 2s per inmate per week, for which he was to provide 'firing, soap and candles', feed the inmates according to the specified Bill of Fare, teach any children in the workhouse for two hours a day, and put the able-bodied paupers to work – any income from their labour going into his own pocket. The workhouse had fifty-six inmates in 1777 but had closed by 1832, when forty paupers were being farmed out.

Cudham's workhouse, also built in 1731, was at the east side of the main road at Leaves Green (TQ415616). The property is now a private residence.

By 1756, Farnborough had a workhouse at Locksbottom.[10]

Beckenham's workhouse stood on Cow Lees, south of the junction of Bromley Road and Oakwood Avenue (TQ381693). The building had two storeys plus attics. The ground floor contained the master's parlour, a committee room, a hall for cooking and eating, and a large ward for male inmates. On the first floor were two bedrooms, a children's room, and a store also used as the female inmates' sitting room. The building also had a wash-house and mangle room, two pantries and a cellar. There were fourteen bedsteads in the establishment, which in 1777 could house up to thirty-five inmates. In 1818, paupers were allowed to bring any furniture they possessed into the house. Male inmates were employed in the garden and in chopping wood, and the females in knitting and domestic duties.[11]

Chislehurst erected a workhouse in 1759 on School Road (TQ442701). In 1777, it could house seventeen inmates, and in 1832 twenty-three were in residence, including ten children. Up to 1808, the inmates worked at spinning then changed to making sails and rope. The property later housed St Michael's Home for Boys.[12]

A Gilbert Union was formed in 1816 by St Mary Cray and Orpington.[13] Its workhouse was at Reynolds Smith, a hamlet near the border of the two parishes.[14]

The Bromley Union workhouse in the early 1900s.

Bromley Poor Law Union was formed in May 1836 and initially retained the existing workhouse premises at Chislehurst (for able-bodied paupers), St Mary Cray (children) and Bromley (the aged and infirm). In 1844, a large new workhouse, designed by James Savage and S.O. Foden, was erected at Locksbottom, 3 miles south-east of Bromley (TQ433650). Its front block had a three-storey central section flanked by two-storey wings. Accommodation for boys or girls, again three storeys high, was placed at each end. A central spine led to a parallel accommodation block to the rear, then continued through to a third parallel block, the original infirmary.

The inmates originally attended services at Holy Trinity Church, but their uniforms and segregation from local worshippers led to a chapel being erected at the workhouse in 1862.[15] In 1872, a new ninety-bed infirmary was erected at the site, and over the years the medical facilities expanded considerably to the north and east.

The main workhouse building had been demolished by the 1930s. Around 1934, the site became Farnborough Hospital, now the Princess Royal University Hospital. The chapel, now a private residence, is the only surviving workhouse building.

CANTERBURY

In 1727, fourteen Canterbury parishes were incorporated under a Local Act, allowing them to jointly operate a workhouse. It occupied a building known as the Poor Priest's Hospital on what is now Stour Street (TR147577). Able-bodied adults were occupied in weaving hop sacks, making their own clothes and beating hemp. Children performed knitting, sewing, and spinning linen and hop bagging. In 1832, there were 237 inmates, including 50 children and 2 infants. The sexes were completely separated and there were separate wards for the aged and for deserted and orphan children, who were taken care of by nurses. Those who were capable were employed in scavenging, weaving, shoemaking and agriculture.

Its Local Act status exempted the Incorporation from the 1834 Act, and it continued in operation until 1881 when it was reconstituted as a Poor Law Union, then becoming a single Poor Law Parish in 1897.

In 1846, the architect S.O. Foden and former Assistant Poor Law Commissioner Henry Parker published their proposed design for a new Incorporation workhouse. Unlike earlier workhouse layouts, which they claimed were based on American prison buildings, their projected scheme for Canterbury aimed to be more humane, particularly for the aged and young,

The now-demolished entrance block of Canterbury workhouse in 2001.

with their exercise yards bounded by open fences rather than high walls, and with covered play-sheds for the children.[16] The design subsequently built by the Incorporation, by local architect Hezekiah Marshall, was somewhat different in style, although with a similar double-courtyard layout. It was erected in 1848–50 at Nunnery Fields (TR150567) and housed over 400 inmates. A seventy-bed infirmary block was added at the west of the workhouse in 1883.

In 1930, the site became a PAI known as The Home. In 1948, it joined the NHS as Nunnery Fields Hospital, providing geriatric care. After its closure in 2001, the main building was demolished but the 1883 infirmary was converted to residential use.

From around 1911, the parish operated cottage homes at 113 Wincheap, Canterbury (TR138567), housing up to fifty children. The site later became the Woodville Homes and in more recent times has been used as a training centre.

CRANBROOK

A workhouse operated at Cranbrook from around 1723.[17] From 1763, it occupied part of Sissinghurst Castle (TQ807383), which had previously housed French prisoners of war. The parish also took over the castle's farm. With inmates providing the labour, the farm provided most of the workhouse's food requirements. By 1777, the establishment could house 100 paupers. In 1832, the inmates numbered 133, of whom 71 were children under 15. All the men and boys were employed on the land.

Hawkhurst built a workhouse in 1726.[18] Its premises on The Moor (TQ755294) could accommodate 100 inmates. In 1832, there were forty in residence.

Frittenden workhouse housed up to forty inmates in the present-day Charity Farm building on Headcorn Road (TQ815412).

The workhouse at Sandhurst occupied what is now Fairview Cottages on Back Road (TQ799283).

Goudhurst had a workhouse from 1725.[19] By 1777, it could house fifty-five inmates and occupied what is now Clayhill Cottages on Clayhill Lane (TQ720375). In 1832, there were 100 paupers in residence.

Benenden opened a workhouse in 1732 in Feoffees Cottages on Walkhurst Road (TQ812330). In 1777, it could house forty paupers.

Cranbrook Poor Law Union was formed in November 1835. In 1838, the union erected a new workhouse on Hartley Road, half a mile to the southwest of Cranbrook (TQ760350). Designed by John Whichcord, the building was broadly based on Sir Francis Head's model courtyard plan.

The Cranbrook Union workhouse in the early 1900s.

On 12 March 1907, a fire caused serious damage at the workhouse. The following year, there was a scandal involving the master, Henry Fincham, and two local suppliers, grocer Charles Fagg and publican James Miles. Fincham had accepted goods of inferior quality and smaller quantity than had been ordered, the difference in value being credited to his account at the two men's establishments. Fincham got six months' hard labour, the other two receiving lesser sentences.

In 1930, Kent County Council took over the site which was redesignated as Hartley House PAI, later becoming an old people's home. The surviving parts of the building are now in private residential use.

DARTFORD

Dartford erected a workhouse in 1729 at the corner of West Hill and Priory Hill (TQ538743). Able-bodied adult inmates were employed in 'domestick or mechanical services' and the children were taught to read and say their catechism and trained for domestic service.[20] Inmates were allowed out for work, their wages going into workhouse funds. Discipline was strict, with serious offences punished by whipping. In 1740, a girl named Betty Pinden was birched after apparently trying to poison the workhouse mistress.[21] Inmate numbers rose from around 30 in 1758 to 105 in 1832.

By 1766, Bexley operated a workhouse on the High Street (TQ494735), where up to forty inmates were housed. In 1787, a new building was erected on the site, now 34–36 High Street.[22] A course of bricks can still be seen bearing the date 1787 and the initials of vestry members. In 1832, the forty-three inmates were aged from 1 to 82 years.

Swanscombe's workhouse occupied a property at Greenhithe, donated to the parish in 1721.[23] It had sixteen inmates in 1777.

At Eynsford, Bower House, on Bower Lane (TQ542655), was once a workhouse housing up to fifteen paupers.

In 1774, a new workhouse at Greensted Green (now Green Street Green) in the parish of Darenth was also used by paupers from Horton Kirby. In 1777, it had thirty-six inmates.

In 1777, workhouses were also in use at Crayford (up to twenty-six inmates), Erith (forty), and Sutton at Hone (forty).

Crayford's workhouse was described in 1816 as a 'wretched building unhealthily placed in the low and wet marshes'.[24]

In 1808, the parish of Wilmington used the sale of annuities to raise money for the erection of a workhouse.[25] In 1832, the inmates comprised twelve adults and ten children. At the same date, Farningham's establishment housed five able-bodied men, six boys and four infirm inmates.

Erith's workhouse was on Sussex Road (formerly Old Workhouse Road), Northumberland Heath (TQ497772).

Dartford Poor Law Union was formed in May 1836. It retained the West Hill site and erected a large new building designed by John Whichcord. The

The long West Hill frontage of the former Dartford Union workhouse.

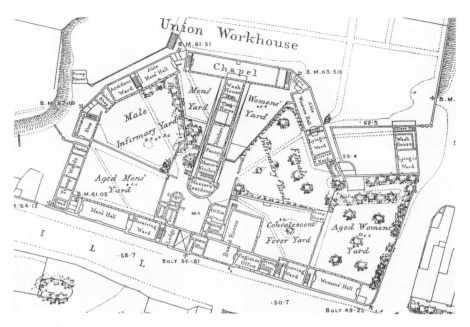

An 1868 map of the Dartford Union workhouse. Women were housed at the east side and men at the west.

long entrance block, facing West Hill, had an archway at its centre, flanked by the porter's lodge and boardroom. The female receiving ward and aged women's quarters lay at the east, mirrored by those for men at the west, with tramp wards at the far west. The semi-circular building at the rear again had men's accommodation to the west and women's to the east, and a chapel at its centre. A range projecting from the side of the chapel contained a wash-house, kitchens and the master's residence, whose windows obtained good views of the inmates' exercise yards. A separate chapel was erected at the north of the workhouse in 1878, and infirmaries at the north and west in 1887–97.

In 1913, the hospital part of the site became known as the King Edward Hospital. During the First World War, the workhouse and hospital were taken over by the Vickers company as accommodation for its munitions workers. In 1930, Kent County Council took over the site, which in 1935 was renamed the County Hospital. After joining the NHS in 1948, it became West Hill Hospital.

In 1986, a project was launched to refurbish the disused workhouse section, now used as business premises. The hospital closed in 2000 and the buildings demolished apart from the now derelict 1878 chapel.

In 1903, the union built the Manor Gate children's home on Common Lane, Wilmington (TQ523725). The building is now a nursing home.

DOVER

In 1777, there was little use of workhouses in the Dover area. Ten inmates could be housed at Buckland's establishment, three at River, and just one at Hougham. The parish of St Mary the Virgin, Dover, had a workhouse at St Katharine's Place, Charlton (TR314421).

The River Gilbert Union was formed in 1793. Its workhouse, at 33 Valley Road, River (TR294432), had 161 inmates in 1802. They were employed in the knitting of hose, shoemaking, spinning, and weaving sacks and woollen and linen cloth.

The Martin Gilbert Union, formed in 1789, had a workhouse on The Street, Martin (TR339470). It housed up to fifty inmates, who were occupied in weaving linen, sacking and sheeting.[26]

The River Poor Law Union, created in April 1835, was renamed Dover Union in 1837. It was initially proposed to extend the existing River workhouse. However, selling the property and building a new workhouse proved a cheaper option.[27]

The new establishment was in an area known as Buckland Bottom, on what became Union Road (now Coombe Valley Road), Dover (TR302420). It was designed by George Lancefield and based on Sir Francis Head's model courtyard plan. The institution began operation in April 1836, providing accommodation for up to 500. One old man, named Young, died while being transferred from the old River workhouse.

The children's block at the former Dover Union workhouse, later Buckland Hospital.

Additions to the buildings from the 1880s onwards included several infirmary blocks, a nurses' home, a chapel and a children's block.

In 1930, the site became a PAI under the control of Kent County Council. A major reconstruction of the buildings took place in 1937–38, with the demolition of some of the buildings fronting Union Road, including the old boardroom.

During the Second World War, the site was used as a casualty hospital and from 1943 was known as the County Hospital. After joining the NHS in 1948, it became the Buckland Hospital. In 2015, the hospital moved into a new building on an adjacent site.

EAST ASHFORD

In 1777, workhouses were in use at Brabourne (for up to thirty inmates), Eastwell (ten), Mersham (twelve) and Wye (forty). The Five Bells public house on The Street in Brabourne (TR100419) was originally built as the parish workhouse.

Chilham had a workhouse by 1811.[28] In January 1822, an inmate named Charles Shornden, who was about to be committed to prison for insubordination in the house, attempted to commit suicide by jumping down a well over 180ft deep. He was rescued and duly imprisoned.[29] In 1832, the workhouse was occupied by 'old persons and families who support themselves, the old people on an allowance'. In the same year, the Wye workhouse had twenty-one inmates aged from 4 to 70 years.

The former East Ashford workhouse, now converted to residential use.

A Gilbert Union was formed by Ruckinge, Orlestone and Warehorne, with its workhouse at Warehorne.[30]

East Ashford Poor Law Union was formed in June 1835 and erected a workhouse for 350 inmates on Willesborough Lees Road (now Kennington Road), Willesborough (TR034423). The two-storey building, constructed in red brick, was designed by John Whichcord and based on Sir Francis Head's model courtyard plan. In 1897–98, a separate infirmary building was added at the west of the site. By 1908, a chapel had been erected to the north.

In December 1884, the workhouse narrowly escaped destruction after a 16-year-old inmate named John Farncombe set fire to the building after locking a fellow resident in a dormitory. The fire spread to the female dormitories and a woman was burned to death. Farncombe later received seven months' hard labour.[31]

In 1930, Kent County Council took over the establishment which became Gill House PAI. In 1948, it joined the new NHS as Willesborough Hospital. After the hospital's closure in 1979, the surviving section of the main workhouse building was converted to residential use. For many years, the chapel was used as a children's nursery.

EASTRY

In 1725, Ash opened a workhouse in rented premises on The Street, opposite the church.[32] The parish erected a 'large and commodious' new workhouse in 1780 on the Sandwich Road. In 1832, forty-seven inmates were aged from 1 to 90 years. The building was later part of the White Post Brewery (TR290583).

By 1710, Deal housed its indoor poor in the Court House on Rectory Road (TR362518), which in 1777 could house 155 inmates. A new workhouse was built in 1782 on West Street, where St Andrew's Church now stands (TR374529).[33] In 1832, the workhouse, now said to operate under Gilbert's Act, had 207 inmates, including a woman in her 90s.

St Mary, Sandwich, established a workhouse in 1725, which the town's other parishes could pay to make use of.[34] In 1735, the parish of St Peter erected its own workhouse, 'in the angle between Love Lane and King Street' (TR331581).[35] In 1777, all three parishes had workhouses, with thirty-six places in St Mary's, twenty-four in St Peter's, and thirty in St Clement's. St Peter's and St Mary's opened a joint workhouse 1798 in Moat Sole. The arrangement ended in 1816 and St Peter's took over the premises, which stood within its bounds. The elderly inmates were subsequently looked after by a woman under the management of an overseer.[36]

In 1777, Wingham's workhouse could house fifteen inmates. In the same year, Nonington opened a workhouse at the north side of Church Street, now Yew Tree Cottages (TR251521). By 1822, its overcrowded state led the vestry to build six cottages for the parish poor further along Church Street, the workhouse itself also being subdivided into eight small dwellings. The establishment continued to have a superintendent and the inmates wove hemp sacks.[37] In 1832, it had sixteen aged and infirm inmates.

In 1793, Eastry became the centre of a Gilbert Union that eventually had sixteen members. It erected a workhouse at the south side of Mill Lane, Eastry (TR308546).

Eythorne, a member of the River Gilbert Union (see page 177) from around 1800, had previously built its own workhouse, which was sold in 1808.[38]

A house at the east end of Northbourne's main street (TR334521) accommodated its parish poor.[39]

Woodnesborough's workhouse, now Street Farm House, was at the east of the village, just off The Street (TR311571). The house and surrounding land were known as Workhouse Farm well into the twentieth century.

Eastry Poor Law Union was formed in April 1835 and erected a new workhouse adjacent to the existing Mill Lane premises. Designed by William Spanton, it was based on Sir Francis Head's model courtyard plan and could house 400 inmates. A three-storey infirmary and detached fever wards were erected to the south of the workhouse in 1871. A chapel was built next to Mill Lane.

The decaying remains of the former Eastry Union workhouse in 2001.

In January 1924, the sole occupant of the vagrants' ward was found in the middle of the night trembling with fear. He related how 'something in white', uttering dreadful, guttural sounds, had approached with long, thin, bony fingers spread out as though to throttle him. It disappeared when he screamed. After the Guardians made it known that a ghost had been seen, there was a falling off in the number of vagrants applying for shelter.[40]

In 1930, Kent County Council took over the site which became Eastry PAI, mainly housing the elderly and chronic sick. After 1948, it joined the NHS as Eastry Hospital, which became a centre for those with learning disabilities. The hospital closed around 1990 and only the chapel and part of the entrance range survive.

ELHAM

By 1777, Elham had a workhouse for up to sixty inmates. In 1789, it moved to the west side of Elham High Street. In 1808, a Gilbert Union was formed based at Elham, using the workhouse and adjacent master's house at what is now 20–22 Elham High Street (TR176440). The union eventually had ten members.

In Newington, a property at the east side of Church Street (TR182374) was once the parish workhouse.

In St Leonard's, Hythe, a workhouse was located on Stade Street.

Folkestone erected a workhouse in 1783 at the corner of Dover Road and St John's Street (TR230363). In 1832, there were sixty-three inmates, aged from 5 months to 84 years. Sweeping the streets had become their sole occupation after the development of mechanised looms had made the workhouse's weaving manufactory obsolete. In 1834, a British School took over the premises. Flats now occupy the site.

At the north side of Lyminge High Street (TR160409), a single-storey building dated 1830 housed the parish poor. A married couple lived there rent-free in return for looking after the inmates.[41] A flying-bomb destroyed the building in 1944.

In 1816, a property known as Swanhouse, on Swan Lane, Sellindge (TR107382), was left to the parish and was used as a workhouse.[42]

Following the formation of Elham Poor Law Union in June 1835, the Guardians erected a new workhouse at 'Each End Hill' (Etchinghill, TR167393) housing up to 300 inmates. It was based on Sir Francis Head's model courtyard plan.

The chapel is now the only surviving part of the Elham workhouse.

In the 1890s, major additions were made to the site including a new administration block at the east side of the workhouse, an infirmary at the south-east, a chapel at the north-east, and casual wards at the north near to the road.

In 1908, workhouse inmate John Keel Shepherd died at the age of 108.

After 1930, the site was taken over by Kent County Council and became Hill House PAI. In 1948, it joined the NHS as St Mary's Hospital and provided geriatric care. The site has now been redeveloped and all the buildings demolished apart from the chapel.

In 1888, the union erected children's cottage homes on Cheriton High Street (TR190369). The site is now used by local social services.

FAVERSHAM

Faversham's first workhouse was opened in 1722 at the south side of Church Street, near the church (TR017615). In 1777, it could house up to seventy inmates. To obtain more space, the workhouse relocated in 1822 to the hospital of a former army barracks at Ospringe, at the north side of what is now

Sheerways (TR001609).[43] In 1832, it housed seventy-five inmates, of whom thirty-one were under 14 years. Those that were able worked on the roads or in the garden. The aged lived apart from the able-bodied and were allowed tea and sugar on top of the usual diet. The weekly allowance for the able-bodied was 6lb 6oz of bread, 4lb of meat, 4lb of suet puddings, and as much soup and vegetables as they could eat. Inmates dined together but, with the exception of married couples, slept in separate apartments. To reduce the expense of accommodating 'distressed travellers', a separate room was built at the workhouse where a night's lodging was provided sleeping on clean straw. After its second week of operation, the number of applicants for the facility had fallen to one.

A building at the north side of Workhouse Road in Throwley (TQ993545) is still known as the Old Workhouse. In 1777, it housed up to a dozen paupers. In the same year, workhouses were also in operation at Boughton-under-Blean (for up to forty inmates), and Sheldwich (sixteen).

A Gilbert Union based at Selling was formed in 1790, eventually having fourteen members. The union had a workhouse at Hogben's Hill, Selling (TR032566). Later converted to cottages, the property was known as Harefield Square, now just The Square.

In 1792, Ospringe erected a workhouse at Painter's Forstal (TQ994594), now known as the Old House.

Lynsted accommodated its poor in a large house now known as Bumpit on Bogle Road, Lynsted (TQ949612). In 1777, it could house 100 inmates. In 1816, Lynsted formed a Gilbert Union with the adjacent parish of Teynham.

Doddington's workhouse, on Dully Hill (TQ929571), was later converted into two cottages which were demolished in 1987.[44] Preston had a workhouse at the corner of Canterbury Road and Slaters Lane (TR017604)

Faversham Poor Law Union was created in March 1835. A new workhouse for 400 paupers was erected in 1836 at Gravel Pit Road (now Lower Road), Faversham (TR001614). Designed by John Day, it was based on Sir Francis Head's model courtyard plan.

In January 1854, a 72-year-old inmate named Thomas Culver died after a pauper nurse inadvertently gave him disinfectant rather than the intended 'house medicine'.[45]

From 1930, the site was run by Kent County Council and known as Gravel Pit House PAI, renamed Bensted House by 1939. In 1948, it joined the NHS as Bensted House Hospital, providing care for geriatric patients up until the 1980s. The former workhouse buildings were subsequently demolished and the Lewis Close housing development (named after Lionel Lewis and his wife, the master and matron from 1945) was erected on the site.

GRAVESEND AND MILTON

In 1777, the parishes of Gravesend and Milton each had a workhouse accommodating up to fifty inmates. By 1783, they were sharing an establishment at the north side of The Terrace, behind the Clarendon Royal Hotel. The property was later known as Grape Vine Cottage.[46] In 1786, the inmates numbered about sixty and were mostly occupied in spinning and knitting.[47]

Gravesend erected a new workhouse in 1797, at what is now 20–23 Stone Street (TQ646739). In 1832, the sixty-seven inmates included sixteen under the age of 14. The men were mostly former watermen, fishermen and labourers. At the same date, Milton's workhouse had twenty-five inmates, who included former labourers, mechanics and watermen.

Gravesend and Milton Poor Law Union was formed in September 1835 and initially continued using the existing Gravesend workhouse. In 1846–47, the union erected a new building at Trafalgar Road, Gravesend (TQ644736). Designed by John Gould, it had an entrance block at the south containing the Guardians' boardroom, master's room and schoolrooms. The T-shaped main block contained the kitchens and dining hall in its projecting central range. Later additions included an infirmary in 1855, a new children's ward in 1882, and accommodation for lunatics in 1891.

Gravesend's former parish workhouse erected in 1797 on Stone Street.

In 1930, the establishment became a PAI run by Kent County Council. It joined the NHS in 1948 as St James' Hospital, finally closing in 1985. The site was then redeveloped as the St James Oaks sheltered housing complex, with the workhouse buildings being demolished.

In 1899, the union opened children's homes at 28–29 (later renumbered as 32–33) Clarence Place, Gravesend (TQ648734), now private residences.

HOLLINGBOURNE

Lenham had a workhouse from around 1730 on Faversham Road (TQ898522). In 1777, it held forty inmates. Only its mortuary (later a village lock-up) survives.

In 1777, workhouses were also in operation at Hollingbourne (for up to forty inmates), Boxley (thirty-six) and Sutton Valence (twenty).

A cottage on Sittingbourne Road, Detling (TQ784577), was used as a workhouse in the early 1800s. The Cloth Hall, on North Street, Headcorn (TQ832442), had a similar function. East Sutton's workhouse premises survive as Workhouse Cottages on Workhouse Lane (TQ824500). Ulcombe had a workhouse on The Street.

Hollingbourne Poor Law Union was formed in October 1835 and initially took over the existing workhouse premises at Hollingbourne, Lenham and Headcorn, with the Ulcombe premises being used as a store. The following year, a new union workhouse was erected at Whiteheath Field on the Maidstone to Ashford Road (TQ820548). It had an H-shaped layout and housed up to 300 inmates. The building was enlarged in 1838 to add a schoolroom, chapel, extra dormitories and a lying-in ward. The infirmary was extended in 1839.[48]

In the 1860s, a fife and drum band was started for the boys in the workhouse. In 1864, the children had an outing to Gravesend. An inspection in 1866 noted that adult male inmates were employed in gardening, while the boys learned tailoring and shoemaking. Women and girls were occupied in oakum picking, domestic work and needlework.[49]

A new washing machine was installed at the workhouse in 1900. The weekly laundry then required the employment of just one woman rather than the four that had previously been needed, and the work was finished by Wednesday at the latest.

In November 1914, nineteen wounded soldiers were treated in the workhouse, the first such institution in the country to house war casualties.

The workhouse was closed around 1921 and the buildings subsequently demolished except for the mortuary, which still stands on the site.

The Hollingbourne Union workhouse in about 1920.

A view just inside the entrance of the Hoo Union workhouse in about 1912.

HOO

In 1777, the Hoo parish of Allhallows had a workhouse housing up to six paupers.

Following the formation of the Hoo Union in September 1835, a workhouse was erected on the Main Road at Hoo St Werburgh (TQ778721). Its design was based on Sir Francis Head's model courtyard plan.

In December 1840, the workhouse master at Hoo, James Miles, was accused of flogging several young female inmates. It was said that he had made them bare the upper parts of their body and beaten them with birch rods. Miles was subsequently given six months' imprisonment. As a result of the affair, the PLC banned the corporal punishment of female workhouse inmates.

The Hoo workhouse was closed around 1921 and later converted for use as council offices. The building was demolished in the 1960s.

ISLE OF THANET

Ramsgate's workhouse was erected in 1724 on a site that now lies under Sussex Street (TR384653). In 1777, it housed up to eighty-four paupers. The number in residence in 1832 was 105, the females being occupied in domestic duties and the males in grinding corn or working for the surveyor of the highways.

The St Lawrence in Thanet workhouse was also erected in 1724, on Chapel Road. The establishment kept pigs and the men received a regular tobacco ration.[50] Forty inmates could be housed in 1777, with the same number resident in 1832 when they included twenty-four aged over 70, together with six idiots and children.

St John's, Margate, had a workhouse from 1727. A large, new building, two storeys high, was erected in 1769 on Prospect Place, now Victoria Road (TR356704).[51] In 1832, there were 203 inmates, aged from 1 to 80 years. A few rooms were fitted up for aged couples.

St Peter in Thanet opened a workhouse in 1753 at the north side of the High Street, Broadstairs (TR383683). A new building was erected in 1810, paid for by Thomas Brown, a London merchant. Its facilities included a linen manufactory. In 1832, there were about fifty inmates. The property was bought in 1836 by the vicar, the Revd John Hodgson, and became Nuckell's Almshouse.[52]

In 1777, the workhouse at Minster in Thanet housed up to thirty inmates.

After many years of boarding out its paupers at the St Peter in Thanet workhouse, Birchington formed a Gilbert Union in 1794 with Monkton, Sarre and

The Isle of Thanet workhouse. A long line of washing can be seen right of centre.

Acol, and erected a workhouse on Park Lane, Birchington (TR304687). The inmates worked at making coarse sheeting and sacking. From 1822–25, the workhouse was run by a contractor, Edward Young, who received 2*s* 6*d* a week 'to victual, lodge, wash and clothe' the inmates.[53] The building is now a private house.

The Isle of Thanet Poor Law Union was created in April 1835 and erected a workhouse at Tothill Street, Minster (TR311655). It adopted Sir Francis Head's courtyard plan and accommodated up to 400 inmates.

In 1839, the Guardians resolved that any 'pauper pregnant with a bastard child' should 'wear a cap without a border and a yellow sleeve to the gown as a mark of disgrace'. A few months later, the PLC banned such practices.[54]

In 1849, a cholera outbreak led to several deaths in the workhouse and all the able-bodied inmates were sent out and given out-relief. After a similar occurrence in 1854, the Guardians rejected a PLB recommendation that they build fever wards, deciding they were unnecessary.[55] In 1863, however, a new infirmary was built, extending east from the south range of the workhouse. A chapel was also erected at the east of the infirmary and a casual ward at the north.

From 1915–20, the workhouse infirmary served as Hill House Military Hospital. In 1930, Kent County Council took over the site which became Hill House PAI. In 1948, the establishment joined the NHS as Hill House Hospital. It closed in 1986 and the buildings were demolished in 1989. Housing now stands on the site.

In 1901, the union opened children's cottage homes at Preston Road, Manston (TR348663). They comprised four pairs of houses and accommodated a total of 120 children. The houses are now private residences.

MAIDSTONE

Maidstone erected a workhouse in 1720 at the west end of Knightrider Street (TQ761554). It was a 'large and handsome building of three stories high, ninety-one feet in length, and twenty-one in depth, with a large kitchin thrown behind'. Over the door was the cautionary text, 'If any would not work, neither should he eat'. In 1724, the inmates comprised seventeen women, five men and eighteen children. Of these, the three women and eight children able to work were employed in spinning worsted. The elderly did housework and taught the children to read. The children had a small play area behind the house.[56] In 1777, the premises housed up to 150 inmates. The following year, the workhouse advertised 'Seven strong hearty boys, from 13 to 15 years of age – and seven girls from 14 to 16 years – to be disposed of as apprentices, by applying to the Master.'[57] A Local Act in 1780 established the Trustees of the Poor to administer poor relief. From around 1822, the workhouse was run by a contractor who in 1832 was paid 3s 9d a head per week. Twine, ropes and sacking were made. Working inmates received 3d a day, while the old and impotent were 'induldged with tea, snuff and tobacco'. From 1842, the site was occupied by the Bluecoat School, then from 1907 by the Baptist church, which still stands there.

A workhouse existed at Linton in 1737, and by 1777 Bearsted had an establishment for twenty-seven inmates.

In 1771, a workhouse was built at Coxheath, south of the junction of Workhouse Lane and Stockett Lane (TQ743517). Its use was eventually shared by a dozen parishes. The inmates manufactured hop-bagging.[58] In 1832, there were 90 inmates although the number was up to 160 in winter. Those who were able were set to agricultural work on the workhouse's 4 acres of land, or to quarry and break stone.

Yalding had a workhouse from around 1734.[59] In 1777, the building could house thirty paupers. In 1795, the workhouse moved to larger premises at what is now Acton Place Cottages on Vicarage Road, Yalding (TQ700502).

Church Cottage, on West Street, Hunton (TQ723497), was once a poorhouse.

Staplehurst opened a workhouse in 1753 at Bly Court, Chapel Lane (TQ787432). In 1777, it could house forty-five paupers.

The Maidstone Union workhouse as seen from its entrance driveway.

Marden's workhouse was built in 1790 on what is now Albion Road (TQ747444). It had three floors, with eight large rooms on the ground floor, eight large bedrooms and four attics. In 1832, there were fifty-two inmates. The site is now occupied by The Allens housing scheme but the workhouse pump survives.

Coxheath Poor Law Union was created in October 1835 from parishes in the Maidstone area, but excluding Maidstone itself, which hoped to retain its Local Act administration. However, the PLC decreed that it should join the Coxheath Union which was then renamed the Maidstone Union.

An initial scheme to enlarge the existing Maidstone workhouse was vetoed by the PLC. Instead, a site was purchased at the south of Heath Road, Coxheath (TQ744509), on which a new building was erected. It was designed by John Whichcord and based on Sir Francis Head's courtyard plan. A separate school building was later erected at the opposite side of Heath Road. An ornate, Gothic-style chapel, dedicated as Holy Trinity, was erected at the north of the workhouse in 1883.

In 1930, the workhouse became a PAI known as the Coxheath Home, then joined the NHS in 1948 as Linton Hospital. The school site later became John Day House, accommodating the elderly mentally infirm. All the buildings except the chapel were demolished in about 1994.

MALLING

From 1749, Birling and Snodland shared the use of a workhouse with Luddesdown and Halling.[60] It occupied the old Bishop's Palace at Halling (TQ705639).

On Common Road, Ightham, a property dating from 1753, now The Old Cottage (TQ557587), was the parish workhouse. It could house twenty inmates in 1777.

By 1777, workhouses were also in use at West Malling (for up to twenty inmates), Aylesford (forty), Birling (twenty-eight), Mereworth (fourteen), East Peckham (forty), West Peckham (twenty), Shipborne (eleven), Wateringbury (fifteen) and Wouldham (five).

A row of cottages near the parish church on St Mary's Road in Wrotham (TQ610590) now bears the name Workhouse Cottages, indicating their former use as a home for up to eighty paupers. Workhouse Lane, at Ryarsh (TQ665600), similarly points to the location of the local institution.

Malling Poor Law Union was formed in October 1835. A new workhouse for 360 inmates was erected in 1836 on King Hill, West Malling (TQ671562). John Whichcord's design was broadly similar to his layout for Dartford workhouse. It had a long entrance range with a central archway, and a T-shaped main block with the leg of the 'T' protruding forward from the main accommodation range at the rear.

In May 1838, three young inmates, boys named Moss, Murdock and Styles, were given three weeks' imprisonment with hard labour by Tunbridge Wells magistrates. The boys had risen early, put bolsters in their beds, let themselves out of a window and scampered for some hours over the countryside, returning at breakfast time.

In 1930, the site became a PAI run by Kent County Council. Later used as short-term accommodation for homeless families, it was the subject of a much-publicised protest in 1965 because of its rules forbidding husbands to stay overnight and a limit of three months on stays there.

The buildings were demolished in the 1980s.

MEDWAY

Rochester had two workhouses, both erected in 1724, with local MPs Sir Thomas Colby and Sir John Jennings each contributing £100 towards their construction. The first, in St Margaret's parish, was erected at the west side of St Margaret's Street (TQ740682). It was managed by twelve annually elected governors who took turns to visit the workhouse each day.[61] In 1777, it could house up to seventy paupers. In 1832, there were about 100 inmates, mostly aged and infirm. The second establishment, in the parish of St Nicholas, situated on The Common, the present-day Corporation Street. The inmates were occupied in spinning worsted and yarn.[62] In 1777, the premises could house ninety inmates.

A workhouse was built in 1725 on Chatham High Street, again with £100 donations from Rochester's two MPs. The inmates picked oakum for the local shipyard, and spun wool and flax, from which their own clothing was made. The children attended school in the morning then in the afternoon were occupied in spinning and sewing or in picking oakum. Boys were apprenticed as fisher-men, carpenters, blacksmiths and other trades, while girls were put into service.[63] In 1832, when there were 317 inmates, the arrangement and management of the workhouse were described as extremely bad. The premises consisted of two long lines of buildings, enclosing a narrow yard, which was the only place of exercise for both sexes, the young and the aged, for prostitutes and for decent females. A number of the day-rooms and workshops were underground. A little oakum picking was the only work required. The inmates were provided with

The west wing of the former Medway Union workhouse main building, shortly before its demolition in 2001.

the finest wheaten bread – an attempt to introduce bread made from second flour had nearly caused a mutiny. Good quality beer was brewed in the house, but the paupers insisted on having porter and gin, which was allowed to them.

In 1764, the former Ship Inn on Church Street, Gillingham, was converted to a workhouse.[64] In 1777, it could accommodate sixty inmates.

Medway Poor Law Union was formed in September 1835 and took over the existing workhouse buildings in Chatham (for the aged, infirm and sick), St Margaret's (for the able-bodied) and St Nicholas (for children). A new workhouse was eventually opened in 1859 at what became 42 Magpie Hall Road, Chatham (TQ763670). The old premises were then sold off. The St Margaret's building is now used by the King's School, Rochester.

The new workhouse, for 650 inmates, was designed by Frederick Peck and Edward Stephens. It comprised an entrance block with vagrants' and receiving wards; a T-shaped main accommodation block with kitchen and dining hall at its rear; workshops and laundry; and an infirmary, at the west of the main building, with itch, fever and smallpox wards. In 1884, a large new infirmary was added at the west of the site. By 1898, a separate chapel stood at the north of the workhouse.[65]

In February 1911, William Hennen, 94, and Fanny Wadhams, 80, took their marriage vows after departing from the workhouse, where they had fallen in love while inmates. A number of such matches followed the introduction of the old-age pension, which offered the possibility of independent living to some of the elderly who previously would have had no other option than the workhouse.

The workhouse site was taken over by Kent County Council in 1930. Two years later it became Medway Hospital, then in 1936 was renamed County Hospital. In 1948, it joined the NHS as All Saints' Hospital. After its closure in 1999, the old buildings were demolished except for the entrance block, now a children's centre.

In 1903, the union opened a children's cottage homes site on Pattens Lane, Chatham (TQ752662). It eventually comprised eight cottages for boys and eight for girls, schools, workshops and a staff house. Only the school block now survives.

MILTON

Sittingbourne's workhouse was on the south side of the High Street, originally just east of Brenchley House (TQ906636), later moving about 100 metres to the west, a site now occupied by 99 High Street.[66] It could house twenty-five inmates in 1777.

Milton's workhouse stood on North Street and had forty places in 1777. At the same date, workhouses were also in use at Borden (for up to eight inmates), Hartlip (ten), Iwade (four) and Rainham (twenty).

A building on The Street in Borden (TQ882629), now Apple Tree Cottage and The Cottage, once served as the parish workhouse. Bredgar's establishment once occupied a house on Swanton Street dating from 1579.

Milton (also known as Milton Regis) Poor Law Union was formed in March 1835. The following May, there were a number of disturbances in various parts of the union caused by angry paupers who were upset as a result of a reduction in their previous out-relief allowances. Members of the Board of Guardians were barracked and stoned, eventually requiring the intervention of police and troops.

A new workhouse, based on Sir Francis Head's model courtyard plan, was erected in 1836 at 1 North Street (TQ903650).

In 1839, workhouse teacher William Weatherhead was dismissed with drunkenness recorded as the reason. He was, in fact, guilty of much more serious offences including the sexual abuse of girls in his care. Information on Weatherhead's conduct had been passed to the PLC by the workhouse chaplain, the Revd George Greaves. However, it was judged unlikely that Weatherhead would be convicted, and no criminal charges were brought.[67]

In 1874, an infectious diseases hospital was erected at the site, later used as an infirmary. In 1887, a two-storey block was built in the central courtyard housing a new dining hall, kitchen and laundry, with men's dormitories on the upper floor.

After 1930, the site was taken over by Kent County Council and became a PAI. In 1948, it joined the NHS as Milton Regis Hospital. The buildings were demolished around 1994 and housing erected on the site.

Around 1905, the union established a home for girls at Church House, North Street, Milton Regis (TQ908653), now converted to offices. A boys' home was opened in 1914 at Langley House, Brewery Road, Milton Regis (TQ904648).

PENSHURST

Cowden had a workhouse by 1769 when its operation was handed over to a contractor, John Dulake.[68] It presumably occupied what became known as Workhouse Cottage on North Street (TQ463406).[69] The establishment had twenty-four inmates in 1777.

Chiddingstone had a workhouse at what is now Old Workhouse Cottages, Somerden Green (TQ503458). It could house thirty inmates in 1777. In 1832, the residents comprised two men, four women and one illegitimate boy.

Leigh's workhouse, where the Saxby Wood development now stands (TQ545463), had twenty-four inmates in 1832, aged from 2 to 84 years.

A workhouse was in operation at Penshurst by 1821.

Penshurst Poor Law Union was formed in March 1835, one of the first in Kent to be created and relatively small in size. A union workhouse was completed early in 1836 at what is variously referred to as Bough Beeches or Bough Beech Green. Its opening was far from welcome in some quarters. On 7 February, the Tunbridge Wells yeomanry were called out when an attack on the building was feared, but it failed to materialise. They were called out again the next day when a large number of people assembled near the workhouse. After local magistrates read the Riot Act the crowds dispersed, with no damage having been done to the building.[70]

In September 1836, the union was absorbed into the adjacent Sevenoaks Poor Law Union. The Penshurst workhouse building was sold off in December 1838.

ROMNEY MARSH

By 1777, a parish workhouse was in use at Lydd, housing up to forty inmates.

Newchurch had an establishment on Norwood Lane, now the site of Louise Cottage (T050303). From 1791–1834, a workhouse operated at what is now 10–16 Mill Road, Dymchurch (TR100292).[71] Another was located at Crockley Green, New Romney. A house known as Well Cottage, on St Mary's Road, St Mary in the Marsh (TR070268), is said to have been used as a local poorhouse.[72] In 1822, the parish of Brookland advertised for a master and mistress to farm the poor in its workhouse, their number being not less than twenty-five.[73]

Romney Marsh Poor Law Union was created in November 1835. Initially, the union retained three existing parish workhouses: Lydd (for the able-bodied), Brookland (for the aged and infirm), and New Romney (for children). Eventually, a large house at the south side of Church Road, New Romney (TR063247), was purchased and converted for use as the union workhouse.

An inmate named Sarah Ann Collick died in the workhouse in May 1890, at the age of 98. While in domestic service, she had entered the Lydd workhouse in 1807 while recovering from an accident and then refused to leave. Though able-bodied, she had remained a workhouse inmate for eighty-three years.

From 1904, birth certificates for those born in the workhouse gave its address as Buttfield House, New Romney.

The workhouse closed in 1930 and the inmates were transferred to other institutions. The building was subsequently demolished and replaced by private housing.

By 1913, the union had also established a children's home known as Glan Morfa on Spitalfield Lane, New Romney.

SEVENOAKS

Otford had a workhouse from around 1730, when around nine inmates were housed in a rented property.[74] In 1777, the establishment had twenty places.

In 1772, the Chevening vestry purchased the building now occupied by 15–21 Chevening Road, Chevening (TQ499561), which had already been in use as a workhouse and poorhouse for many years.[75] It housed up to twenty inmates in 1777 and had twenty in residence in 1832.

Edenbridge had a poorhouse on Church Street (TQ444461). In 1777, it could accomodate forty paupers. The fifteen inmates in 1832 were mostly old people. The remodelled building later housed a school then a library.

The Sevenoaks workhouse stood at the south-west corner of the junction of St John's Hill and Camden Road (TQ531562). In 1777 it could house up to eighty inmates. In 1832, it was described as 'an old an inconvenient building', surrounded by more than 2 acres of garden, which provided employment for the inmates.

By 1777, workhouses were also in use at Brasted (for up to twelve inmates), Halsted (six), Kemsing (thirteen), Sundridge (forty) and Westerham (fifty).

Westerham's workhouse was at the junction of Vicarage Hill and Hosey Hill, where Quebec Cottages now stand (TQ449539). In 1832, the forty-nine workhouse residents were the elderly and children. The establishment was said to be remarkable for its neatness and cleanliness and had a room for the solitary confinement of miscreants.

Sevenoaks Poor Law Union was formed in April 1835 and the following year absorbed the small adjacent Penshurst Union (see page 194). The Guardians decided against building a new workhouse and instead enlarged the St John's Hill premises.

The management of the institution at this time was somewhat lacking. In 1837, the inmates were said to be dirty and vermin-ridden, with many suffering from 'the itch' (scabies). The master and matron were forced to resign and the porter

The boarded-up main building of the former Sevenoaks Union workhouse, prior to its conversion to residential use.

was dismissed for drunkenness and violence.[76] An inspection of the building by the PLC in 1841 revealed massive overcrowding and other defects. In the boys' bedrooms, sixty-two boys and two men occupied just seventeen beds. Fifteen of these were 6ft long by 4½ft wide, in each of which four boys slept; in the two others, which were about half the size, a man and a boy slept. At one end of each room, the wall and floor were soaked from a tub used as a common urinal. In the girls' dormitories, the inmates also slept four to a bed. In the adults' bedrooms, they generally slept two to a bed, or two women and a child.

The PLC subsequently required numerous improvements to be made. After some consideration, the Guardians decided that they would, after all, erect a new workhouse. A site was found on what is now Church Road, a mile to the south of Sundridge (TQ482537). The building, designed by Mr Mason, was completed in 1844. It had a T-shaped, corridor-plan main block, three storeys high, with the dining hall and kitchen in the rear wing. There was a separate infirmary at the rear of the main building, and an isolation block further to the north with a burial ground beyond. Vagrant cells were erected at the east of the workhouse in 1896.[77]

The workhouse later became Sundridge PAI, also known as Birchfield House, catering for patients with mental difficulties. Under the NHS, it operated as Sundridge Hospital until its closure in the late 1990s. The buildings have now been converted to residential use.

From 1911, the union operated a children's home known as Rock House at 96 Chipstead Lane, Riverhead (TQ510561).

SHEPPEY

The parish of Minster had a poorhouse as early as 1630. Financed by a charity set up by Sir John Haywood, it provided shelter for the old and homeless until any of those that were able could find work or accommodation.[78] By 1777, a workhouse was in operation housing twenty-six inmates. A new building was erected in 1784 on what is now Wards Hill Road (TQ955733). It burned down five years later but was rebuilt.

In 1777, the Eastchurch workhouse housed up to forty inmates.

Sheppey Poor Law Union was formed in March 1835 and took over the existing Minster workhouse. Around £1,000 was spent on the enlargement of the building. A new infirmary was erected at the west of the site in 1869. In 1889, the workhouse buildings were again damaged by fire.

The workhouse had its own school at the north of the site which was in use until 1895. From that date, the workhouse children attended the local village school, although they had to sit in their own part of the classroom. From 1904, birth certificates of children born in the workhouse gave its address as Cliff House.

A 2005 view of the jumble of buildings forming the frontage of the former Sheppey Union workhouse, later Minster Hospital.

In 1930, the institution became a PAI run by Kent County Council. In 1938, the site was redesignated as Minster Hospital with its facilities then including a maternity unit and operating theatre. It later became Sheppey Hospital, which closed around 2002. Most of the buildings have now been replaced by modern housing.

STROOD (NORTH AYLESFORD)

In 1721, a workhouse was erected in Strood at the north-east of St Nicholas' churchyard (TQ735693). The plain building had a hipped roof in which were four dormer windows. An inscription over the door proclaimed it as a place 'in which the sick and aged are taken care of; the ignorant instructed; such as are able to work, employed; and a comfortable maintenance provided for all.' In 1777, it could house sixty-three inmates. A Local Act was obtained in 1812 creating the Strood Trustees to manage the decaying building. It was eventually demolished in 1853.

Meopham had a workhouse from 1724 on The Street (TQ644660). The building is now known as Elizabeth House.[79] In 1796, it contained six old people and eleven children. Their diet was generally broth or milk for breakfast, beef for dinner, and bread and cheese or butter for supper every day.

From 1749, Luddesdown and Halling shared the use of workhouse with Birling and Snodland. It occupied the former Bishop's Palace at Halling (TQ705639).

In 1777, workhouses existed at Cobham (for thirty inmates), Northfleet (forty) and Shorne (twenty). The Northfleet building, located at Perry Street, was sold in 1794.[80] In 1796, the poor at Chalk were 'mostly farmed in a workhouse with Northfleet'.[81] In 1819, the Northfleet workhouse moved to a former manor house at the east end of the High Street, a site now occupied by Granby Place (TQ624742).[82] In 1832, the workhouse had eighteen male and seven female inmates, mostly aged.

Frindsbury's workhouse stood on Church Green, Frindsbury. Cliffe's establishment was at he west side of Church Street (TQ736766).

North Aylesford Union (renamed Strood in 1884) was formed in September 1835, initially using the old workhouses at Strood and Frindsbury.

A new workhouse for 442 inmates was erected in 1837, at 2 Gun Lane, Strood (TQ735695). Males were housed at the east and females at the west. The front block had a central entrance archway. To its right were the master's quarters, boys' accommodation and male probationary ward. At the left were

The men's wing of the former Strood workhouse in 1957.

the porter's lodge, boardroom, girls' accommodation and female probation-ary ward. To the rear, a T-shaped, three-storey block housed the men's and women's accommodation. The forward-projecting leg of the 'T' contained a laundry and kitchen. The area between the entrance and rear blocks was divided by a further laundry on the women's side and by workshops on the men's side. An infirmary was added at the east of the site in 1869. Around 1893, a large new block was erected at the centre of the site and linked to both the entrance and rear buildings.

In 1930, the site became a Kent County Council PAI, but it closed around 1938. The premises were later used for a variety of purposes. A block at the rear of the building was used as a local authority clinic, while the 1869 infirmary was used as offices by the War Pension Welfare Service. The latter subsequently housed a teachers' centre and in more recent times has been used as a doctor's surgery and school accommodation.

TENTERDEN

Tenterden had a workhouse from 1724 at Borough Place on the High Street (TQ88233). In 1832, it had forty-four inmates, most aged under 16 or over 50. The building is now a row of private residences.

In 1777, parish workhouses also existed at Biddenden (for up to fifty-two inmates), Rolvenden (fifty), Stone (twenty) and Wittersham (twenty).

At the former Biddenden workhouse, on Sissinghurst Road (TQ846383), an annual distribution of bread and cheese on Easter Monday mornings commemorates the 'Biddenden Maids', the twins Eliza and Mary Chulkhurst, born in the year 1500 and joined at the hips and shoulders. After living joined together for thirty-four years, one of them died. The other, refusing to be separated, died six hours later. The two women left their property to the poor of the parish.

Stone-in-Oxney's workhouse, now two cottages, was on The Street (TQ939278).

In 1832, the High Halden workhouse had thirty inmates, 'chiefly children and extremely old people'.

Stocks Mill House, on Stocks Road, Wittersham (TQ900273), originally the mill-house of the Stocks windmill, later became the parish poorhouse.[83]

In 1814, Appledore's workhouse was noted as being on Appledore Heath.[84]

At the west side of Rolvenden's High Street, a row of red-brick cottages, bearing the date 1804, was once the parish workhouse.[85]

Tenterden Poor Law Union was created in November 1835 and initially took over the Borough Place workhouse, with £1,100 spent on its enlargement. However, the premises proved unsatisfactory and in 1843 a new building was erected on Plummer Lane, to the west of Tenterden (TQ874328).

A 2001 view of West View Hospital, formerly the Tenterden Union workhouse.

Designed by James Savage, it had a T-shaped main building, three storeys at the centre, joined by two-storey wings to three-storey cross-wings at each end. The rear wing of the main block contained the dining hall. A two-storey infirmary stood at the west of the site.

After 1930, the establishment housed patients with mental conditions, then after 1948 it joined the NHS as West View Hospital, providing geriatric care. The buildings were demolished around 2002 and a health centre now occupies the site.

TONBRIDGE

A workhouse was erected in 1726 at Bank Street, Tonbridge (TQ590467). In 1732, it housed about forty inmates, nearly half of whom were old people. Children were employed in spinning and knitting, providing clothing for the whole establishment. They were taught to read by female inmates and on reaching the appropriate age were apprenticed or went into service.[86] There were 130 inmates in 1777. Later used as a school, the somewhat altered building is now office accommodation.

Speldhurst workhouse opened in 1755, north-east of the junction of the present-day Manor Road and Rusthall Road (TQ561396). It housed thirty inmates in 1777, with forty-five in residence in 1832. The building was demolished in 1900.

Brenchley's workhouse, at 1–3 High Street (TQ677418), had sixty inmates in 1777 and seventy-three in 1832. The building has now been converted to three cottages.

The workhouse at Horsmonden could house twenty inmates in 1777 and had forty-two in 1832. In the latter year, the Pembury workhouse, occupying what is now Stanton House, on Romford Road (TQ635409), was home to thirty paupers.

A property now known as Grays House, at the south of Hadlow's High Street (TQ633497), was once the parish's workhouse. In 1777, it housed up to sixteen inmates. At the same date, the workhouse at Bidborough could hold six inmates.

In 1805, the parishes of Tudeley and Capel formed a Gilbert Union. The location of its workhouse is uncertain.

Tonbridge Poor Law Union was formed in November 1835 and erected a new workhouse at Newbars Wood, Tonbridge Road, Pembury (TQ615413). The new building, for 400 inmates, was designed by John Whichcord and completed in December 1836. Labour for the construction work was provided by inmates from the former parish workhouses still operating in the union. The building had a two-storey entrance block, with a three-storey main accommodation block to its rear. The space between the two was divided up by outbuildings containing kitchens, workshops, etc. to create exercise yards for different classes of inmate.

The first master, George Gittins, died in January 1837. A temporary master took over until June, when ex-Grenadier Guard Sergeant John Harrison and his wife became master and matron. Within two months, Harrison resigned after being charged with drunkenness and other improper conduct.[87]

A smallpox epidemic at the workhouse in the winter of 1837/8 led to the building of an isolation block. A hospital building was added at the north of the site in 1856. In the same year, 12 acres of land at the south-east of the workhouse were acquired for the cultivation of vegetables by the inmates.

Originally, religious services were held in the workhouse dining hall. In 1861, two boys were punished for 'breaking wind' and talking during a service. A separate chapel was erected in 1870. It had two entrances, one for men and one for women.

In 1872, a new vagrants' block at the east of the workhouse contained the labour-master's quarters at its centre, with six sleeping and labour cells at each side.

A larger infirmary was added to the east of the earlier hospital block in 1890. Despite the increase in hospital accommodation, the workhouse was criticised in 1894 for having only one fully trained nurse – a temporarily employed night nurse.[88]

The Tonbridge Union workhouse at Pembury – the main building is centre left, the infirmary centre right, and the vagrants' block centre foreground.

In 1922, the hospital part of the premises was renamed Sandhill Hospital. In 1930, the site was taken over by Kent County Council and the workhouse section became a PAI. Medical facilities were further developed and the site, by then known as Pembury Hospital, joined the new NHS in 1948.

All the old buildings, with the exception of the chapel, were demolished in September 2011 and replaced by the new Tunbridge Wells Hospital.

WEST ASHFORD

Ashford's parish workhouse was established in 1705, at the end of New Rents (TR007428).[89] In 1777, it housed up to seventy paupers. By 1797, the inmates were employed in a bleachery for Irish linen. It was said that the poor in most of Kent at that date seldom tasted meat in winter, except in a poorhouse. They drank tea at all their meals, which, with bread, potatoes and cheese, constituted their main diet.[90]

In 1777, workhouses were also in operation at Bethersden (for up to twenty inmates), Charing (two), Kingsnorth (twelve) and Westwell (ten).

A plaque on a house on Charing's Market Place identifies it as the old workhouse (TQ953494). A poorhouse, now The Old House, stood on Station Road (TQ949490).

A view of Hothfield Common with the West Ashford Union workhouse behind.

A 2001 view of the former West Ashford Union workhouse, now a care home for the elderly.

The Bethersden workhouse was at 4–8 Bateman's Corner (TQ 933405), now a row of private houses.

Westwell's workhouse (TQ991469) had closed by 1797 and its poor were maintained at home.[91] In 1832, however, the parish again had a workhouse containing twenty-three inmates who were all either under 16 or over 65.

Great Chart had a workhouse by 1797. The vestry expected a labourer to be able maintain three children. They allowed 1*s* a week for every child above the third or allowed the parents to place it in the workhouse.[92]

In 1832, Egerton's workhouse had thirty-two inmates from 2 to 90 years of age.

The West Ashford Poor Law Union was formed in June 1835 and erected a workhouse at Chapel Lane, Hothfield Common (TQ968464). It housed up to 240 inmates and was based on Sir Francis Head's model courtyard design.

A major renovation costing £5,000 took place in 1902 with the creation of an infirmary and a school for thirty-three children.

In 1930, the site became Hothfield PAI run by Kent County Council. In 1941, the premises were taken over as a 150-bed military hospital. At one point, following the evacuation of Dunkirk, approximately 15,000 men were camping on nearby Hothfield Common, with those needing treatment attending the out-patients' department each day.

After 1948, the institution joined the NHS as Hothfield Hospital. After its closure around 1979, the premises were converted for use as a private nursing home.

6

MIDDLESEX

BRENTFORD

Chiswick's workhouse was built in 1725 on the north side of Chiswick High Road at Turnham Green (TQ210785), where a Poundland store is currently located. The building was enlarged in 1759, taking its capacity to ninety places.[1] In 1832, the inmates comprised twenty-one men aged from 46 to 86, mostly market gardeners and fishermen; twenty-seven women aged from 20 to 87, widows and servants; and ten orphan children aged from 2 months to 14 years. Men capable of labour were employed in the workhouse garden. Women did household work and nursed the sick. Men and women were not allowed communication with each other.

Twickenham's workhouse, also established in 1725, adjoined some almshouses at the north side of what is now The Green, just east of Briar Road (TQ151730).[2] In 1777, the workhouse could house up to ninety inmates. By 1817, the building had been enlarged by incorporating some of the adjacent almshouses, then was altered again in 1826 to separate the male and female inmates.

Ealing's workhouse was erected west of St Mary's Lane around 1728.[3] In 1777, it could hold up to 100 inmates. In 1797, it was said to be 'a small inconvenient building, very ill adapted to the purpose', with inmates sleeping up to four to a bed.[4]

A workhouse existed at Heston by 1734 and could house thirty inmates. A new building was erected in about 1786 at the south end of Sutton Lane, on the west side of the road.[5] In 1832, there twenty-three adult inmates, aged from 72 to 91 years, and six children, including one infant. A few of the men and boys were employed in agricultural labour and received extra food and beer.

Isleworth had a workhouse from around 1738 at the west end of Brentford Bridge (TQ172772), which in 1777 housed 110 inmates. It fell into disrepair and was replaced in 1821 by a new building on what is now Linkfield Road (TQ159762).[6] In 1832, there were seventy-seven inmates aged from 10 to 103 years. Males that were capable were occupied in cultivating land, collecting manure or working for local employers, while women made clothing for the use of the house, and children made pottle baskets.[7] The inmates were said to be so comfortable and well-fed that many applied for entry, especially at the start of winter, and were difficult to get out again. The building was later converted to almshouses.

New Brentford opened a workhouse in 1757 on the Ham at Brentford Bridge (TQ173771). The inmates worked at spinning and in 1760 received three meat dinners a week and up to 3½lb of meat per head. Gin, however, was banned from the premises. In 1777, the establishment could accommodate fifty inmates. In 1787, a riot by inmates led magistrates to propose that a 'room of confinement' be set up at the workhouse for troublemakers. In 1791, the master, Joseph Smith, was dismissed for having an improper relationship with a young woman inmate who then revealed she thought she was pregnant. Four years later, the master and matron were discharged for not keeping order in the workhouse.[8]

In 1777, Acton had a workhouse for sixteen inmates. The establishment, for the old and infirm poor, appears to have occupied the almshouses built in 1725 in the Steyne, where Steyne Road now runs (TQ199805).[9]

Brentford Poor Law Union was formed in June 1836 and initially took over the parish workhouses at Ealing, Isleworth and Twickenham. A new workhouse on Twickenham Road, Isleworth (TQ164764) was opened in 1839. The architect was Lewis Vulliamy whose design was based on the PLC's model cruciform layout.

A workhouse school, known as Percy House, was built alongside Twickenham Road in 1883. The buildings included a chapel, dining hall and swimming bath.

In 1895-1902, a new infirmary was built on the workhouse site and a much larger workhouse erected to its south-east, on land adjoining the Percy House School. The new premises, designed by W.H. Ward of Birmingham, had a pavilion-style layout with separate buildings for the different categories of inmate and for the dining hall, chapel, laundry, workshops, etc. In its day, the scheme was considered the epitome of workhouse design providing spacious, modern accommodation for a wide range of inmates, including the able-bodied, aged and infirm, expectant mothers and those with young children, married couples, the mentally deficient and the mentally ill.

The Brentford Union's first workhouse, opened at Isleworth in 1839.

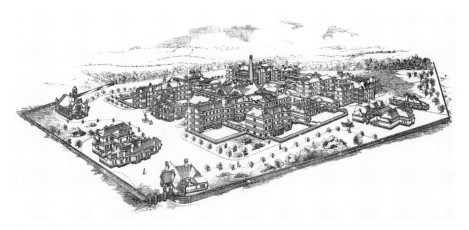

The architect's design for Brentford's new state-of-the-art workhouse, opened in 1902.

In 1915, Percy House was taken over as an auxiliary military hospital where a total of almost 5,000 wounded soldiers were treated.

From around 1920, the workhouse was known as Warkworth House and the infirmary part of the site as the West Middlesex Hospital. In 1935, the two sections were merged to create the West Middlesex County Hospital, with most of the pauper inmates then being transferred to Percy House. In 1948, the site again became West Middlesex Hospital. Almost all of the old buildings have now been demolished.

EDMONTON

In Enfield, a workhouse was opened in 1719 at Chase Side (TQ326976). It housed up to seventy inmates in 1777. From 1806, children from the establishment were sent to work at a silk factory at Sewardstone in Essex.[10] The workhouse was rebuilt on the same site in 1827.

Cheshunt, just into Hertfordshire, opened a workhouse in 1722, perhaps on Marsh Lane (now Trinity Lane). In 1753, it moved into leased premises on the east side of Crossbrook Street. Seventy inmates could be housed in 1777. The establishment relocated to the west side of the High Street in 1781.[11] A 'large substantial brick building' housing 100 paupers was erected at Flamstead End around 1822.[12]

Hornsey had a workhouse on Priory Road, opened in 1730.[13] It accommodated thirty inmates in 1777. The ninety-two residents in 1832 included twenty-three boys and twelve girls.

In 1731, Edmonton erected a workhouse on Church Street, at the west of All Saints' Church. It provided seventy-six places in 1777, then in 1832 was home to thirty-three males and forty-five females. Thirteen of the men had been agricultural labourers and five had been gentleman's servants; three of the women had been housekeepers and thirty had been servants.

In 1734, Waltham leased a building near the Green Yard (TL380005) for use as a workhouse.[14]

Tottenham's parish workhouse was erected on Tottenham High Road in about 1763 and in 1777 could house sixty inmates. The building was extended in 1818. Its inmates in 1832 were fifty-four aged men and women and sixteen children. The property was later known as Coombe's Croft House.[15]

Edmonton Poor Law Union was formed in February 1837, with Hampstead (see page 84) among its members until 1848. The union initially retained three former parish workhouses, housing able-bodied adults at Edmonton, the aged and infirm at Hampstead, and the children at Enfield. Before long, however, the old Edmonton and Hampstead premises were replaced by a new building at Edmonton.

The new workhouse was erected in 1840–41 at Tanners End, Edmonton (TQ335923), with its entrance at what became known as 77 Bridport Road. Intended to accommodate 500 inmates, it was designed by George Gilbert Scott and William Bonython Moffatt.

In 1910, a large infirmary was erected at the east of the workhouse, separated from it by a long iron fence. From 1915–20 it operated as Edmonton Military Hospital, then became known as the North Middlesex Hospital.

In 1930, Middlesex County Council took over the whole site. The work-house section, then known as Edmonton House, closed in 1938 and its buildings were absorbed by the hospital which joined the NHS in 1948. Little remains of the old buildings although part of the 1910 infirmary survives.

The old Enfield building continued to house the union's children for many years but their health was a regular cause for concern. In a twelve-month period in 1837–38, there were outbreaks of conditions including smallpox, scarlet fever, ophthalmia, measles, tuberculosis, 'the itch' (scabies) and ring-worm. Over that time, there were seventeen deaths out of a total of 150 children.[16] By the 1880s, overcrowding at Enfield resulted in new children's accommodation being opened at Chase Farm. The Enfield site was then used as a union infirmary until 1910, when it became accommodation for the elderly. Up until 1948, it was known as Enfield House, then became part of the NHS as St Michael's Hospital, specialising in geriatric care. Modern housing now occupies the site.

The Chase Farm Schools, on The Ridgeway, Enfield (TQ312980), were opened in March 1886 and housed 350 children. In 1900, the local Catholic priest, Father O'Gorman, complained that the Catholic children from Chase Farm were not attending his church. An investigation led to allegations by three boys that the priest had assaulted them and that they wished to change their religious affiliation. Although the Guardians eventually decided not to

An aerial view of the Edmonton Union workhouse in the 1920s.

take proceedings against the priest, he was barred from visiting children at the school. Catholic parents were also told that their children would be given Protestant instruction unless a written request was made to the contrary.[17]

In the early 1900s, the union began to buy houses to use as scattered homes. Children in these homes attended local schools as, increasingly, did those at Chase Farm. In 1930, Chase Farm was taken over by Middlesex County Council, who expanded the scattered homes policy. In 1938, the site was used to house inmates transferred from the former Edmonton workhouse. Ten years later, it joined the NHS as Chase Farm Hospital.

HENDON

A workhouse, or 'House of Maintenance', was opened at Harrow on the Hill in 1724. The purpose-built premises, now 33–35 West Street (TQ151872), held up to fifty inmates. Breakfast consisted of milk porridge, broth or water -gruel. Dinner included meat three times a week, and pea soup once. Dinner on other days and supper each day comprised 2oz of butter or 4oz of cheese with bread. Each inmate was allowed three pints of beer a day.[18] In 1832, the residents comprised thirteen men aged from 60 to 81, nine women aged from 30 to 80, and nine children. Tasks given to the inmates included picking oakum and working a corn mill.

Hendon had a workhouse from 1735 at the south end of the Burroughs, where Quadrant Close flats now stand (TQ227889).[19] In 1777, it could house thirty inmates. The thirty-five residents in 1832 were either very old and infirm, or very young and destitute.

In 1777, Pinner had a workhouse for thirty inmates, although it may have been rather more like a poorhouse for the aged and infirm. In 1789, the prem-ises, beside the River Pinn, near the George Inn (TQ121894), were enlarged for use as a workhouse.[20] In 1832, the average number of inmates was thirteen, generally old and infirm, who had previously been employed in farm work. If able, they were occupied in working the garden, while strong and healthy paupers were sent to dig gravel.

Great Stanmore erected a workhouse in 1788 on the east side of Stanmore Hill (TQ167926). Two years later, it was fenced in and the inmates required permis-sion to go outside.[21] In 1832, the establishment contained ten males and thirteen females. Able-bodied males were employed in digging gravel on the Common.

Hendon Poor Law Union was created in May 1835 and three years later erected a new workhouse at Burnt Oak on the east side of the Edgware Road

A tram runs along the Edgware Road past the Hendon Union workhouse in the early 1900s.

(TQ200908). An infirmary was added in 1868 and padded rooms for lunatic inmates in 1890.

The workhouse site was taken over by Middlesex County Council in 1930 and became Redhill PAI. From 1948 it was an old people's home known as Redhill House. The buildings no longer exist.

In 1859, a union school for 150 children was erected a little way up Edgware Road, to the north-west of the workhouse (TQ197911).

In 1925–27, a large union infirmary was erected at the rear of the school, one of the last such establishments to be built. It comprised a central administrative block flanked by two-storey ward pavilions, plus a receiving block, and an operating theatre.

After 1930, the infirmary was taken over by the Middlesex County Council and became Redhill County Hospital, later renamed Edgware General Hospital. The former union school became a men's home later known as Redhill Lodge. The school and much of the former infirmary were demolished as part of a major redevelopment of the site, now known as Edgware Community Hospital.

STAINES

In September 1774, a public meeting in Harmondsworth agreed to the erection of a workhouse for the parish. The building was located at the north side of the Bath Road, between the present-day Sipson Road and New Road (TQ080769). In 1777, it housed up to forty inmates. The labour of the inmates was sold on an annual basis to local employers. The able-bodied went out to neighbouring farms, while children over the age of 8 worked for up to seven hours a day at the workhouse. In 1832, there were twenty-one inmates aged from 1 to 83 years. The building, later known as Devonshire Place, survived until the 1950s.[22]

Staines had a workhouse by 1759, probably near Pound Mill, just east of the former Staines West station. In 1777, it housed up to fifty inmates. The parish also used a property at Hale Bridge (TQ034718). At various times, workhouse inmates were occupied in oakum-picking, sack-weaving and basket-making. The Pound Mill premises were replaced in 1824 by a new building on Shortwood Common.[23]

Sunbury's workhouse was built around 1765 on the common to the west of Green Street.[24] In 1777, it housed up to twenty-five paupers. In 1832, the inmates comprised sixteen adults and seven children. Those that were able were occupied in household work or gardening. There were three meat dinners a week, with bread and cheese or soup on other days. Beer was given every day.

Shepperton had a workhouse by 1777, when it could house up to thirty-five inmates. In 1834, it was located in leased premises in Watersplash Road.[25]

By 1813, Stanwell had a workhouse on Hithermoor Road (TQ039743). The building was demolished around 1934 and replaced by Cheltenham Villas.[26]

Staines Poor Law Union began operation in June 1836 and initially retained the former parish workhouses at Staines, Stanwell and Sunbury. In 1840–41, a new union workhouse was built at Ashford, at what is now the junction of Town Lane and London Road (TQ062724). It accommodated up to 300 inmates.

In September 1898, it was discovered that John Lewis, aged 67, of Harmondsworth, who had recently been admitted to the workhouse in a destitute state, had a bank balance of £1,600. He was ordered to pay 10s 6d a week for board and lodging.[27]

By 1914, a boys' home had been added at the east of the workhouse. It was later converted for use as a nurses' home.

In 1930, the workhouse site was taken over by Middlesex County Council and became a PAI known as The Hall. In 1941, it was renamed Staines County Hospital, then joined the NHS in 1948 as Ashford Hospital. All the old workhouse buildings have now been demolished.

The entrance drive to the Staines Union workhouse in the early 1900s.

UXBRIDGE

In 1744, the Hillingdon vestry resolved to 'pull down the Parish Houses adjoining to St John's Churchyard and the material employed in the building of a Workhouse'. By 1747, the new building had been erected at the corner of Royal Lane and Pield Heath Road, Colham Green (TQ069821). It comprised nine rooms, together with a kitchen, dining room, hospital room and brewhouse. From 1758–68, John Hill was paid £300 a year to maintain the parish's poor and could also keep any income from the inmates' work. In 1768, a room for spinning had been set up. By 1810, a schoolroom and a workroom for cobblers had been added. In 1830, the premises were enlarged to provide separate male and female accommodation.[28]

In 1777, Ruislip had a workhouse for thirty inmates. It was situated on the east side of Duck's Hill Road (TQ083891).[29] Harefield's U-shaped workhouse was erected in 1782 on Breakspear Road North (TQ055903).[30] In 1832, it had fifteen inmates, six of whom were males under the age of 15, the rest being aged. Those able to work were employed in the workhouse gardens. The Ruislip and Harefield properties are both now private residences.

By 1803, Norwood had opened a workhouse on Featherstone Road, Southall Green, with twelve inmates in residence.[31]

Hayes had a workhouse by 1803 on the south side of Botwell Lane, near Printing House Lane (formerly Workhouse Lane), usually having about twenty-four inmates. The old men worked in the 2-acre garden and the women in the house.[32]

In 1806, Northolt built a workhouse at the east side of Mandeville Road (TQ133845). The building's nine rooms included a shop and brewhouse. It later housed the Load of Hay pub. A replacement building dating from 1930 is now a restaurant.[33]

By 1815, a building at the north of the Green, on Church Road, West Drayton (TQ059795), was used as a workhouse.[34] The property is now retail premises.

Ickenham had a poorhouse that stood in front of the churchyard on Back Lane (TQ079861).[35]

Uxbridge Poor Law Union began operation in June 1836 and bought the existing Hillingdon workhouse site for £300, together with a further 4 acres of land. A new workhouse building was erected, designed by William Thorold, and part of the old parish workhouse was converted into an infirmary block. A chapel was added in 1875 and other buildings including a female infirmary in 1907.

An aerial view of the Uxbridge Union workhouse, with an inset view of the main entrance. (Courtesy of Howard Wingfield)

An inspection report in 1867 recommended that a padded room be provided for lunatic inmates; that the women should not sleep two in a bed, especially as there were plenty of beds to allow them to sleep singly; that the flock in the bedding should be carded as it was lumpy; and that iron-enamelled basins should be provided to replace the troughs in which inmates were washing.[36]

In 1931, the workhouse site became Hillingdon County Hospital, then joined the NHS in 1948 as Hillingdon Hospital. The old buildings have now been demolished.

WILLESDEN

In 1835, the parish of Willesden joined the new Hendon Poor Law Union. By 1895, the union's workhouse at Edgware had become extremely overcrowded. Since a large proportion of its inmates came from Willesden, a local campaign was mounted to set up a separate workhouse at Willesden. In 1896, the LGB decided that Willesden should separate and operate as an independent Poor Law District.

Initially, the Willesden Guardians contracted with the Hendon Union to continue making use of the Edgware workhouse. In 1900, when Hendon gave notice that no more space was available, the Guardians boarded out inmates at the Winslow Union workhouse and at Hackney's Well Street workhouse. They also hired two mansions from the Midland Railway Company at Cricklewood Broadway.

In order to provide their own accommodation, the Guardians acquired a 60-acre site on the north side of Acton Lane (TQ202828), where construction work began in 1900. The development of the site reversed the usual pattern, with an infirmary being erected first, in 1900–02, and then a workhouse at its rear, in 1907–08. Both were designed by Alfred Saxon Snell. When the infirmary came into use in 1902, only 150 of its 400 places were occupied by the sick, the remainder being given over to ordinary workhouse inmates until the workhouse buildings were constructed.

The infirmary had a central administrative block flanked at each side by two double ward-blocks of two storeys, all linked by covered corridors. Generators provided electric light and power, while heating was by open fires supplemented by hot water pipes.

The workhouse phase of construction comprised male and female pavilions, each holding 100 able-bodied inmates, a receiving block and a dining hall.

From 1904, the birth certificates of those born in the workhouse recorded its address as Twyford Lodge, and later as 494 Acton Lane.

The now-demolished clocktower entrance to the Central Middlesex Hospital, formerly the Willesden workhouse and infirmary.

During the First World War, much of the workhouse accommodation was taken over as hostel accommodation for female munitions workers and military personnel.

In 1914, the infirmary was renamed Willesden Institution, then in 1921 became Park Royal Hospital.[37] In 1930, the institution was taken over by Middlesex County Council and renamed the Central Middlesex County Hospital. It joined the NHS in 1948 as the Central Middlesex Hospital. Most of the old buildings have now been demolished to make way for a new hospital.

The Guardians erected children's homes at the north of the workhouse on Barret's Green Road (TQ203830). By the early 1920s, sixteen scattered homes at various locations in Cricklewood and Harlesden accommodated a total of 230 children.

7

SURREY

ASH

Ash Gilbert Union was formed in 1790 by the parishes of Ash and Normandy and Puttenham. Its workhouse was at the east of Ash on what is now Foxhills Lane (SU902512). By 1806, Long Sutton and Seale and Tongham had joined the union.

Ash's Gilbert Union status allowed it to remain in operation until 1869. Its member parishes were then distributed among the Farnham, Hartley Wintney and Guildford Unions.

The workhouse building no longer exists and modern housing stands on the site.

CHERTSEY

Chertsey erected a workhouse in 1726–27 at the east side of Fox Lane (TQ038664), now the site of Chertsey railway station. By November 1728, there were fifty-four inmates including three men 'infirm and incapable of doing any thing', twelve women 'most of them very antient, and two blind', and thirty-nine children.[1] Those who were capable were employed in washing, baking, brewing, nursing and cleaning the workhouse, while the children knitted hose for the inmates. In 1777, the establishment could house seventy inmates. There were typically forty-five in residence in 1832, including ten children who were taught to read and write.

In 1733, Walton-on-Thames leased a property at Hole Corner for use as a workhouse.[2] In 1777, its premises could house fifty inmates. In 1797, the workhouse was run by a contractor. The inmates usually had meat for dinner, and bread and broth for breakfast and supper.[3]

Windlesham erected a workhouse in 1761 adjoining the New Road alms-houses at Bagshot (SU916631).

In 1777, Weybridge had a workhouse for up to twenty inmates. At the same date, Chobham's workhouse housed thirty paupers in a building on Red Lion Lane (SU972628).[4] In 1784, the establishment had fourteen bedsteads. Rebuilt after a fire in 1790, the workhouse had twenty-nine inmates in 1832, almost all being either children or the aged and infirm. The property is now known as Jubilee Cottages.[5]

The location of Byfleet's workhouse now lies under Stream Close, off Rectory Lane (TQ059610). The building survived until the 1970s.[6]

Horsell's workhouse was at the east of the village, behind St Mary's Church. Pyrford's establishment, now Glebe House at Pyrford Green (TQ048588), had twelve inmates in 1777.[7]

Chertsey Poor Law Union was formed in November 1835 and erected a workhouse at Ottershaw, at the south of Murray Road (TQ02663). It was designed by Sampson Kempthorne and based on his model hexagonal plan. Its entrance block faced the road, and at the rear three wings radiated from a

The front block of the former Chertsey Union workhouse, one of Sampson Kempthorne's hexagonal designs.

central hub. A chapel was erected at the west of the workhouse in 1868. Fever wards were added in 1871 and a mortuary and casual wards in 1883. A separate infirmary was built in 1894, together with children's quarters.[8]

In 1930, the workhouse was taken over by Surrey County Council and later became Murray House Certified Institution for the Mentally Defective. It became part of Botleys Park Hospital and joined the NHS in 1948, continuing in operation until 1984. Most of the former workhouse buildings have now been demolished. The entrance block and chapel survive, both converted to residential use.

By 1924, the union had opened a children's home at Ottershaw.

CROYDON

A workhouse was erected in 1727 at the corner of Duppas Hill Lane and Duppas Hill Terrace, Croydon (TQ319649). By 1777 it could house eighty inmates. The inmates worked from 6 a.m. to 7 p.m. in summer, and 7 a.m. to 6 p.m. in winter. They had to 'sit at meals in a decent manner with hands and faces washed, hair combed and clothes brushed'. There was to be 'no tobacco to be smoked in their lodging-room' nor any 'distilled liquors to come into the House'.[9] In 1832, the inmates comprised fifty-nine men, forty-four women, twenty-eight boys and sixteen girls. The young boys and girls were employed in spinning hair. The aged and infirm were allowed tea instead of beer for supper, and mutton.

Mitcham had a workhouse from around 1742 overlooking Figge's (or Pigg's) Marsh. It was replaced in 1782 by new premises at the east side of Mitcham Common (TQ291681). In 1832, there were around 100 inmates, mostly aged and infirm, together with twenty children. Six looms, mainly worked by the children, produced matting and sacks. Some willow-plaiting was also carried out and the 3-acre garden was cultivated by the inmates. Adults slept two to a bed, some receiving a weekly ration of tea, tobacco or snuff. The building later became a factory making waterproof clothing for troops in the Crimean War.[10]

Beddington's workhouse had ten inmates in 1777. It was located between Church Lane and Guy Road (TQ299651).[11]

Penge, then a hamlet in the parish of Battersea, had a workhouse which in 1832 had just six inmates, all aged between 60 and 82 years.

Coulsdon's workhouse was a flint-faced building now known as Newland Cottages, at the rear of Old Fox Close (TQ319568).[12]

Croydon Poor Law Union was formed in May 1836 and took over the Duppas Hill and Mitcham workhouses. To save money, the latter was closed in

The Croydon Union's new workhouse opened in 1866 on Queen's Road.

1838 and the inmates transferred to Croydon. In 1866, the increasing number of paupers that had accompanied the growth of Croydon led to the opening of a new workhouse for 350 inmates on Queen's Road, Croydon (TQ320673). Designed by John Berney, the Italianate main building was three storeys high with a central tower.

The Duppas Hill building was then converted for use as an infirmary, until its replacement in 1885 by a new facility at a site between Eridge Road (now Woodcroft Road) and Mayday Road (TQ316674). The new infirmary had a pavilion-plan design with a central administration block flanked at each side by two ward-blocks, each three storeys high and containing 104 beds. A corridor linked the ward pavilions and the administration block. A chapel, dedicated to St Barnabas, was added in 1895.

The workhouse and infirmary were taken over by Croydon Borough Council in 1930. The workhouse became a PAI known as Queen's Road Homes, whose rules still prohibited the possession of alcohol, knives, razors, heavy belts, dice or playing cards. Everyone was searched on admission, and any money or valuables were taken away for safekeeping. The main part of the building was badly damaged by bombing in April 1941.[13] The establishment joined the NHS in 1948 as the Queen's Hospital, specialising in geriatric care. It finally closed in 1987. In 2008, most of the main block was illegally demolished during a redevelopment of the site. All that survives is the central tower of the main block, now incorporated into a modern residential building.

The infirmary joined the NHS as the Mayday Hospital, now Croydon University Hospital. Many of its original buildings survive.

The union erected cottage homes for boys in 1897 on Mayday Road (TQ317671) and in 1905 on Pawson's Road (TQ321674). A girls' home was opened at Nonington Hall, Bingham Road, Addiscombe, later moving to Lower Addiscombe Road (TQ333663). Girls' cottage homes were also erected at 218–220 London Road, West Croydon (TQ318665). None of the homes survive.

DORKING

A workhouse was built at Ockley in 1741. It had a large garden where beans and cabbage were grown.[14] In 1777, it could house twenty-five inmates. In 1832, they comprised nine aged, infirm or widowed adults and twelve children.

Dorking had workhouse on South Street.[15] In 1777, it could hold eighty inmates. There were seventy-three residents in 1832, mainly old or infirm, and a few boys. Seven of the inmates were described as idiots.

In 1777, workhouses were also in operation at Abinger (for up to thirty inmates), Effingham (six families) and Wotton (twenty-five).

Abinger had a workhouse and a poorhouse at Abinger Bottom, on the site of 'St John's' and the corner opposite (TQ126448).[16] The workhouse had just six inmates in 1832, ranging from 7 to 67 years of age.

An aerial view of the Dorking workhouse, later Dorking General Hospital.

Effingham's establishment was located on Effingham Common Road, on part of what is now Indian Farm.[17]

A building from the 1790s, now 1–2 Brook Cottages, Parkgate Road (TQ200429), was home to the Newdigate workhouse.[18]

Dorking Poor Law Union was created in June 1836. Initially, the union took over the Dorking and Ockley workhouses, but a new building was erected in 1840–41 at the eastern side of the Horsham Road (TQ165487), Dorking. It was designed by William Shearburn and accommodated 250 inmates. It had an entrance block at the west of the site, with an H-shaped main building to the rear. The entrance block was unusually stylish with a neo-Grecian design faced in white-painted stucco.

In the latter part of the nineteenth century, a chapel was added at the north of the site. In 1897, a new infirmary was added at the rear of the workhouse.

In 1930, the workhouse became Dorking PAI under the control of Surrey County Council. In 1936, the council acquired St Anne's, a large property at Redhill, previously occupied by the Foundling Hospital. Fifty-three elderly and infirm inmates were transferred to St Anne's from the Dorking Institution, which then became Dorking County Hospital. The hospital joined the NHS in 1948, subsequently becoming known as Dorking General Hospital. Only the entrance block now survives, used in recent times as a children's nursery.

EPSOM

Epsom's workhouse stood on Dorking Road (TQ203599). In 1777, it housed sixty inmates. A 1779 inspection found that the children were dirty, louse-ridden, half-naked and unable to read; the beer tasted bad, and a lunatic named Thomas Scriven was partly naked and chained up.[19] In 1797, the inmates were occupied in spinning coarse woollen or linen yarn. Breakfast was either broth, milk porridge or gruel; dinner every day was meat and bread, and supper was bread and cheese or butter. Each person had a pint of small beer at dinner and supper.[20] In 1824, the parish advertised that several healthy workhouse boys were available to be apprenticed as shoemakers or tailors with a premium of 40s.[21] The eighty inmates in 1832 were generally old people, imbecile persons and children.

Ewell had an early workhouse at the west side of what is now the West Street recreation ground (TQ214622). By 1760, a second workhouse was established nearby, at the south side of West Street (TQ213621). It incorporated a former 'pest house' – a building used to isolate cases of infectious diseases.[22] In 1786, able-bodied inmates were required to card and spin 18lb of wool per day.[23]

Cobham's workhouse, housing forty inmates, is said to have occupied what is now 9–10 Korea Cottages on the Upper Tilt, Cobham (TQ120591).[24]

Carshalton had a workhouse in a building later known as Leicester House at the east of Wrythe Green (TQ276652). In 1777, it housed twenty inmates. At the same date, Cheam's workhouse had fourteen places and Stoke D'Abernon's twelve.

In Leatherhead, a 'House of Industry' was erected in 1808 on Kingston Road, in the vicinity of the present-day Dilston Road (TQ164577).[25]

In 1832, Great Bookham's workhouse inmates comprised seven adults and six children.

Epsom Poor Law Union was formed in May 1836 and initially retained parish workhouse premises at Epsom (for the aged and infirm), Ewell (for able-bodied men and boys over 13), Carshalton (for girls under 16, boys under 13) and Leatherhead (for aged and infirm women). Able-bodied women were distributed among the latter three establishments.

A new building, housing 250 inmates, was erected at the rear of the old Dorking Road premises. The design, by William Mason, was chosen because its Tudor-style features gave the appearance of an almshouse rather than a prison. Following its opening in 1838, the old buildings were disposed of. A new boardroom and pavilion-plan infirmary were added in 1882, followed in 1888 by a three-storey block for aged men, receiving wards, a dining hall, and a sixty-bed vagrants' ward.[26]

After being taken over by Surrey County Council in 1930, the workhouse became a PAI, also known as Middle House, while the infirmary section became Epsom District Hospital, dealing with surgical and acute cases. After 1948, the main workhouse building became The Oaks old people's home, while the infirmary became an NHS hospital. The Oaks was demolished in the mid-1970s and the site was renamed Epsom General Hospital in 1991.

By the 1920s, the union had established a children's home at 38 Wilmerhatch Lane (now Woodcote Green Road).

FARNHAM

Farnham had a workhouse by 1777 which housed sixty-five inmates. It stood in the town and was said to have been 'most wretched'.[27] In 1791, after adopting Gilbert's Act, the parish erected a new workhouse on a site between Hale Road and Guildford Road (SU850475). The establishment was noted as being 'on a good plan and in a good situation' and having decreased mortality rates among the poor.[28] Infirm inmates were occupied in picking wool, while children attended the carding machine, spun and were taught to read. Breakfast for the inmates was either onion pottage or bread and broth; dinner was either meat pudding and vegetables, or bread, cheese and beer; supper was bread and beer, with cheese sometimes included. In 1832, the workhouse had fifty-five inmates.

The parishes of Frensham and Frimley each adopted Gilbert's Act. Frimley had a workhouse by 1811 at the north-west corner the Frimley Fuel Allotments, now occupied by the Tomlinscote playing field (TQ890588).[29]

Farnham's Gilbert Parish status placed it largely outside the 1834 Act. In 1846, however, Farnham and the adjacent Gilbert Union of Aldershot and Bentley were persuaded to join with four other parishes in the area to form the new Farnham Poor Law Union. The union took over the existing Farnham workhouse and extended the building with a central dining hall and kitchens, infirmary and a block for the aged.

After the Aldershot army camp opened in 1856, the workhouse infirmary treated many syphilitic cases, a large proportion of which were fatal.[30]

In 1867, a *Lancet* report on the workhouse found much to criticise. Many of the buildings were said to be dark and poorly ventilated, with bare dirty walls and narrow beds. Sanitary facilities were poor, only two towels a week being provided for each ward and no toilet paper. Only one nurse was employed and there was no nursing cover at night. Inmates were not given forks with which

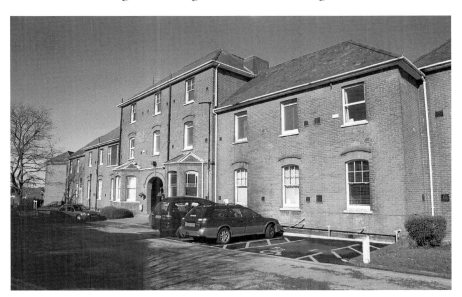

The now-demolished 1900 infirmary at the former Farnham Union workhouse was one of its last buildings to survive.

to eat their food. The casual wards were described as being like rabbit hutches and the vagrants given no food. The lately departed workhouse master, James Sargeant (the great-great-grandfather of British politician Jeremy Corbyn), who had held the post for fourteen years, was said to have been despotic.[31] A subsequent LGB inquiry concluded that while some aspects of the article were matters of concern, others were disproved or exaggerated.[32]

In 1930, under the control of Surrey County Council, the main workhouse block became Farnham County Institution, later known as St Andrew's old people's home. The infirmary buildings became Farnham Hospital, joining the NHS in 1948 and later incorporating the whole site, which was completely redeveloped in 2006–07.

In 1849, the Farnham and Hartley Wintney Unions established a District School for their children. Initially located in a former workhouse at Aldershot (SU861511), it moved in 1856 to purpose-built premises at Crondall (SU802468).

GODSTONE

In 1777, parish workhouses existed at Bletchingley (for up to fifty inmates), Horne (twenty), Limpsfield (thirty) and Oxted (fifty).

Limpsfield's workhouse, which dated back to at least the mid-1760s, stood at the north end of what is now Wolf's Row (TQ407526).[33] The establishment was known for the white rose ointment it produced from the blooms that grew over the building.

Horne's workhouse stood near its parish church, as did that in Bletchingley, which was on the west side of Church Lane (TQ328509).

A property now known as The Old Lock-up on Oxted High Street is said to have been the parish workhouse in the 1820s.[34] It had closed by 1832.

Godstone had a workhouse at 60 High Street (TQ349518), later occupied by the White Swan Inn, now converted to flats known as White Swan House. In 1832, the workhouse housed twelve males, aged from 11 months to 74 years, and twelve females, aged from 4 to 86.

Warlingham's establishment was located on Workhouse Lane, now Hillbury Road, in the garden of what is now The Grange (TQ351582).

The Chelsham workhouse was on the edge of Bull Green (TQ372590).[35]

Godstone Poor Law Union came into being in October 1835 and continued to use existing parish workhouse premises at Bletchingley. Four years later, the Guardians purchased the workhouse site, then owned by the clerk of the parish, and substantially enlarged the building under the direction of architect John Whichcord. A separate school block was erected to the north of the workhouse. In the latter part of the nineteenth century, considerable expansion took place at the north of the workhouse and an infirmary and separate infectious block were added at the west of the site.

In July 1907, an inmate who had inherited a large fortune expressed his desire to repay the money expended on him during his six years in the workhouse. A meeting of the Guardians was told that a cheque for £124 had been received.[36]

In 1930, Surrey County Council took over the site, which then became Clerk's Croft Mental Deficiency Institution. After 1948, it joined the NHS as Clerk's Croft Hospital. The site was redeveloped in the 1980s and is now occupied by the Clerks Croft housing estate.

GUILDFORD

A workhouse was established by Archbishop George Abbot in 1630 at the east end of North Street, Guildford (SU998495), where unemployed cloth-workers were occupied in producing linen, then later woollen cloth. After it ceased operation in 1656, the building was divided into cottages for the poor.[37]

By 1777, Guildford's three parishes had their own workhouses: Holy Trinity (for twenty inmates), St Mary (twenty-four) and St Nicholas (twenty). By 1832, St Mary's, which incorporated the old North Street manufactory, served all three parishes. Its thirty-seven inmates included two insane men, five girls who attended the Quaker school and eight boys who went to the National School. The inmates had three meat dinners a week, with broth or pudding on other days. Adults received a daily pint of beer, children half a pint.

Shere's workhouse, now Western Cottages, was erected in the 1720s on Ewhurst Road, Peaslake (TQ086446), and housed forty paupers. It had its own bakehouse and brewhouse. A 15ft dining table was used for communal meals which were eaten off wooden trenchers with spoons.[38] In 1794, the parish burial register noted that Susan Honey had spent forty years in the workhouse.[39]

Send and Ripley had a workhouse from 1738 at what is now 42–46 Newark Lane, Ripley. In 1777, it housed thirty inmates. The parish later adopted Gilbert's Act.

Albury's workhouse, now known as Heath Lodge, was erected in 1732 on Park Road at Albury Heath (TQ064469). In 1777, it housed up to eighteen inmates. At the same date, there were also workhouses at West Clandon (for up to four inmates), Godalming (seventy-six), Pirbright (thirty), Wisley (eight) and Woking (forty).

Godalming adopted Gilbert's Act in 1786 and had a workhouse on Moss Lane (SU969439), where a school now stands. In 1832, inmates received four meat dinners a week, one meat soup and two bread and cheese. Beer was allowed at dinner. The older boys worked in local leather mills, and the girls in silk mills.

Woking's workhouse was at the northern edge of Westfield Common (TQ004565).[40] It later housed the Old Cricketers Inn.

West Horsley established a workhouse at the east side of The Street, in a property now known as the Old House (TQ079531).

Guildford Poor Law Union was formed in April 1836 and initially retained the workhouse premises at Send and Ripley, Godalming and Worplesdon. After discussing various schemes for enlarging the existing buildings, the Guardians obtained plans for a new workhouse from architects Scott and Moffatt. It was originally to be built at Worplesdon but was subsequently erected at a new site on what is now Cooper Road, Guildford (TQ008495). The building, housing 300 inmates, was opened in 1838. It was a typical Scott and Moffatt design, with a low entrance range, three-storey main block and infirmary at the rear. The facilities included a bone-crushing mill, worked by cranks from the able-bodied men's yard.

In 1856, a new hospital was added at the south-east of the workhouse and a school with attached casual wards at the south-west. A large pavilion-plan infirmary was added at the east of the workhouse in 1893, together with an infectious block, a married couples' block, and a large casual ward on what is now Warren Road.

In 1906, it was reported that the workhouse was so overcrowded that inmates were being accommodated at night in the chapel of the institution.[41]

During the First World War, the workhouse was taken over for use as a military hospital, providing 445 beds for 'other ranks'.[42]

After 1930, the site was taken over by Surrey County Council. The workhouse became a PAI known as St Luke's Home, while the medical facilities became Warren Road Hospital. The whole site joined the NHS in 1948 as St Luke's Hospital, finally closing in 1996. Most of the old buildings were then demolished. The former casual ward-block now houses a workhouse museum.

The entrance to the Guildford Union workhouse during its First World War deployment as a military hospital.

The former casual ward at Guildford Union workhouse. The largest surviving building of its type, it now houses a workhouse museum.

HAMBLEDON

In 1777, parish workhouses existed at Chiddingfold (for up to twelve inmates), Hambledon (eight), Haslemere (thirty) and Witley (thirty).

Around 1786, Hambledon, Bramley, Chiddingfold and Dunsfold formed a Gilbert Union and erected a workhouse on Wormley Lane, Hambledon (SU957381). Elstead, Hascombe, Haslemere and St-Martha-on-the-Hill (Chilworth) joined later.

In 1793, Cranley (renamed Cranleigh in 1867 to avoid handwritten confusion with Crawley) also adopted Gilbert's Act.[43] Its ambitious workhouse, at the south of Cranley Common (TQ049392), could house 250 inmates. Able-bodied men worked at grave-digging, stone-breaking and cracking flints, while the women did housework, sewing and laundry. Both sexes also made shoes and sorted bones. Husbands and wives below the age of 60 lived in opposite wings of the building. Outings were limited to twice-weekly church services, workhouse inmates being segregated from the rest of the congregation.[44] The building no longer exists.

Ewhurst adopted Gilbert's Act in 1799. In 1832, its workhouse housed nine men, two women and two girls.

In 1832, Witley's workhouse had twenty-five inmates though it could house eighty. The one able-bodied man worked for a nearby farmer, the parish receiving 3s a week for his labour. There were ten children below the age

The former Hambledon Union workhouse. Inset is a view of its 1776 foundation stone.

of seven who all went to school. The inmates had six meat dinners a week. Smoking was banned.

Hambledon Poor Law Union was formed in March 1836 and took over the Hambledon Gilbert Union workhouse. The square building, two-storeys high plus attics, enclosed a courtyard divided by a central dining hall and kitchen. Females occupied the east of the building and males the west. A separate infirmary was later added to the north of the site and a new board-room was erected in 1882.

In 1930, Surrey County Council took over the site which became a PAI, with the infirmary known as Hambledon Hospital. In 1940, the children's accommodation was converted for use as a nursery for twenty young children and six nursing mothers. From 1942–49, the premises were home to King Edward's School, Witley, whose own building had been requisitioned by the Admiralty. The site was then an old people's residence, Hambledon Homes, until the 1970s. The surviving buildings have now been converted for residential use.

KINGSTON

The first workhouse in Kingston was set up in 1725 in rented premises near the site now occupied by Surrey County Hall.[45] In 1777, it could house 288 inmates. In the late 1700s, the workhouse moved to London Road, opposite the junction with Coombe Road (TQ189695). In 1832, the average number of inmates was eighty.

Esher built a workhouse in 1740 at the south of the village green (TQ138647). In 1777, it could hold thirty-four inmates. Its operation was contracted out to a 'renter of the poor' who often proved unreliable. In 1773, William Collier had 'greatly neglected clothing the poor'. In 1781, Jonathan Buller simply disappeared.[46] From 1837, the premises housed a National School, replaced in 1858 by a new building, now used for adult learning.

Wimbledon's parish workhouse, erected in 1752, stood at the north side of what is now Camp Road (formerly Workhouse Lane, TQ231711). Almshouses now occupy the site.

Thames Ditton had a workhouse from 1760.[47] It occupied rented premises, which in 1777 could house up to thirty inmates.

In 1777, workhouses were also in use at Malden (for up to twelve inmates), Hampton Town (thirty) and Hampton Wick (six).

Hampton's workhouse stood on what is now Roy Grove (TQ137709). It was used to mark the south-eastern end of a base measured by General Roy

The entrance drive to the Kingston Union workhouse where a number of inmates and staff are enjoying the sunshine.

in 1784, which laid the foundations of the Ordnance Survey. The location is identified by half-buried cannon.

East and West Molesey established a joint workhouse in 1822 in what is now known as the Old Manor House on Bell Road, East Molesey (TQ145677).[48]

The Kingston Poor Law Union was created in June 1836 and retained the Kingston, Hampton and Esher workhouses. The following year, construction began of a new workhouse on Coombe Road, Kingston (TQ195697). William Mason's double-cruciform design (two linked, cross-shaped blocks) housed 320 inmates. The Tudor-style building lay at the end of a long, tree-lined driveway. Water came from a 90ft well which provided the institution's supply until 1910.[49]

Soon after the workhouse opened in the summer of 1839, a torrent of complaints against the master and matron, Mr and Mrs William Smith, led to an inquiry by the Guardians. Smith was found to be using handcuffs and leg-irons to ill-treat the inmates. Although initially only reprimanded, the pair were dismissed in 1840.[50]

An H-shaped 100-bed infirmary was built at the north-east of the workhouse in 1843 and a larger one at the south-west in 1868. An even larger infirmary complex was added at the north in 1899, with its entrance on Kingston Hill. From 1902, the northern part of the site operated as Kingston Infirmary.

During the First World War, the Red Cross took over the infirmary to house military casualties. In 1920, it was renamed Kingston and District Hospital.

After 1930, the workhouse section became the Kingston Central Relief Institution, then in 1948 was integrated into Kingston Hospital. Steady redevelopment since the 1960s has seen the demolition of most of the old buildings.

By the early 1900s, the union ran a number of scattered homes, with a central home at 163 Kingston Road, New Malden and a receiving home at Moira House, 13 Old Bridge Street, Hampton Wick.

REIGATE

Reigate Borough set up a workhouse in 1730 on Park Lane, then named Workhouse Lane.[51] It had thirty inmates in 1777. In 1832, the seventeen residents were aged, infirm or infants.

The Foreign (rural) part of Reigate also had a workhouse from around 1730. It was located at Shaw's Corner, on what is now Hatchlands Road, Redhill (TQ269502). There were forty inmates in 1777. The building survives as the rear part of The Hatch pub (former Foresters' Arms).[52]

At Chaldon, around 1740, the Lord of the Manor built five cottages, collectively known as Beggars Lodge, for use as a poorhouse, on what is now Chaldon Common Lane (TQ323551). The premises were later used as a workhouse.[53] The establishment had twelve inmates in 1777.

Workhouses also existed in 1777 at Betchworth (for up to thirty inmates) and Burstow (fifteen). Betchworth had two establishments – one on Gadbrook Common (TQ215486), the other where Bovey Cottage stands on what is now Station Road (TQ20950). Burstow's workhouse was located on what is now Wheeler's Lane, Smallfield, in the vicinity of Centenary Hall (TQ315430).[54]

In 1793, Reigate, Buckland, Nutfield, Headley and Horley formed a Gilbert Union and erected a workhouse at Earlswood Common, Redhill (TQ272491). The establishment was 'a large fair brick building', square in shape, around a central courtyard. The inmates' breakfast was either water-gruel with pottage, or broth and bread. Dinner on Sunday, Tuesday and Thursday was ox beef or mutton, vegetables and bread; on Monday and Saturday it was stewed ox cheek or legs or shins of beef; on the other days, its was suet pudding or rice milk, sweetened with sugar. Supper every day was bread and cheese or bread and butter. 'Small beer' was also served at dinner and supper.[55] A fulling mill was installed and the inmates were occupied in making blankets and coarse woollens.[56] In 1832, there were eighty-four inmates.

Buckland also had a workhouse on Lawrence Lane (TQ226513) in what is now Orchard Farm Cottages.[57] Brockham's was at what is now 18-20 The Borough (TQ194497).

Charlwood had a workhouse on Charlwood Street. In 1836, a workhouse also existed at Merstham.[58]

Reigate Poor Law Union was formed in March 1836. It adopted the existing Gilbert Union workhouse and spent £2,000 on alterations and repairs.

In March 1837, Peter Bews was appointed master of the workhouse but was dismissed the following October as not 'fit and suitable' for the post.[59]

The buildings were gradually expanded over the years, most notably with a new infirmary erected at the east of the workhouse in 1915–16, immediately taken over by the Red Cross for wartime military patients.

In 1930, the establishment was taken over by Surrey County Council and became a PAI. In 1936, the inmates were transferred to St Anne's, Redhill, previously occupied by the Foundling Hospital. The Reigate site then became Redhill County Hospital. It joined the NHS in 1948, renamed Redhill General Hospital. After its closure in 1991, the site was redeveloped for residential use, now known as Abinger Drive. Most of the old workhouse and hospital buildings have been demolished.

By 1908, a children's cottage home had been opened at 25–27 Hardwick Road, Meadvale, Redhill (TQ265491). It accommodated fifteen boys and fifteen girls.[60]

RICHMOND

Barnes opened a workhouse in 1758, where all those receiving parish pensions were then sent to be clothed, fed and put to work. The inmates were employed from 6 a.m. to 7 p.m. in summer, and from 8 a.m. to 6 p.m. in winter. Their breakfast was milk porridge, water-gruel, broth or bread and beer; midday dinner was pudding, beef or broth, rice milk, or bread and cheese; supper was bread and cheese, hasty pudding or milk porridge. Swearing or other disorderly behaviour was punished by a day's loss of meals, while those refusing to work, or damaging or stealing workhouse property could end up in the Bridewell prison.[61]

In 1778, Barnes erected a larger workhouse at the southern edge of Barnes Common (TQ222754). William Mears and his wife from the Wandsworth workhouse were appointed as master and matron, at a salary of £20 plus 21*s* to Mrs Mears for tea and sugar. Twelve new beds, 4ft 6in wide with flock mattresses, were bought to supplement the two best bedsteads transferred from the old premises. A further three old bedsteads were kept for the new workhouse's 'foul wards', which housed those with venereal conditions. The inmates' work included the spinning and carding of wool and, from 1812, the dressing of hemp and flax. Among the tasks given to children was the scaring away of birds from a field where peas were being grown. After its closure in 1836, the workhouse building became known as the Manor House until its demolition in 1961.[62]

A workhouse was established in Richmond in 1729, initially using temporary accommodation, probably in cottages to the south of what is now Clarence Street (TQ180752).[63] The next year, it moved to Rump Hall, a large house on Petersham Road (TQ180741). A new building, paid for by George III, was erected in 1786–87 on Grove Road, Richmond (TQ188742). The H-shaped, two-storey building was in use by October 1787, by which date the vestry had decided to add a new infirmary and accommodation for lunatics and disorderly persons.

Mortlake's workhouse was erected 1733 at the east side of what is now Mullins Path (TQ207758). In 1774, William Ross was appointed as contractor at a fee of 2s 10d per head per week. The inmates were to receive three hot and one cold meat dinners per week.[64] In 1832, the inmates comprised seventeen adults and fifteen children. The building was subsequently used as a National School and is now occupied by the Capel Court flats.

Richmond Poor Law Union was created in June 1836 and took over the Grove Road workhouse, which was altered to meet the requirements of the 1834 Act. By the 1880s, a chapel and a cellular casual ward had been added alongside Grove Road. As well as a sleeping compartment, the casual ward cells included a stone-breaking section. At this date, the workhouse also had a section known as the Irish Ward.

In 1901–02, a large infirmary was erected at the south-west of the workhouse. The ward-blocks were three storeys high, each floor having a twenty-four bed 'Nightingale' ward plus a separate three-bed ward. The infirmary also included a lying-in ward, nurses' home, lunatic wards and a combined ambulance house and mortuary.

In 1915, the site became Richmond Military Hospital, providing 514 beds for 'other ranks'.[65] In 1930, it became a PAI under the control of Surrey County Council. In 1948, the infirmary section joined the NHS as Grove Road Hospital, with the old workhouse building known as Kingsmead. After its closure in 1974, the main block and entrance lodge were converted to residential use.

The oldest part of the former Richmond Union workhouse. Inset is a view of a stone recording King George III's financial contribution to its building.

In the 1890s, the union operated a cottage home at 11–13 Cleveland Road, Barnes. From around 1901, there were several scattered homes on St Leonard's Road, Mortlake.

8

SUSSEX

ARUNDEL

Arundel had a poorhouse from at least 1682, probably sited on the east side of Park Place (TQ014070). In 1713 it was recorded as housing poor children and widows. A new workhouse was built in its garden in 1779–80.[1]

Sometime after 1782, Arundel adopted Gilbert's Act. In 1831, the parish erected a new building on the existing workhouse site at the south end of what had become Poorhouse Hill, now Mount Pleasant, Arundel. In 1832, it had fifty inmates, including twenty-six children.

The former Arundel Gilbert Parish workhouse, now converted to flats.

Arundel's status as a Gilbert Parish largely exempted it from the 1834 Act and the workhouse continued in operation until 1869, when all remaining Gilbert administrations were abolished. Arundel then became part of the East Preston Poor Law Union.

In 1871, the old workhouse was used as a temporary smallpox hospital. In the first part of the twentieth century, it became a clubhouse, then in 1985–86 was converted into flats.

BATTLE

Langton House on the High Street, Battle (TQ748158), is said to have served as a poorhouse or workhouse from 1718 to 1724, and again from 1805 onwards.[2] A separate establishment operated in premises just south of Battle railway station, near the present-day Senlac Hotel (TQ753153). In 1777, Battle's workhouse housed up to fifty-five inmates. In 1832, the residents comprised twenty-five adults aged from 30 to 90, and thirty-two children aged from 1 to 18 years.

Bexhill erected a workhouse in 1755 on Bexhill Down, where King Offa School now stands (TQ737081).[3] It held forty inmates in 1777. In 1832, the residents were all aged between 60 and 70 years.

Ewhurst's workhouse housed forty-five inmates in 1777. The residents in 1832 were fourteen adults and twenty children. The workhouse was the subject of a dismal report in 1835 by Assistant Poor Law Commissioner William Hawley:

> In the day-room I found a group of children sitting in listless idleness, uninstructed in either moral or useful duties. One of the bedrooms was appropriated to the reception of an aged man and woman and three girls; a third room was the sleeping-place of a young woman affected with a certain loathsome disease, and in company with her were several boys and girls; in another a violent female maniac, fastened with cords to a chair, was disturbing all the inmates of the house by loud and obscene exclamations. In a low dark garret, hot to suffocation, I discovered eight beds closely packed together, on one of which was sitting a lame pauper, inhaling as much air as an aperture intended for a window would admit; on another was stretched a poor wretched being in the last stage of consumption, emaciated and exhausted by disease.[4]

Westfield's workhouse was located on what is still known as Workhouse Lane (TQ813155), where thirty-six paupers could be housed in 1777. The inmates in 1832 comprised ten aged adults and twelve boys and girls.

Other workhouses in the area in 1777 were Brightling (for up to forty inmates), Hollington (twenty-four), Mountfield (thirty) and Sedlescombe (thirty).

Sedlescombe's workhouse (referred to as a poorhouse prior to 1770) began life in a property known as Guns (now Spilsteads Cottages) on Stream Lane (TQ771188). It then successively occupied Magpie Cottage (Q780182) and Riverbridge Cottages (TQ782177), both on the Street, and finally Brede Lane Cottages.[5] In 1832, it had ten inmates.

In 1832, the inmates of Mountfield workhouse were six males, aged from 4 to 60 years, and four females aged from 8 to 50 years.

The parish of Catsfield had a workhouse in operation by 1812.

Battle Poor Law Union was formed in June 1835. Initially, the union retained the workhouse at Battle to house able-bodied paupers, the Catsfield and Sedlescombe workhouses for the aged and infirm, and the Bexhill workhouse for children.

A new workhouse for up to 440 inmates was opened in 1840 on North Trade Road, Battle (TQ732159). The building was designed by Hastings-born Frederick Thatcher who, in 1834, was one of the first Associates of the Institute of British Architects. It had a separate front block, three storeys high at its centre, where an entrance archway was located. To the rear, the main building formed

An early 1900s view of the Battle Union workhouse.

an inverted 'T', with a three-storey octagonal hub at its centre. Two-storey ranges ran to the east and west, with a three-storey range to the north. Outbuildings across the arms of the 'T' gave the workhouse a semi-hexagonal perimeter. There was an isolation hospital at the north-west of the site, later used as a nurses' home.

In 1930, the site became Battle PAI, run by East Sussex County Council. In 1948, it joined the NHS as Battle Hospital, specialising in geriatric care. Following the hospital's closure in the late 1990s, the buildings were converted to residential use.

BRIGHTON

In 1727, Brighton (then known as Brighthelmstone) erected a workhouse on the site of the former St Bartholomew's convent at the west side of Market Street (TQ310039). It could house up to thirty-five paupers and included a kitchen, workroom, pantry, brew-house, bedrooms and two cellars. The inmates picked oakum and, in the winter, collected and crushed oyster shells, the resulting mixture being sold as a fertilizer.[6] By 1777, the workhouse had seventy places and in 1800 was enlarged to house up to 150 inmates, who now wore heavy brown uniforms.

In 1810, the town obtained a Local Act and administration of poor relief passed to a board of thirty Directors and Guardians of the Poor elected by the town commissioners. Following a second Act in 1825, the board were elected by all the inhabitants of the town. One of the board's first tasks was to try to make the poorhouse diet more economical by reducing the consumption of bread and substituting rice or herrings in its place.[7]

In 1818, the Guardians decided that a new workhouse was needed to cope with the increasing number of inmates. A site was purchased on Church Hill (TQ306046), at the south-east of the junction of the present-day Buckingham Road and Dyke Road. A competition to design the new building was won by William Mackie.[8] The H-shaped layout provided separate accommodation for different classes of inmate, with the administrative functions placed at the centre. The inmates were employed in making 'whitening' (ground chalk used for whitewashing), ropes, doormats, rugs and sacking. They also ground their own flour and made their own clothes. In 1832, the workhouse had one of the most generous diets in the country. The three meals a day had no limits on quantity. There were six meat dinners in the week and the inmates were served at table by the master and matron. Men received two pints of beer a day, children one pint, and women a pint of beer and a pint of tea.

Brighton's Local Act status made it largely immune from the 1834 Act and it continued to operate as a Local Act parish until 1930.

In April 1839, two absconding inmates, Sophia Clifton, 17, and Olive King, 16, were found guilty of stealing their workhouse uniforms and the attempted theft of alternative clothing. The two were transported to Australia for fourteen years.[9]

In 1854, the Guardians decided to replace the Church Hill workhouse with a new building on Race Hill (TQ328052), together with an industrial school for juveniles at Warren Farm, Rottingdean (TQ354057). However, they were reluctant to pay for piped water to supply the new establishments, so workhouse labour was used to dig a well at the Warren Farm site. Progress was slow and the lack of water resulted in a long postponement of the building work on the new workhouse. Finally, in March 1862, after four years of digging to a world record depth of 1,285ft, water was finally reached. Construction of the new workhouse then progressed, with the building completed in September 1867 at a cost of £41,000. The Church Hill site was then sold off, usefully raising a total of £42,000.

The new workhouse was designed by J.C. & G. Lansdown of Charing Cross, in conjunction with local man George Maynard. Its impressive T-shaped main block had a four-storey frontage with a central clocktower. The building was divided into male and female sections by means of iron gates in the corridors.

The massive frontage of the Brighton workhouse is partly hidden by the institution's casual ward.

An infirmary and lunatic block were placed at the south of the main building. In 1880, additional land was purchased to the west of the site. New casual
wards were erected at its northern end in 1885, followed by additional infirmary pavilions at the south.

From 1904, the birth certificates for those born in the workhouse gave its
address as 250 Elm Grove.

From 1915–20, the premises were used as the Kitchener Indian Hospital,
treating sick and wounded Indian soldiers. In 1930, the site became Brighton
Municipal Hospital, then joined the NHS in 1948 as Brighton General
Hospital. Medical use of the now listed building ended in 2009.

The Warren Farm School opened in August 1862 when seventy-five boys
and sixty-five girls processed there from the old Church Hill workhouse. The
site was later occupied by the Fitzherbert School. The buildings were demolished in the early 1990s.

CHAILEY

Ringmer had a workhouse by 1733.[10] It was at the centre of the village on
a site now known as Corner Green (TQ445124). In 1777, it could house
twenty-four inmates who were occupied in carding and spinning wool, hemp
and flax. In 1832, there were about twenty inmates. Nearly half were boys, the
others being old men and women and 'simple' children.

In 1777, parish workhouses were operating at Chailey (for forty inmates),
Ditchling (twenty) and Wivelsfield (sixteen).

Chailey's workhouse was located at North Common, Chailey (TQ383210).

Ditchling's workhouse was at the corner of South Street and Lewes Road
(TQ326151). In 1832, it had twenty-six inmates ranging in age from infancy
to 81 years. It was demolished around 1874 for the widening of South Street.

Wivelsfield's workhouse stood on Church Lane (TQ338208). A surviving
part now houses the offices of a local school.

An L-shaped building, now known as Cuttings, at the east side of Cricketfield
(T417216), was used as Newick's workhouse.

In 1832, Barcombe's workhouse inmates comprised eleven males and ten
females.

Chailey Poor Law Union was formed in March 1835. The union initially
retained the three parish workhouses at North Common, Ditchling and
Ringmer. Able-bodied inmates were placed at Chailey, the aged at Ditchling,
and children at Ringmer.

The former Chailey parish workhouse at North Common which continued to be used by the Chailey Union until the 1870s.

The new Chailey Union workhouse opened at East Chiltington in 1873.

In 1873, all the old premises were replaced by a single new workhouse on Honeypot Lane at East Chiltington (TQ383173). Designed by Henry Card, the building accommodated 250 inmates and included a substantial infirmary.

The north-eastern entrance to the site was flanked by single-storey blocks probably containing a porter's lodge, boardroom and receiving wards. The main block was a long two-storey building facing to the east.

In 1898, the Chailey, West Firle and Lewes unions merged, with the new body continuing under the name of Lewes Union. The former Lewes and Chailey workhouses were closed and their inmates transferred to East Chiltington.

In 1930, the East Chiltington site was taken over by East Sussex County Council and became a PAI known as Lewes Institution. It joined the NHS in 1948, becoming known as Pouchlands Hospital. The buildings were redeveloped for residential use around 1991.

The old Ditchling workhouse was demolished around 1874. From 1875–1902, the North Common premises housed the Brighton and Preston Industrial School for Boys. The building was subsequently occupied by the Heritage Crafts School.

CHICHESTER

In 1625, almshouses for 'twelve decayed tradesmen' were erected on the east side of Broyle Road, Chichester (SU861056). They were funded by a gift from William Cawley, noted for having signed the execution warrant of Charles I. Mention of the building's use as a workhouse was made in 1681.[11]

A Local Act in 1753 created an Incorporation of eight Chichester parishes and the Cathedral Close for maintaining the poor, with thirty Guardians elected annually by the inhabitants. At the same time, the almshouse was formally converted into the Incorporation's workhouse. The building was extended by the addition of new wings and the wall around the garden. A spinning shop was established, and a room with an unglazed, barred window became a 'bridewell' for punishing miscreants.[12]

The workhouse had extensive rules. Liars were deprived of their dinner and placed on a stool in the dining hall with a paper pinned to their breast bearing the words 'Infamous Lyar'. Anyone given permission to leave the premises but returning late could not go out again for two months. Smoking in bed could earn two hours in the stocks and the loss of one meal's meat. In 1765, the 'pernicious and scandalous practice' of tea-drinking was banned after two young

The original portion of the Chichester workhouse.

inmates had been scalded. In 1803, several badly behaved women were ordered to attend church twice each Sunday wearing 'a Chip Hat and Linsey Woolsey Gown with the Letters B.C. [Bad Conduct?] on their Right arm with Yellow, with a Checked Handkerchief'.[13]

Chichester's Local Act status largely exempted it from the 1834 Act and the Incorporation continued in operation until 1930. Over that period, the workhouse buildings were extended at various times.

In 1930, West Sussex County Council took over the site which became a PAI. After 1948, the premises were used as NHS offices, with a hospital laundry operating at the rear.

The original almshouse block and chapel still survive, but later additions at the rear of the site were demolished in 2001.

In 1913, the Guardians established a children's cottage home on Trumley Road, Lavant (SU850083). The building, known as Lavant House, had previously been a home for orphan girls. The property is now occupied by a school.

CUCKFIELD

In 1738, the Bull Inn in Ockenden Lane, Cuckfield (TQ302245), was converted for use as a workhouse. In 1777, it could house sixty inmates. It was rebuilt in the early 1800s as a manufactory of woollen and linen cloths. In 1832, the inmates carried out a 'coarse manufacture of linen and woollen' from which clothing was made and distributed to pauper families.

Cowfold's workhouse, at the north of the churchyard (TQ212226), could house fifteen inmates in 1777. In 1803, its residents were occupied in carding or spinning flax or hemp. The building later became a private house then in 1929 was converted into almshouses still known as Margaret Cottages.[14]

Slaugham had a 'Workhouse for Women' in a property now known as Poyningshurst on Coos Lane, Slaugham (TQ251285).[15] In 1777 it could house twenty-four inmates.

In 1777, workhouses were also in use at Ardingly (for up to twenty inmates), Bolney (fifteen), Horsted Keynes (sixty), Hurstpierpoint (twenty-five), Lindfield (thirty-two) and New Timber (nine).

Ardingly's workhouse was in a property known as Jordans, at the corner of Church Lane and Street Lane (TQ340298).[16] In 1832, Ardingly was described as 'the worst parish in the worst county'. The workhouse was an old house for up to thirty-nine inmates, for whom no employment was provided. The sick and aged were neglected, clothed in tattered garments and had no comforts allowed them.

The Horsted Keynes workhouse is said to have been located at the north side of The Green, where the Green Man pub now stands (TQ384282).

Hurstpierpoint's workhouse was on the west side of Pitt Lane (TQ 282l62). The establishment had its own bakery and brewhouse.[17] In 1832, there were forty-eight inmates aged from 1 to 70 years.

Old Place, on Lindfield's High Street (TQ349258), served as a workhouse.[18] A small building nearby (TQ348257) was also used as a workhouse or poorhouse.[19]

Cuckfield Poor Law Union was formed in March 1835. Initially, the union continued to use the existing Cuckfield workhouse. In 1843, a new building was erected to the west of the Ardingly Road. It was designed by S.O. Foden in collaboration with Assistant Poor Law Commissioner H.W. Parker. Foden and Parker objected to the prison-like appearance of earlier workhouses. Their own designs placed yards for the old and for children in front of the main building and surrounded them by open fences rather than by high walls.

The entrance to the Cuckfield workhouse was flanked by a lodge to the east and vagrants' accommodation to the west. The main workhouse build-

The main block of the Cuckfield workhouse. The yards for the elderly and children were separated by railings rather than the more usual high walls.

ing was a substantial three-storey structure in which the wards for different classes were placed back-to-back, facing either the front or rear of the building. A small chapel in Gothic style was built to the west of the main building in 1858. A separate infirmary block was added at the north of the workhouse by 1877, and a further one to its north in 1890.

The site was taken over by East Sussex County Council in 1930 and later renamed Cuckfield Hospital. During the Second World War, it was a military hospital for Canadian troops, then joined the NHS in 1948. After its closure in 1991, the buildings were converted to residential use.

EAST GRINSTEAD

East Grinstead had a workhouse from 1725. Its location is uncertain but in 1742 it had seven rooms on the ground floor, seven on the first floor, a garret, a cellar, nine feather beds, nineteen 'chaff beds', shoemaking tools and seven spinning wheels.[20] In 1747, the establishment moved to new premises on London Road. In 1832, there were about 100 inmates in the workhouse which was said to be 'altogether inefficient'. No work was done and twenty single men placed in the house the previous winter had refused to even draw a bucket of water. After being reprimanded by a magistrate they returned to the workhouse and spent their time in 'lolling over the pales and smoking their pipes'.

Lingfield erected a workhouse in 1729 on Newchapel Road (TQ380436). In 1832, it housed thirty inmates aged from 18 months to 82 years. The property is now known as The Garth.

Withyham had a workhouse by the 1730s on Lye Common. This building burned down and, in 1738, another property was rented near Withyham station.[21] In 1777, the workhouse could house forty-three inmates and in 1832 there were forty-six in residence.

Crawley's workhouse occupied what is now Fir Tree Cottage on London Road (TQ269376). In 1777, the establishment housed up to eight inmates.

The Worth workhouse could house twenty inmates in 1777. A new building was erected in the 1790s at the junction of Church Road and Turners Hill Road (TQ299368). In 1832 it had thirty-three residents whose ages ranged from 7 to 90 years. Later known as Khyber Cottages, the building was demolished in 1967.

Hartfield's workhouse had thirty-three inmates in 1832, two-thirds of them under 14 years. The building, on Church Street (TQ478357), survives as the Anchor Inn.

East Grinstead Poor Law Union was formed in September 1835 and initially retained five existing workhouses. East Grinstead received able-bodied adults, with any overflow going to Withyham. The aged and infirm were placed at Worth, girls at Hartfield and boys at Lingfield. The Lingfield inmates knitted stockings and made moleskin waistcoats and straw hats and bonnets.[22]

In 1859, a new workhouse accommodating 260 inmates was erected at the south side of Glen Vue Road, East Grinstead (TQ390382). Designed by Frederick Peck, it had a T-shaped main block, with a separate entrance block at the north facing Glen Vue Road, and an infirmary at the south. The institution later adopted the address 98 Railway Approach.

In 1930, under West Sussex County Council, the site became a PAI, later St Leonard's House old people's home. The building was demolished around 1980.

EAST PRESTON

In 1777, workhouses were in operation at Angmering (for up to twenty inmates), Littlehampton (twenty), Poling (twelve) and Rustington (ten).

The East Preston Union workhouse in the early 1900s.

In January 1791, a Gilbert Union was formed by East Preston, Burpham, Goring, Littlehampton and Ferring, and erected a workhouse on The Street, East Preston (TQ070023). It was enlarged in 1806 and had a large square yard at its centre. The union had grown to nineteen parishes by 1832, when the number of workhouse inmates averaged fifty in summer and seventy in winter, mostly the old and infirm, children, or pregnant single women. The inmates made sacking, rope and bedding. The weekly diet included six meat dinners and one bread and cheese, with a daily pint of beer. Some of the old people received an allowance of tea or tobacco. The men slept two to a bed.

Its Gilbert Union status largely exempted East Preston from the 1834 Act. The workhouse was enlarged in 1853 by the addition of a schoolroom and an infirmary.

In September 1869, following the abolition of all the remaining Gilbert Unions, the East Preston Poor Law Union was created. A new workhouse was built on the existing site in 1872–73. It was designed by G.B. Nichols and had a T-shaped main building. An infirmary was added at the south-east in 1906.[23]

From 1904, the birth certificates of those born in the workhouse gave its address as North View, East Preston.

In 1930, the establishment was taken over by West Sussex County Council and became the North View Institution, later old people's home. The building was demolished in 1969 and the Fairlands housing estate was erected on the site.

EASTBOURNE

Eastbourne's first workhouse was opened in 1737 in a rented property known as Pillory House, presumably in the vicinity of Pillory Barn on Bradford Street (TV596994).[24] Around 1755, a new building housing up to fifty paupers was erected on what is now Grove Road (TV608989). It was later described as a tenement divided into six dwellings, with a garden attached.[25] In 1817, the establishment moved a short distance to Church Street, into premises built as a barracks during the Napoleonic Wars (TV596994). Its inmates in 1832 comprised fourteen men, fourteen women, eighteen girls and seventeen boys. There had been a manufactory of coarse woollens and linens in the workhouse, with labour partly provided by children from large families attending by day to earn something for their support. However, mounting debts had led to the ending of the scheme.

In 1743, Alfriston established a workhouse at Cross House, Waterloo Square (TQ520031). It moved in 1790 to 10–11 North Street (TQ520032).[26]

In 1777, the workhouse at West Dean had eighteen places and that at Wilmington eight places.

From around 1780, Seaford had a workhouse on Blatchington Road, on the site of the medieval leper hospital of St John's. The master and his assistant resided in Twyn House and Twyn Cottage, with the inmates in a long building at the rear. The establishment closed in 1810 and the inmates were transferred to Eastbourne.[27] However, it had apparently resumed operation in 1832.

Eastbourne Poor Law Union was formed in March 1835 and took over the Church Street workhouse. The main building stood at the west of the site. Various outbuildings were placed around the large central yard where a chapel was erected in 1857. An infectious hospital was erected at the east of the site in 1877, and converted to an infirmary in 1887. A master's house was added in 1913. In 1927–28, a new ward-block was built at the centre of the site, requiring demolition of the chapel.[28]

From 1929, the infirmary was known as St Mary's Hospital. In 1948, the whole site joined the NHS under that name. Following the closure of the hospital in 1989, the buildings were demolished and replaced by a housing development.

By the early 1900s, the union had established a home for up to twenty children at 2–4 Birling Street, Eastbourne. The property is now in private residential use.

HAILSHAM

Hailsham had a workhouse by 1762. The timbered building, at the corner of Vicarage Road and Market Street (TQ591094), housed up to forty inmates who were occupied in spinning wool. The establishment also possessed a cider press.[29]

Heathfield's workhouse, on Church Street (TQ598202), was established in 1757.[30] In 1777, it could house twenty-five paupers. In 1832, thirty-six were in residence. Part of the building is now a cottage.

In 1777, workhouses were also in use at Chiddingly (twenty-five places), Herstmonceux (forty-five), Hooe (thirty), Ninfield (fifteen), Warbleton (sixty) and Wartling (forty).

Chiddingly's workhouse was located at Nash Street, Golden Cross (TQ548123). In 1832, it had twelve male inmates and ten female. The property is now a private residence variously known as the Old Workhouse or Robin Mead.

Hooe's workhouse was at the north side of Hooe Common (TQ694106). The property is now known as Elizabethan Cottages.

What in now Whitehouse Farm, on Hooe Road, Russell's Green (TQ703116), was once the Ninfield parish workhouse.

The Warbleton workhouse, situated opposite the parish church (TQ609181), later became a school and is now three cottages.[31]

Laughton's workhouse was on Church Road (TQ501125). The building is now three cottages named Meadowside, Beech Cottage and Church Cottage.[32]

Hellingly had a workhouse at Upper Horsebridge at the west side of what became Union Road (now Hawks Road, TQ588112). In 1832, it had forty-two inmates aged from 1 to 80 years.

In 1832, Herstmonceux's workhouse, at Gardner Street, had twenty-three inmates. The inmates' diet included meat on five days a week, while – it was said – the industrious labourer in his cottage had no such fare.

Hailsham Poor Law Union was formed in April 1835 and initially continued using the workhouses at Hellingly (for men), Warbleton (boys), Arlington (women and small children), Herstmonceux (girls) and Hailsham (the aged and infirm).

In 1835–36, the Hellingly workhouse was substantially extended with Sampson Kempthorne as architect. It adopted a cruciform layout and could accommodate up to 270 inmates. The other workhouses were then closed, apart from Hailsham which continued in use until 1854.

At Hellingly, the infirmary at the west of the site was enlarged in 1870, and a new boardroom was erected on the opposite side of Union Road in 1878.

A view of the severe-looking main building of Hailsham Union workhouse.

In 1930, the site was taken over by East Sussex County Council. After briefly operating as Hellingly House PAI, it was closed in May 1932 then was demolished. Housing now occupies the site.

HASTINGS

In 1753, three Hastings parishes (All Saints, St Clement's and St Mary in the Castle) jointly funded a new workhouse, which was erected on the site now occupied by 42 George Street (TQ822094). After St Mary and All Saints withdrew from the scheme in 1773, St Clement's continued using the George Street premises, which in 1777 could house sixty paupers. There were fifty-three inmates in 1832, aged from 1 to 80 years. Some worked in the streets as scavengers.

All Saints subsequently operated workhouses at 125 All Saints Street (TQ827097) and at Paul's Field, now the site of 135 Old London Road (TQ829104).[33] The twenty-five inmates in 1832 were aged from 18 months to 86 years. The men were mostly former fishermen.

St Mary in the Castle opened a workhouse at Baldslow.[34] In 1777, its establishment housed up to twenty inmates. There were fourteen in residence in 1832, only four of whom were able to work.

In 1777, Fairlight had a workhouse for thirty inmates.

A view of the Hastings Union workhouse. The original cruciform building is nearer to the camera, while the later pavilion blocks run across the upper part of the picture.

In the 1830s, workhouses were also in use at Guestling, Pett, and the Hastings parishes of Holy Trinity, St Leonard and St Mary Magdalen.

Hastings Poor Law Union was formed in July 1835. As an interim measure, the All Saints workhouse was assigned to receive able-bodied paupers and St Clement's the aged and infirm. A new workhouse was erected at the east side of Cackle Street (now Frederick Road, TQ832113). It opened its doors on 10 July 1837, with 160 paupers being transferred from the old parish work-houses in the union.[35]

The new building, designed by Sampson Kempthorne and Annesley Voysey, followed Kempthorne's model cruciform plan and accommodated 300 inmates.[36] A long two-storey infirmary was erected alongside Cackle Street in 1868.

In 1899, work started on a new workhouse at the opposite side of Cackle Street, designed by Alfred W. Jeffery and William Skiller.[37] The foundation stone was laid by Alderman Frederick Tuppenney, after whom Cackle Street was renamed Frederick Road in 1904. The new building had a pavilion-plan layout. The central administrative block contained the master and matron's and medical officer's quarters, dining hall, kitchen and stores. At each side were three-storey ward-blocks, one for men and one for women, each housing

171 inmates. An entrance block with vagrants' cells was located towards the road, and a chapel was placed at the south of the site. A subway under the road connected the old and new sites.

In 1929, future novelist Catherine Cookson became head laundress at the workhouse.

In 1930, the site was taken over by Hastings Borough Council and became Hastings Municipal Hospital. It joined the NHS in 1948 as St Helen's Hospital. After its closure in 1994, the 1903 buildings were replaced by a housing development. Much of the 1837 building survives, now in residential use.

By 1908, the union had established several children's scattered homes in Hastings.

HORSHAM

Horsham opened a workhouse in 1727 on the south side of Normandy, where St Mary's almshouses now stand. In 1777, it could house eighty inmates. In 1832, there were forty-nine residents, all old people or children, apart from one lunatic who was kept in manacles. The children attended the local infant or National schools.

From 1730, Warnham had a workhouse for twenty paupers, located in three tenements where 7–21 Church Street now stands (TQ158335).

The Rusper workhouse was opened in 1731 in a former almshouse at Venters, a mile to the east of the village. In 1777, it could house forty inmates.[38]

In 1763, West Grinstead leased a house south of Dial Post for use as a poorhouse.[39] In 1777, the parish workhouse had thirty inmates. In 1794, the establishment had eighteen rooms. In 1832, there were forty inmates, all children or old people. Employing the inmates in weaving had been discontinued as uneconomic.

Beeding had a workhouse by 1768, which may have stood at the north side of the High Street.[40] In 1777, it could house fourteen inmates.

In 1777, workhouses were also in use at Ifield (for up to twenty inmates), Itchingfield (four), Shipley (twenty-six) and Slynfold (thirteen).

Ifield's workhouse was erected in 1747 on Tweed Lane, Ifield Green (TQ249380). In 1832, it had fifteen inmates. The property is now known as The Tweed.

Shipley's first workhouse may have been Renche's Farm (now Cottage) near Dragons Green (TQ146235). By the early 1800s, it occupied a property on Pound Lane, now known as Whitehart Cottages (TQ149226). The building had a 'Black Hole' used for punishing miscreants. The rules prohibited smoking, except in the day room, and required that 'any female being in the family way shall be degraded by wearing a party coloured or workhouse dress'. In 1833, a fine house called New Buildings Place was rented to house additional paupers. However, the inmates tore down old panelling in one of the rooms for firewood.[41]

Horsham Poor Law Union was formed in September 1835. Initially, the old Horsham workhouse was used to house able-bodied paupers, with Shipley used for children, and Warnham for the aged and infirm. A new workhouse for 250 inmates was erected in 1838–39 at the south side of the Crawley Road, Horsham (TQ189317). Designed by London architects Hallett and Newman, the building had a large central courtyard with an arched entrance at the north.[42] A large pavilion-plan infirmary block was added in 1903.

In 1930, the site was taken over by West Sussex County Council and became Horsham PAI. During the Second World War, military casualties were treated at the site. After 1948, as Forest Hospital, it provided care for patients with severe learning disabilities. The hospital closed around 1990 and the buildings have now been converted to residential use.

By 1924, the union had opened a children's home at 5–7 Bedford Road, Horsham.

The former Horsham Union workhouse.

LEWES

The Lewes parish of St John sub Castro had a poorhouse, later workhouse, from 1633 at what is now 7 Castle Banks (TQ414102). In 1832, it had twenty-nine inmates, including eighteen children.

All Saints, Lewes, built a workhouse in 1730 at what is now 31 High Street. By 1758, it had become rundown and a replacement was erected on the west side of St Nicholas Lane (TQ416100). In 1777, the establishment could house thirty inmates, with thirty-two in residence in 1832, ranging in age from 1 month to 90 years. One man worked as a scavenger and five boys as errand boys. The aged received extra-nutritious food, and those who went to work, an extra pint of beer a day.

St Thomas à Becket at Cliffe, Lewes, had a workhouse on South Street (TQ422101). In 1777, it accommodated thirty inmates.

St Anne's, Lewes, operated a workhouse on the High Street. In 1832, it was described as a poorhouse with up to forty inmates ranging in age from a month to 90 years. At the same date, the workhouse of St Michael, Lewes, was home to eighteen paupers. The eldest was the parish's beadle.

The Lewes Poor Law Union was formed in August 1835 from Lewes's six parishes plus South Malling. The union took over the existing workhouses on South Street and St Nicholas Lane, both of which were altered and enlarged. The St Anne's premises on the High Street were used to house the union's pauper children.

The Lewes Union workhouse, used in the early 1900s to house female inebriates.

In 1868, a new workhouse for 205 inmates was built at the north side of De Montfort Road, Lewes (TQ407103). Designed by Henry Currey, it had a single-storey entrance block and a corridor-plan main building with numerous gables. A separate infirmary was placed at the north-west of the main building. A school block accommodating forty children was added at the north-east in 1875.

In 1898, Lewes merged with the adjacent Chailey and West Firle Unions, the new body being named the Lewes Union. The West Firle and Lewes work-houses were closed and their inmates transferred to the former Chailey Union workhouse at East Chiltington.

From 1902–10, the former workhouse at Lewes housed the Southern Counties Reformatory for Female Inebriates. It then had various uses and was leased to a tractor company in 1920 before being converted to flats. The buildings were demolished in the 1950s to make way for the Abergavenny Road flats.

The children's block at the Lewes workhouse site, renamed Avenue House, continued in use as an East Sussex Council children's home until the 1950s.

MIDHURST

In 1777, workhouses were in use at Chithurst (for up to six inmates), Easebourne (twenty-six), Fernhurst (sixteen), Midhurst (thirty), Rogate (eighteen), Terwick (five) and Trotton (twenty-four).

In 1792, Easebourne and fifteen neighbouring parishes formed a Gilbert Union and erected a workhouse at Dodsley Lane, Easebourne (SU890232), which opened in October 1794. The buildings, three storeys high at the front and two storeys at each side, enclosed a large courtyard. On the ground floor, the front portion, facing towards the road, contained the governor's room and committee room, with the inmates' dining rooms to their rear. The south wing included a kitchen, bakehouse, wash-house, brew-house and stables. The north side contained a workroom, weavers', tailors' and shoemakers' workshops, and a 'room for old people to pick wool in'. At the west of the courtyard were an ash-house, dead-house, bathing room and two 'prison' cells.[43] The building could house 180 inmates and by October 1795 there were 159 in residence. In line with Gilbert's Act, these were mostly under 14 or over 60 years of age, although exceptions could be made to admit the physically or mentally infirm, or women with infant children. The women performed domestic work, while men were employed in gardening, or were hired out for farm work.[44]

The former Easebourne Gilbert Union workhouse, later adopted by the Midhurst Poor Law Union.

Harting had a workhouse in Harting Place, an old manor house near the church, but this was dismantled by 1800.[45] In 1832, there was a workhouse for eighty paupers, although the average number was about twenty, all of whom had separate rooms.

In 1832, Midhurst's workhouse had twenty-six inmates, including seventeen children. Those capable of work were employed in the workhouse garden, in household work and in husbandry. Those going out to work had meat every day. The aged and others had meat four times a week and were allowed tea.

Rogate's workhouse in 1832 comprised several small cottages joined together. Its inmates were four old men, one old woman and five children.

Midhurst Poor Law Union was formed in May 1835 and took over the Easebourne workhouse, which was enlarged in 1836. A single-storey board-room was later added at the front of the building.

In 1930, the site was taken over by West Sussex County Council and became known as Budgenor Institution. In the mid-1970s, the council used the premises, renamed Budgenor Lodge, as temporary accommodation for homeless families. In 2006, the building was converted into apartments.

NEWHAVEN

In 1777, a workhouse was in use at Rottingdean for up to seventeen inmates. It was closed by 1832.

Rodmell had a workhouse or poorhouse at the north-east of the village (TQ420063), now part of a row of cottages which includes The Old Poor House.

Newhaven Poor Law Union was formed in February 1835, one of the first to be created under the 1834 Act, and erected a new workhouse on Church Hill, Newhaven (TQ440011). The building, intended to accommodate up to 150 inmates, was designed by Sampson Kempthorne. It had a somewhat unusual layout, with the three-storey main building having the form of a large block, going against Kempthorne's usual approach to ventilation. Around 1900, a two-storey infirmary was added at the north-east of the workhouse.

In 1930, the site was taken over by East Sussex County Council and became Hill House Institution. In 1948, it joined the NHS as Newhaven Downs Hospital. The building has latterly been occupied by the Newhaven Rehabilitation Centre.

The main building of the former Newhaven Union workhouse. Its box-like design was atypical of both the period and Kempthorne's other work.

PETWORTH

Workhouses were in operation by 1777 at Petworth (for up to seventy inmates), Kirdford (sixty), Wisborough Green (eighty), Billingshurst (forty-five) and Rudgwick (thirty).

Petworth workhouse stood on North Street. At some date after 1782, the parish adopted Gilbert's Act. A new workhouse was erected in 1820, again on North Street (SU976226).[46] In 1832, the number of inmates averaged about fifty – 'entirely old people, young children, or females to be confined of bastard children'. The inmates were occupied in making sacking and rope. The younger children were taught to read in the house, while the older ones attended the national school.

The Wisborough Green workhouse was situated on School Road (TQ052258). In 1832, it had thirty-four inmates, chiefly the aged and children. Some able-bodied men who had entered the establishment the previous winter were said to have proved noisy and troublesome, insulting passers-by over the low wall.

The Kirdford workhouse was located to the north of St John's Church (TQ17265). In 1832, there were about fifty inmates of all classes and ages, including twenty children. The boys were sent to work for local farmers, but there was a surplus of labour in the area and men were working at boys' wages.

The workhouse at Petworth, one of the three operated by the Petworth Union.

Billingshurst had a workhouse by 1732. Located on East Street (TQ89259), it had fifty inmates in 1832. A few ropes were manufactured.

Rudgwick's workhouse occupied what is now the Fox Inn on Guildford Road, Bucks Green (TQ077330). The North Chapel (Northchapel) workhouse, now Forge Cottage, was at the east side of Main Street (SU952295).

Petworth Poor Law Union was formed in September 1835 and took over the workhouses at Petworth (for able-bodied adults), Wisborough Green (for children) and Kirdford (for the old and infirm).

The Petworth building had a U-shaped layout, open to the east. Men were housed in the south wing and women in the west. The master's accommodation was at the north-west corner, and the north wing contained a wash-house, boiling room, bake-house, laundry and female casuals' block. A male casuals' block and stone-breaking yard lay at the south-west of the site.[47] The establishment was taken over by West Sussex County Council in 1930 but was closed in 1933 and the building demolished.

The Wisborough Green workhouse was an L-shaped building. The three-storey east wing, now The Old Workhouse, housed a boardroom and two school rooms. The north wing, now the village hall, contained a wash-house, the master's room, and a hall. The area between the wings, now a car park, was the boys' exercise yard. A small building in The Old Workhouse's garden may have been a mortuary.[48]

The Kirdford workhouse closed in 1885 and the building is now in private residential use.

RYE

Rye's first workhouse opened in 1724 in a warehouse on what is now Rope Walk (TQ920205).[49] It was donated to the parish by Allan Grebell and enlarged in 1735. A separate 'pest house' for smallpox victims was added in 1762. In 1777, the workhouse could house sixty inmates. In 1783, it moved to Gun Garden (TQ922203) and received only the elderly and children. There were forty-six residents in 1835.

In 1777, workhouses were also in use at Brede (for thirty inmates), Iden (twenty) and Winchelsea (twenty-four).

Brede, one of the hotspots of discontent that spawned the Swing Riots in 1830, had a workhouse at the junction of Cackle Street and Pottery Lane (TQ822186). It had thirty inmates in 1832. In 1835, it was noted that 'the house is offered to all the single men, and such as contract improvident marriages, where stone-breaking is provided for them.'[50] The property, later known as Alpha Place, no longer exists.

Winchelsea's workhouse occupied an old building on Tanyards Lane (TQ907175). Only the aged and infirm were admitted. The property, formerly known as Strand House, is now used as a hotel.

In 1787, Udimore built a workhouse to the east of Cock Marling (TQ889189).[51] Now known as Woodside Cottages, the property is surrounded by Workhouse Wood.

Northiam had a workhouse consisting of five cottages on what is now Station Road, adjacent to Workhouse Pond (TQ828254). In 1832, it had fifty-six inmates. Three of the cottages, known as Knelle View Terrace, survived until the 1960s.

In 1832, the workhouse at Beckley had thirty-four inmates of all ages.

At various times, workhouses also existed in the area at Peasmarsh, Playden and on Workhouse Lane, Icklesham.

Rye Poor Law Union was formed in July 1835 and initially used the workhouses at Rye (for the aged and infirm), Brede (able-bodied males), Peasmarsh (able-bodied females) and Northiam (children). By 1837, only Rye and Brede were in use.

In 1845, a new workhouse for 436 inmates was opened at Rye Hill (TQ919214). Designed by S.O. Foden and H.W. Parker it had a T-shaped main building. A central hub housed the master's quarters, with the dining hall

The former Rye Union workhouse and (inset) an inmate in front of the main entrance. (Pictures courtesy of Nick Chillingworth, Les Bearman and Alan Dickenson.)

to the rear. Female accommodation was at the east side and male at the west. An infirmary was erected to the north of the workhouse in 1847.[52]

In 1930, the site was taken over by East Sussex Council and became a PAI known as The Retreat. In 1941 it was requisitioned for military use, with the inmates evacuated to Socknersh Manor. Immediately after the war, the building provided temporary housing for evicted families. In 1949, it joined the NHS as Hill House Hospital, providing care for the mentally and physically handicapped. The hospital closed around 1980, and the main block is now in residential use.

STEYNING

In 1729, Steyning purchased a medieval timber-framed building on Mouse Lane (TQ173115) for use as a workhouse. In 1777, it could house up to eighteen inmates. The building still exists, now converted to cottages.

Henfield's workhouse, now Cedar View, was built in 1736 at the south of Nep Town Road (TQ213156).[53] It had sixty places in 1777 and around thirty inmates in 1832, all elderly, infirm or children. An acre of garden supplied vegetables.

New Shoreham established a workhouse in 1754, housing twenty inmates.

By 1768, Beeding had a workhouse which may have stood on the north side of High Street.[54] It could accommodate fourteen inmates in 1777. In the same year, workhouses were also in use at Poynings (for up to twenty inmates) and Sompting (fifteen).

Preston had a workhouse at the rear of what is now the Crown & Anchor pub on Preston Road (TQ302064). The small thatched building, with flint and brick walls, was demolished in 1844.[55]

Steyning Poor Law Union was formed in July 1835. Its initial plans to house children in the Steyning workhouse, the able-bodied at Henfield, and the elderly at Shoreham, caused a riot requiring military intervention.[56]

In 1836, a new workhouse, designed by a Mr Elliot, was built on a 2-acre site at Ham Road, Shoreham-by-Sea (TQ218052). Later additions to the site included infirmaries, vagrants' wards and a chapel. By the 1890s, the accommodation was deemed inadequate and plans were made for larger premises.

In 1896, the Guardians acquired a 23-acre site on Upper Shoreham Road, Kingston-by-Sea (TQ227060). The new building, designed by Clayton and Black, was completed in 1901. The pavilion-plan layout had a central administrative block containing the master's quarters, offices, kitchens and dining hall. This was linked by covered walkways to the men's pavilions at the west, and women's at the east.

The abandoned dining-hall block of the Steyning Union workhouse, prior to its demolition.

An arched entrance block stood by the road at the north of the site, with vagrants' wards to its west, and a receiving ward for new inmates to its east.

Great efforts were made to keep men and women segregated, with 'unclimbable' fencing installed in 1905. However, men were still caught climbing over the barrier and a female inmate had a second illegitimate child while in the workhouse. An inquiry discovered that male and female inmates were passing messages to one another just using the general postal service.[57]

In 1906, four new hospital blocks were opened at the east of the site and a chapel at the west. During the First World War, the hospital facilities were used by the military. In 1918, German prisoners of war cultivated vegetables in 16 acres of the workhouse gardens.

In 1930, the site was taken over by East Sussex County Council and became a PAI known as Shoreham Institution, renamed Southlands Hospital in 1933. By the end of the twentieth century, the old workhouse blocks had become disused. The site has now been redeveloped for housing, although the old receiving and casual ward buildings still survive.

After the move to Kingston-by-Sea, the old Shoreham workhouse site became a union children's home, known as St Wilfrid's. The union also operated cottage homes nearby on Gordon Road and Rosslyn Road.

SUTTON

In 1777, workhouses were in operation at Bersted (for up to twenty-five inmates), Heyshott (twelve) and Slindon (ten).

A house now known as Farriers on The Street in Heyshott (SU897180) was once the parish workhouse.

A Gilbert Union based at Sutton was formed in 1791, eventually having seventeen members. The Incorporation established a workhouse at Sutton End (SU983165).

Over the years, the inmates were occupied in tasks such as the making of woollen blankets, hemp sacks and horse-hair cider cloths.[58]

Its Gilbert Union status largely exempted Sutton from the 1834 Act. It continued in operation, with a declining number of members, until 1869 when all remaining Gilbert Unions were abolished. Its member parishes were distributed between the East Preston, Petworth and Westhampnett Poor Law Unions.

The former workhouse is now a private residence known as the Old Poor House.

THAKEHAM

West Chiltington had a poorhouse from 1704 in a cottage on Broadford Bridge Road (TQ094201). It later became a workhouse and in 1777 could house fifteen inmates. In 1832, the residents comprised one old man, two old women and two orphan children. A house now called Gobles now occupies the site.[59]

Washington had a workhouse from 1739, possibly located north of The Street.[60]

In 1777, workhouses were also in use at Ashington (up to eight inmates), Findon (fifteen), Pulborough (forty-six), Storrington (thirty-four) and Thakeham (twenty).

A property known as Goar Cottages, at the bottom of Bost Hill, Findon (TQ125075), was once home to the parish's workhouse.

The Pulborough workhouse was at the south side of Lower Street, east of the building known as Henleys (TQ056185). In 1832, it had about thirty inmates, chiefly the aged and infirm, or pregnant single women.

The Storrington workhouse was in Cootham, where Duke's Row now stands (TQ074145).[61]

Thakeham's workhouse once occupied a row of cottages on The Street (TQ107173), of which Mouse Cottage and Bottom Cottage survive. Cumberland House, where The Street meets Cray's Lane (TQ109172), was also used.[62]

In 1789, a Gilbert Union was formed by Thakeham, Ashington, Findon, Sullington, Washington and Wiston. The union opened a workhouse in 1791 at Rock Road, Heath Common (TQ101149).

In 1851, a property on Church Street, Amberley, was referred to as the Old Workhouse.[63]

Thakeham Poor Law Union was formed in May 1835 and took over the existing Gilbert Union workhouse. The building was enlarged in 1853 and could then accommodate 250 inmates. The building had a double-courtyard layout.

In 1930, the establishment became a PAI under the control of West Sussex County Council. After its closure in 1936, it was replaced by a new school, known in more recent times as Rydon Community College.

TICEHURST

Salehurst had acquired a poorhouse or workhouse by 1730, now School Terrace on Northbridge Street (TQ740242).[64] It could house 100 paupers in 1777 and had 40 inmates in 1832.

A workhouse was opened at Lamberhurst in 1740 in a property on School Hill known as Wealden Hall House, now The Charity (TQ676363). In 1777, it could hold twenty-four inmates.

A policeman stands at the entrance to the Ticehurst Union workhouse – another of Sampson Kempthorne's hexagonal designs.

In 1777, workhouses were also in operation at Burwash (for up to seventy inmates), Ticehurst (forty) and Wadhurst (thirty).

Burwash's workhouse was at Burwash Weald, at the rear of what are now Pooks Hill View and Church House (TQ650231).[65] In 1832, the establishment had thirty-three inmates of all ages.

In 1778, Wadhurst purchased workhouse premises near the church, where a doctor's surgery now stands (TQ641317).[66] In 1832, it had thirty-five inmates.

Frant's workhouse had forty-two residents in 1832, including nineteen children under the age of 10. At the same date, Ticehurst's had thirty-seven, including twenty-one children.

Ticehurst Poor Law Union was formed in September 1835 and initially used the existing parish workhouse premises at Ticehurst, Salehurst and Lamberhurst. A new workhouse was erected in 1836–37 at Union Street, Flimwell (TQ705313). It was designed by Sampson Kempthorne, based on his model hexagonal plan. Later additions included infectious wards in 1885 and an iron chapel at the south of the workhouse.[67]

After 1930, the establishment was taken over by East Sussex County Council and became The Furzes PAI, later Furze House old people's home. The buildings were demolished around 1980.

UCKFIELD

In 1739, Mayfield purchased the Old Star Inn (now Stone Court, TQ586269) for use as a workhouse. Female inmates worked in textile production.[68] In 1777, there was accommodation for just five inmates. In 1832, the residents comprised forty-seven aged men and women and orphan children. They were employed in spinning and weaving. The diet was meat puddings three times a week, meat soup three times a week, bread and cheese on Saturdays, and beer every day.

Rotherfield had a workhouse, location uncertain, as early as 1580.[69] It later moved to premises at the west side of the High Street (TQ556296). In 1777, the establishment held up to fifty inmates, with thirty-two there in 1832. The building now comprises the White Cottage, Olinda House and the Old Almshouse.

Uckfield's workhouse, now Bell Farmhouse, was at the south end of Belmont Road (TQ469211). It could house thirty inmates in 1777. In 1832, it was criticised as being excessively comfortable. Three days a week, inmates had hot dinners of meat puddings or boiled beef, with beer, and on the other days meat soup.

Fletching had a workhouse, now converted to two cottages, at Splaynes Green (TQ430243). It had thirty-eight places in 1777, with forty-two in residence in 1832, all aged under 20 or over 70.

Other workhouses active in 1777 were Buxted (with twenty-five places), Maresfield (twenty) and Waldron (thirty). Buxted's workhouse, later Workhouse Farm, stood on Pound Lane, half a mile to the south-east of the village (TQ513227). Maresfield workhouse, later Old Workhouse Farm, now Paddock Farm, was near the junction of Nursery Lane and Old Forge Lane (TQ464263). Waldron's workhouse occupied what is now Grove Cottages at the west of the village (TQ546195).[70] In 1832, its twenty-nine inmates were aged from 1 to 80 years.

Framfield had a workhouse on Sandy Lane, now Bretts Cottages (TQ495210). In 1832, the average number of inmates was about thirty.

Uckfield Poor Law Union was created in March 1835. It initially retained the workhouses at Maresfield and Mayfield (both used for able-bodied men), Framfield (women), Uckfield (girls), Buxted (boys), Waldron (the sick), and Rotherfield and Fletching (both for the elderly and infirm). A new workhouse to house 350 inmates was built in 1838–39 at Ridgewood, to the south of Uckfield (TQ478197). The building, mostly three storeys high and constructed in red brick, was designed by H.E. Kendall and based on the PLC's model cruciform layout.[71]

In 1930, the site was taken over by East Sussex County Council and became High View PAI, later High View House old people's home. The building was demolished in the 1980s and housing now covers the site.

The main building of the Uckfield Union workhouse.

WESTBOURNE

Westbourne's workhouse was erected in 1773 at Westbourne Common (SU759083). A 'springing house' for sack manufacture was added in 1775.[72] The establishment had ninety inmates in 1777.

Workhouses were also in operation in 1777 at Bosham (for up to twenty-six inmates), West Dean (eighteen) and Stoughton (fifty). Bosham's parish workhouse, now Harbour Cottages, was situated on the village's quay (SU803038).[73]

Funtington had a workhouse at West Ashling (SU804072). Chidham's workhouse, now The Poor Cottage, was on Chidham Lane (SU794040).

Westbourne Poor Law Union was formed in March 1835 and initially used the old workhouses at Westbourne (for the able-bodied and children) and Bosham (for the aged and infirm). However, following criticism by an inspector about the lax regime at Bosham, it was closed down. Westbourne became the union's only workhouse and £2,000 was spent on enlarging it to house 220 inmates.

By 1915, the union had a home for eighteen children at Stein Road, Southbourne. From 1925–33, the workhouse was used as a children's home. The buildings were then demolished although parts of the surrounding walls survive.

WEST FIRLE

In 1812, the parishes of Glynde, West Firle and Beddingham obtained a Local Act for the 'Better Employment and Support of the Poor'. The Act, which was modelled on Gilbert's Act, allowed the union to provide a workhouse, although it is unclear whether one was ever established.[74]

In 1832, Berwick had a workhouse whose inmates comprised one old man, three old women, seven boys, and seven girls under 18.

West Firle Poor Law Union was formed in March 1835 and built a workhouse for 140 inmates at Burgh Lane, West Firle (TQ484081). The H-shaped main building was constructed in flint and enclosed two yards, one bounded by lower outbuildings to the east and a long, detached block at the west.[75]

In 1898, West Firle merged with the Chailey and Lewes Unions, the new body continuing under the name of Lewes Union. The Lewes and West Firle workhouses were closed and their inmates transferred to the former Chailey Union workhouse at East Chiltington.

The West Firle premises were subsequently converted to residential use and became known as Stamford Buildings. The property suffered severe

An early 1900s view of the West Firle Union workhouse.

damage during the Second World War when a Spitfire crashed into it. All that now remains is the northern part of the 'H' which has been converted into two houses.

WESTHAMPNETT

In 1745, Yapton opened a workhouse in a property later known as Rope Cottages, next to the former Black Dog pub on North End Road (SU976033).

Pagham opened a workhouse on Church Lane around 1750.

In 1777, workhouses were in operation at Aldingbourne (for up to thirty inmates), Barnham (fourteen), Mid Lavant (twelve), North Mundham (sixteen), Oving (twelve) and Selsey (thirty-five).

Sometime after 1782, Westhampnett and ten other parishes formed a Gilbert Union. Its workhouse, which could house up to 300 inmates, was an old manor house, formerly known as Westhampnett Place, on Stane Street, Westhampnett (SU879059). In 1832, the average number of inmates was fifty-seven including around twenty children who were taught to read in the establishment. Some of the older boys went out to do farm work. Able-men were admitted for a short period until they could find work. The inmates' weekly diet included six meat dinners and one suet pudding.

In 1791, another Gilbert Union in the area was formed by the parishes of Yapton, Felpham and Walberton, using the workhouse at Yapton. A larger building, now Laburnum Cottages, was erected behind the existing premises in 1818.[76]

A property just off Graffham's main street is still known as the Old Poor House (SU926173). A similarly named house on Mill Lane, Sidlesham (SZ858971), was built from timbers reclaimed from a ship, possibly from the Spanish Armada. Sidelsham formed a Gilbert Union whose other members in 1833 included Appledram, Birdham, Itchenor and Selsey.[77]

Westhampnett Poor Law Union was formed in March 1835. It initially intended to use the existing Gilbert workhouse at Westhampnett for able-bodied paupers, Aldingbourne for the children, and Pagham for the aged and infirm. When this arrangement proved too complicated, the Westhampnett premises were enlarged to house all the inmates apart from the children, who were placed at Yapton. Yapton, too, was eventually dispensed with.

In November 1899, most of the building was destroyed by a fire which broke out at midnight during a gale. Although parts of the structure were four storeys high, the presence of fire escapes resulted in virtually all the 115 inmates escaping without injury. The only fatality was Thomas Gilbert, a 72-year-old with a weak heart. The inmates were distributed among neighbouring institutions, including the workhouses at Chichester, Westbourne, Midhurst, Petworth, East Preston and Thakeham. Westhampnett never rebuilt its workhouse and continued to pay for its paupers to be maintained by other unions, especially Chichester.

Some of the surviving workhouse outbuildings were later used as an isolation hospital and then as a council depot, but none of these still exist.

9

WORKHOUSE RECORDS

Prior to 1834, administration of poor relief, including poorhouse and workhouse operation, was primarily carried out by individual parishes. Their records include:

Board of Guardians' minute books
Poor rates collection and distribution
Settlement and removal records
Vestry minutes
Workhouse inventories, rules and admission books, etc.
Bastardy records such as examinations, maintenance orders, etc.

Following the 1834 Poor Law Amendment Act, extensive records were kept by the Boards of Guardians in each area. Workhouse-related records included:

Admission and discharge registers
Indoor pauper lists (six-monthly summaries)
Registers of births, deaths and burials
Religious Creed registers (1869 onwards, also includes admission details)

The Workhouse website (www.workhouses.org.uk) includes a summary of the records surviving for every New Poor Law institution and where they are held. It also lists the parishes encompassed by each Poor Law Union.

The survival of local Poor Law records is very uneven and, for some unions, virtually zero. There are usually restrictions on access to records less than 100 years old which contain personal information.

Most repositories produce research guides relating to their poor relief records and have online catalogues of their holdings. A list of printed guides relating to poor law records in the region is also included at the end of this chapter.

For simplicity, in the rest of this section, the term 'union' is used to cover all of the various flavours of post-1834 poor relief administration.

LONDON AND MIDDLESEX

The London Metropolitan Archives (LMA – cityoflondon.gov.uk/lma) has records relating to the city's poor going back to the fifteenth century and covers the City and County of London, plus the non-metropolitan parts of Middlesex. Many of the LMA's holdings relating to workhouse inmates (e.g. admission and discharge registers) are now also available online to subscribers of ancestry.co.uk. The LMA also hold the records of the Metropolitan Asylums Board. An online guide to the LMA's poor law records holdings is available at bit.ly/LMAPoorLawRecords.

Westminster City Archives (westminster.gov.uk/archives) has poor relief records for the City of Westminster, whose parishes include St Clement Danes, St George Hanover Square, St Martin in the Fields, St Mary le Strand, St Paul Covent Garden, St James, and St Margaret & St John. However, post-1869 records for Westminster unions are mostly at the LMA. Many Westminster archives are now also available online to subscribers of findmypast.co.uk.

BERKSHIRE

Berkshire Record Office (berkshirerecordoffice.org.uk) is the main repository for Poor Law records in the county, including those for union areas which now form part of Oxfordshire.

KENT

Kent Archives (kent.gov.uk/archives) holds the surviving records for most Kent unions. The main exceptions are those for the Bromley Union (held at Bromley Archives – www.bromley.gov.uk/info/200111/records_and_archives) and for the Medway Union (at Medway Archives Centre – medway.gov.uk/archives).

SURREY

Surrey History Centre (surreycc.gov.uk/heritage) holds most of the county's surviving workhouse-related records. The main exceptions are those for the Croydon Union (held at Croydon Archives – croydon.gov.uk/leisure/archives) and those for the Richmond Union (held at Richmond Local Studies Library – richmond.gov.uk/local_studies_collection). Some poor relief records from the Chertsey, Dorking, Farnham, Guildford, Hambledon and Richmond Unions are now available on findmypast.co.uk.

SUSSEX

West Sussex Record Office (westsussex.gov.uk/leisure/explore_west_sussex/record_office_and_archives.aspx) holds the surviving workhouse-related records for the Arundel, Chichester, Cuckfield, East Grinstead, East Preston, Horsham, Midhurst, Petworth, Steyning, Sutton, Thakeham, Westbourne and Westhampnett Unions.

East Sussex Record Office (thekeep.info) holds the records covering the Battle, Brighton, Chailey, Eastbourne, Hailsham, Hastings, Lewes, Newhaven, Rye, Ticehurst, Uckfield and West Firle Unions.

IMAGES AND TRANSCRIPTIONS OF LOCAL RECORDS

A growing number of local workhouse records, particularly those relating to inmates, are now available online, as images and/or transcriptions. Most active in this area are the commercial genealogy companies such as Ancestry and Findmypast. The free website familysearch.org has browsable images of Kent workhouse records (1777–1911).

Many family history societies have transcribed Poor Law records relating to their area and made them available for purchase in print or on CD via suppliers such as Genfair (genfair.co.uk), or online to their members. Free online access to such records is less common, notable examples being the West Sussex Poor Law Records database (sussexrecordsociety.org/dbs/pl). A recent project at the Surrey History Centre has resulted in free online access to over 100,000 names from Richmond relief records (bit.ly/2Ln4BJG).

The London Family History Centre (www.londonfhc.org) has a collection of microform copies of union workhouse records from around the country.

CENTRAL AUTHORITY RECORDS

The central authority overseeing Poor Law administration after 1834 was successively the Poor Law Commissioners (1834–47), the Poor Law Board (1847–71), the Local Government Board (1871–1919), and the Ministry of Health (1919–48). The main repository of records from these bodies is the UK National Archives (TNA – www.nationalarchives.gov.uk). Its workhouse-related holdings include:

- Architectural plans of workhouses (1861–1918)
- The voluminous correspondence between each Poor Law Union and the central authority – some now digitised including that for the Rye Union (1834–43).
- Registers of staff appointments/departures at each workhouse (with dates, salaries, reasons for leaving).

The TNA's Poor Law holdings are mostly filed in their MH (Ministry of Health) series of records as that was the government department administering the system in its latter years. A useful online guide to these records is available at nationalarchives.gov.uk/help-with-your-research/research-guides/poverty-poor-laws.

The TNA's online search facility (discovery.nationalarchives.gov.uk) covers not only their own holdings but those of many local repositories around the country.

The central authority's annual reports, etc. contain a vast amount of material about the poor relief system, including much about individual unions and their workhouses. These publications form part of the UK Parliamentary Papers (see page 277).

OTHER RECORDS

Civil registration of births and deaths (1837 onwards) – indexes are widely available online, e.g. freebmd.org.uk, fndmypast.com and bmdindex.co.uk.

Census returns – widely available online, e.g. freecen.org.uk and ancestry.co.uk.

Baptism records – workhouse baptisms often took place in the local parish church and form part of its records.

Burial records – pauper burial details are occasionally found in the records of parish churches or municipal cemeteries. From the 1850s, many London unions buried paupers at privately run facilities such as the New Southgate Cemetery or the Brookwood Cemetery, Woking (see www.workhouses.org.uk/Brookwood).

PRINTED GUIDES

Coleman, J.M. (1960), *Sussex Poor Law Records: A Catalogue.*

Gibson, J., Rogers, C. & Webb, C. (2005), *Poor Law Union Records: 1. South-East England and East Anglia.*

Melling, E. (1964), *Kentish Sources: IV The Poor.*

Webb, C. (1999), *A Guide to Surrey Parish Documents.*

Webb, C. (2005), *London, Middlesex and Surrey Workhouse Records: A Guide to their Nature and Location.*

Webb, C. (2006), *A Guide to Middlesex Parish Documents Including Poor Law Records.*

10

USEFUL WEBSITES

Access to the websites listed below is free except for those marked (£). Some non-free sites may be accessible without payment via local libraries or record offices, or by members of educational or other institutions that hold subscriptions.

workhouses.org.uk – a vast collection of information on the institutions run by the poor relief authorities across the British Isles.

londonlives.org – London Lives (1690–1800) has 240,000 searchable manuscripts including poor relief records from several City of London parishes.

british-history.ac.uk – a digital library of core printed sources for the history of the British Isles, e.g. volumes of the Victoria County History.

visionofbritain.org.uk – 'A vision of Britain between 1801 and 2001. Including maps, statistical trends and historical descriptions.'

parlipapers.proquest.com – (£) UK Parliamentary Papers searchable online – includes publications by the successive central Poor Law authorities. (See also archive.org below.)

britishnewspaperarchive.co.uk – (£) a huge archive of nineteenth-century British newspapers. (Access also included with Findmypast subscriptions.)

connectedhistories.org – search multiple online historical sources (1500–1900) including some of the above sites.

nationalarchives.gov.uk – the official archive for the UK Government, and for England and Wales.

maps.nls.uk – historical Ordnance Survey maps of Great Britain.

romanticlondon.org – detailed maps of London in 1792 and 1819.

maps.thehunthouse.com/Streets/Street_Name_Changes.htm – London street name changes (1857–1945).

leicester.contentdm.oclc.org/cdm/landingpage/collection/ p16445coll4 – a large collection of historical trade directories of England and Wales from the 1760s to the 1910s.

archive.org – historical books including local history, periodicals, some official papers, e.g. PLC annual reports.

www.builderindex.org/?q=node/385 – *The Building News* architecture journal.

www.bodley.ox.ac.uk/ilej/ – *The Builder* architecture journal (1843–52).

catalog.hathitrust.org/Record/006883391 – online volumes of *The Builder* architecture journal (some only searchable not viewable).

11

PLACES TO VISIT

Many former workhouse buildings still exist, often now converted to residential or other use. A few workhouse sites have now become home to museums, where visitors can get an insight into their use in former times, although some cover a much wider range of topics in their displays.

The Workhouse, Southwell, Nottinghamshire
nationaltrust.org.uk/workhouse
Ripon Workhouse Museum, Ripon, North Yorkshire
riponmuseums.co.uk/museums/workhouse_museum_gardens
Gressenhall Farm and Workhouse, near Dereham, Norfolk
museums.norfolk.gov.uk/gressenhall-farm-and-workhouse
Vestry House Museum, Walthamstow, London,
vestryhousemuseum.org.uk
Guildford Spike Guildford, Surrey
guildfordspike.co.uk
Red House Museum, Christchurch, Dorset
dorsetmuseums.co.uk/red-house-museum-and-garden
Nidderdale Museum, Pateley Bridge, North Yorkshire
nidderdalemuseum.com
Thackray Medical Museum, Leeds, West Yorkshire
thackraymedicalmuseum.co.uk
Weaver Hall Museum and Workhouse, Northwich, Cheshire
weaverhall.westcheshiremuseums.co.uk
Llanfyllin Workhouse, Llanfyllin, Powys
the-workhouse.org.uk

NOTES

ABBREVIATIONS

HEA   Building reports held at Historic England Archive, Swindon
LGB   Local Government Board
PLB   Poor Law Board
PLC   Poor Law Commissioners
PP   Parliamentary Papers

Online references are followed by date of consultation, e.g. (23/1/2018)

CHAPTER 1

1. McConville, 1981, p. 32.
2. Davies, 2004, p. 7.
3. Leonard, 1900, p. 226.
4. Higginbotham, 2008, p. 14.
5. Morrison, 1999, p. 5.
6. Anonymous, 1653.
7. Morrison, 1999, p. 8.
8. *ibid.*, p. 9.
9. Webb & Webb, 1927, pp. 106-7.
10. Bellers, 1695.
11. Anonymous, 1732, p. 53.
12. Strype J., 1720, p. 198.
13. Anonymous, 1732, pp. 3-4.
14. www.british-history.ac.uk/vch/middx/vol7/pp228-232 (10/1/2018).
15. Melling, 1964, p. 83.
16. Anonymous, 1732, p. 25 abridged.
17. Blincoe, 1832, p. 9.
18. Hitchcock, 2004, p. 133.
19. PP, 1804, pp. 716, 728.
20. www.londonlives.org/statis/workhouses.jsp (1/3/2018).
21. Archbishop's Palace, Bearsted, Birchington, Deal, Eastry, Elham, Harbledown, Martin, Waltham/Petham, St Mary Cray & Orpington, River, Selling, Teynham & Lynsted, Tudeley & Capel, Warehorne and Whitstable.

22. Easebourne, East Preston, Sidelsham, Sutton, Thakeham, Westhampnett and Yapton.
23. Gilbert Unions: Ash, Hambledon and Reigate. Gilbert Parishes: Cranleigh, Ewhurst, Farnham, Frensham, Frimley, Send & Ripley and Godalming.
24. Wallingford Union and Faringdon Parish.
25. Higginbotham, 2012, p. 305.
26. PP, 1804, p. 714.
27. Higginbotham, 2007, pp. 12-13.
28. Nicholls G., 1854, p. 271.
29. Poor Law Unions: City of London, East London, West London, Greenwich, Hackney, Holborn, Kensington, Lewisham, Poplar, St Olave, St Saviour, Stepney, Strand, Wandsworth & Clapham, and Whitechapel. Single Poor Law Parishes: Bermondsey, Bethnal Green, Camberwell, Lambeth, Rotherhithe, St George in the East, St Martin in the Fields, and Southwark St George the Martyr. Local Act administrations: Clerkenwell, St George Hanover Square, St Giles in the Fields & St George, St James Westminster, Islington, Newington, St Luke, St Marylebone, St Pancras, Shoreditch, St Margaret & St John Westminster, and St Sepulchre Middlesex.
30. PP, 1867, p. 464.
31. PP, 1834, *PLC First Annual Report*, p. 104.
32. Lansberry, 1984, p. 110.
33. Kempthorne's other commissions were at Bradfield, Chertsey, Hailsham, Hastings, Newbury, Newhaven, Ticehurst and Wantage.
34. PP, 1836, *PLC Second Annual Report*, p. 56.
35. Higginbotham, 2008.
36. Twining, 1893, pp. 112-18.
37. Rogers J., 1889.
38. Longmate, 1974, p. 203.
39. *The Lancet*, 27 January 1866.
40. The Poor Law Board succeeded the Poor Law Commissioners in 1847.
41. Ayers, 1971, pp. 61-2.
42. Powell, 1930, p. 71.
43. Ayers, 1971, p. 277.
44. PP, 1839, *Report on the Continuance of the PLC*, p. 34.
45. PP, 1839, *PLC Fifth Annual Report*, p. 99.
46. Including Brentford, Bromley, Eastbourne, Edmonton, Gravesend, Guildford, Hastings, Kingston, Lewisham, City of London, Maidenhead, Maidstone, Malling, Mile End Old Town, Reading, Richmond, Staines, Stepney, Strood, Wallingford, Whitechapel and Willesden.
47. The Local Government Board succeeded the the Poor Law Board in 1871.
48. Gaston, 2009, p. 12.

CHAPTER 2

1. Anonymous, 1732, pp. 74-5.
2. discovery.nationalarchives.gov.uk/details/r/D518422 (18/12/2017).
3. Hitchcock, 1985, p. 270.
4. *ibid*.
5. *ibid*.
6. *ibid*.
7. Anonymous, 1732, p. 23.
8. Tomlinson, 1907, p. 364.
9. Hitchcock, 1985, p. 270.
10. Anonymous, 1732, p. 21.
11. 'Noyl' is short-fibred wool, a by-product of the combing process.

12. *ibid.*, pp. 6-7.
13. *ibid.*, pp. 17-20.
14. Hitchcock, 1985, p. 270.
15. PP, 1804, pp. 300-1.
16. Hitchcock, 1985, p. 270.
17. PP, 1804, p. 300.
18. Hitchcock, 1985, p. 270.
19. PP, 1804, pp. 274-5.
20. Hitchcock, 1985, p. 270.
21. Pigot, James & Co., 1824, p. 143.
22. www.londonlives.org/static/StBotolphAldgate.jsp (22/5/2018)
23. *The Examiner*, 26 October 1828, p. 12.
24. Anonymous, 1732, p. 22.
25. *Morning Advertiser*, 14 September 1810.
26. Anonymous, 1732, pp. 22-3.
27. *Morning Advertiser*, 10 July 1838.
28. Anonymous, 1732, p. 26.
29. *ibid.*, p. 25.
30. Hitchcock, 1985, p. 271.
31. PP, 1804, pp. 300-301.
32. .Denton, 1883.
33. Anonymous, 1732, p. 28.
34. Hitchcock, 1985, p. 271.
35. Cox J. E., 1876, p. 151.
36. *ibid.*, p. 156. The compter was a prison.
37. *ibid.*, p. 165.
38. PP, 1804, pp. 300-1.
39. Anonymous, 1732, p. 55.
40. Hitchcock, 1985, p. 271.
41. *ibid.*, p. 143.
42. PP, 1776.
43. Anonymous, 1732, p. 58.
44. PP, 1804, pp. 276-7.
45. Anonymous, 1732, p. 64.
46. *ibid.*, p. 65.
47. Hitchcock, 1985, p. 271.
48. Anonymous, 1732, p. 66.
49. Rocque, 1746.
50. Hitchcock, 1985, p. 271.
51. PP, 1776, pp. 280-1.
52. Hitchcock, 1985, p. 271.
53. *ibid.*
54. *ibid.*
55. Anonymous, 1732, p. 72.
56. *Morning Post*, 18 December 1838.
57. Tanner, 1999, p. 191.
58. *ibid.*, p. 200.
59. *London*, 14 March 1897.

CHAPTER 3

1. Anonymous, 1732, p. 66.
2. *The Lancet*, 4 November 1865.
3. www.british-history.ac.uk/vch/middx/vol11/pp190-202 (18/12/2017).
4. *ibid.*
5. PP, 1837, *PLC Third Annual Report*, p. 87.
6. *Morning Post*, 13 August 1842.
7. *The Lancet*, 27 January 1866.
8. Anonymous, 1732, p. 28.
9. *The Lancet*, 23 September 1865.
10. *ibid.*
11. HEA 101170.
12. Faulkner, 1829, pp. 25-6.
13. Anonymous, 1732, p. 51.
14. Cromwell, 1828, pp. 256-7.
15. *Staffordshire Advertiser*, Saturday, 29 November 1947 ('150 Years Ago').
16. Cromwell, 1828, p. 257.
17. *The Lancet*, 9 September 1865.
18. Feret, 1900, p. 95.
19. *ibid.*, p. 97.
20. *ibid.*, p. 96.
21. *Illustrated London News*, 4 August 1849.
22. PP, 1908-09, *LGB Thirty-eighth Annual Report*, p. xxviii.
23. Anonymous, 1725, pp. 31-2.
24. Anonymous, 1732, p. 24.
25. www.british-history.ac.uk/survey-kent/vol1/pp441-454 (7/1/2018).
26. Guillery, 2012, p. 49.
27. Browne, 1844.
28. *The Lancet*, 26 August 1865.
29. *Illustrated London News*, 25 January 1902, p. 131.
30. Montair, 1995, p. 13.
31. *ibid.*, pp. 13-14, 40.
32. *ibid.*, p. 13.
33. Hitchcock, 1987, p. 275.
34. Montair, 1995, p. 52.
35. *The Lancet*, 1 July, 1865.
36. PP, 1866, pp. 153-6.
37. *British Journal of Nursing*, February 1931, p. 50.
38. Denny, 1995, p. 77.
39. Faulkner, 1813, p. 232.
40. Denny, 1995, p. 78.
41. *The Building News*, 8 December 1905.
42. Anonymous, 1732, p. 50.
43. Wade, 1989, p. 48.
44. www.british-history.ac.uk/vch/middx/vol9/pp130-138 (4/1/2018).
45. HEA 101089.
46. *The Builder*, 2 February 1884.
47. Anonymous, 1732, p. 21.

48. discovery.nationalarchives.gov.uk/details/r/6cf992c0-0471-40ab-84d5-bb771748870c (7/1/2018).

49. *The Builder*, 1 March 1879.

50. *The Builder*, 23 October 1886.

51. www.british-history.ac.uk/vch/middx/vol8/pp76-82 (19/1/2018).

52. *ibid.*

53. *The Lancet*, 29 July 1865.

54. *The Holloway & Hornsey Press*, 20 July 1900.

55. Hitchcock, 1985, p. 273; Faulkner, 1820, p. 246.

56. www.british-history.ac.uk/survey-london/vol42/pp343-364 (17/1/2018).

57. Faulkner, 1820, p. 251.

58. PP, 1909, p. 1064.

59. Anonymous, 1732, pp. 56-7.

60. 'A Night in a Workhouse', *Pall Mall Gazette*, 12-15 January 1866.

61. *The Lancet*, 17 February 1866.

62. Morrison, 1999, p. 122.

63. HEA 101038.

64. *The Builder*, 24 January 1874, p. 69.

65. Allen, 1826, p. 434.

66. Waghorn, 1984, p. 271.

67. *The Lancet*, 26 August 1865.

68. Anonymous, 1732, p. 69.

69. Cleminson, 1983, pp. 2-3.

70. *ibid.*, p. 10.

71. Hitchcock, 1985, p. 278.

72. PP, PLB Fourth Annual Report, p. 7.

73. *South London Press*, 6 December 1902.

74. Hitchcock, 1985, p. 143.

75. www.british-history.ac.uk/vch/middx/vol9/pp241-246 (12/1/2018).

76. Neate, 1967, p. 33.

77. www.british-history.ac.uk/survey-london/vols43-4/pp77-90 (23/1/2018).

78. *ibid.*

79. PP, 1804, p. 298.

80. Brewer, 1816, p. 285.

81. PP, 1866, *Metropolitan Workhouse Infirmaries, etc.* pp. 316-7.

82. www.british-history.ac.uk/survey-london/vols43-4/pp77-90 (23/1/2018).

83. Anonymous, 1732, p. 67.

84. *The Lancet*, 23 September 1865.

85. www.british-history.ac.uk/survey-london/vol40/pt2/pp316-319 (24/1/2018).

86. Anonymous, 1732, pp. 26-7.

87. www.british-history.ac.uk/survey-london/vol40/pt2/pp316-319 (24/1/2018).

88. *The Globe*, 19 August 1834.

89. *Morning Post*, 3 September 1856.

90. Anonymous, 1732, pp. 70-1.

91. PP, 1866, pp. 172-5

92. *East London Observer*, 26 October 1895.

93. *The Builder*, 8 April 1876.

94. *The Builder*, 2 March 1878.

95. *BMJ*, 20 July 1895.

96. Anonymous, 1732, pp. 75-7.

97. *London and Westminster Review*, January 1837, p. 364.
98. *The Lancet*, 15 July 1865.
99. Dobie, 1829, pp. 232-3.
100. Anonymous, 1732, pp. 31-44.
101. *The Lancet*, 15 July 1865.
102. *The Builder*, 21 April 1888, p. 286.
103. Anonymous, 1732, p. 54.
104. Powell, 1930, p. 87.
105. *Anonymous 1732, pp.29-31.*
106. *The Builder*, 11 January 1879, p. 51.
107. search.lma.gov.uk/scripts/mwimain.dll/144/LMA_OPAC/web_detail/ REFD+H19~2FSM?SESSIONSEARCH (28/1/2018).
108. Anonymous, 1732, p. 60.
109. www.british-history.ac.uk/survey-london/vol42/pp343-364 (3/2/2018).
110. *The Lancet*, 7 April 1866.
111. www.british-history.ac.uk/survey-london/vol20/pt3/pp112-114 (29/1/2018).
112. Rogers, 1928, pp. 243-4.
113. McMaster, 1916, p. 222.
114. *The Lancet*, 9 September 1865.
115. Neate, 1967, p. 3.
116. *ibid.*, p. 4.
117. *ibid.*, pp. 6-8.
118. *ibid.*, p, 18.
119. *The Lancet*, 23 December 1865.
120. Neate, 1967, p. 29.
121. *ibid.*, p.28.
122. Monnington & Lampard, 1898, pp. 86-90.
123. Anonymous, 1732, p. 71.
124. *Morning Advertiser*, 11 March 1831 and 2 April 1831.
125. Hitchcock, 1985, p. 278.
126. PP, 1804, p. 510.
127. Saxon Snell, 1881, pp. 5-6.
128. *The Builder*, 21 July 1900.
129. Brown, 1905, p. 11.
130. *Morning Post*, 17 February 1817 p. 1 auction notice.
131. Brown, 1905, p. 13.
132. *ibid.*, p. 17.
133. PP, 1856, *Report on the Accommodation in St. Pancras workhouse.*
134. *The Lancet*, 23 December 1865.
135. Whittington Hospital History Project, 1992, p. 15.
136. HEA 101106.
137. Anonymous, 1732, p. 67.
138. Concanen & Morgan, 1795, p. 252.
139. *The Builder*, 26 February 1887, p. 316.
140. Anonymous, 1732, p. 73.
141. *ibid*, p. 59.
142. HEA 101225.
143. *The Lancet*, 29 July 1865.
144. *The Builder*, 9 December 1871.
145. *Morning Advertiser*, 23 August 1851.

146. Monnington & Lampard, 1898, pp. 58-62.

147. Anonymous, 1725, pp. 13-14.

148. Rocque, 1746.

149. Anonymous, 1732, p. 70.

150. Horwood, 1792-9.

151. Anonymous, 1732, p. 71.

152. Horwood, 1792-9.

153. Horwood & Faden, 1819.

154. *The Times*, 23 January 1860, p. 10.

155. 'The Uncommercial Traveller' in *All Year Round*, 18 February 1860.

156. Davenport-Hill, 1889, pp. 48-9.

157. 'The Short-Timers', in *All Year Round*, 20 June 1863.

158. *Tower Hamlet News*, Volume 2, No. 2, August 1966.

159. www.british-history.ac.uk/survey-london/vols33-4/pp190-192 (3/2/2018).

160. Rocque, 1746.

161. 'Workhouse Locations' (Westminster Archives Information Sheet 12).

162. *ibid*.

163. *ibid*.

164. Richardson R., 2012.

165. Twining, 1893, pp. 112-18.

166. Rogers J., 1889, pp. 3-14.

167. *The Lancet*, 12 August 1865.

168. Information board at Millfield House.

169. Anonymous, 1841, pp. 132-8.

170. Saint, 2013, p. 74.

171. Wandsworth Historical Society, 1973, p. 51.

172. Morden, 1897, pp. 271-4.

173. HEA 101085.

174. Anonymous, 1841.

175. *London*, 1896, p. 1251.

176. HEA 101189.

177. Gibson, 2006, p. 252.

178. HEA 101074.

179. Anonymous, 1732, p. 67.

180. *ibid*., p. 24.

181. www.british-history.ac.uk/survey-london/vol27/pp265-288 (4/3/2018).

182. www.british-history.ac.uk/survey-london/vol27/pp89-93 (4/2/2018).

183. PP, 1838, *PLC Fourth Annual Report*, pp. 87-8.

184. *Woolwich Gazette*, 21 June 1873.

CHAPTER 4

1.   Leonard, 1900, p. 226.

2.   Cox M., 1999.

3.   PP, 1804, p. 18.

4.   *Official Circulars of Public Documents and Information* (1849), vol. 8, p. 94.

5.   Personal reminiscence of former workhouse clerk, Laurie Liddiard.

6.   Darby, 1899, p. 51.

7.   *Reading Mercury*, 19 May 1894, p. 8.

8. Thomas, 1971.
9. Hitchcock, 1985, p. 126.
10. www.hungerfordvirtualmuseum.co.uk/index.php/8-places/313-workhouses (6/5/2018).
11. www.british-history.ac.uk/vch/wilts/vol16/pp8-49 (17/5/2018).
12. www.british-history.ac.uk/vch/wilts/vol16/pp215-222 (17/5/2018).
13. Croucher, 1986, p. 206.
14. www.british-history.ac.uk/vch/wilts/vol16/pp50-69 (17/5/2018).
15. Bunt, 1988.
16. Railton & Barr, 2005, p. 3.
17. PP, 1835, *PLC First Annual Report*, pp. 132-3.
18. Hitchcock, 1985, p. 259.
19. Tighe & Davis, 1858, pp. 518-19.
20. Rogers A.G., 1928, pp. 139-40.
21. www.datchethistory.org.uk/Link%20Articles/link_workhouse.htm (16/6/2018).
22. *Windsor and Eton Express*, 23 October 1841, p. 1.
23. *ibid.*, 26 March 1864, p. 4.
24. *The Lancet*, 28 September 1867.
25. Dearlove, 1990.

CHAPTER 5

1. HEA 101179.
2. *Kentish Gazette*, 23 July 1833.
3. PP, 1844, p. 1.
4. Lansberry, 1984, pp. 109-11.
5. *Kentish Gazette*, 5 April 1864, p. 6.
6. Weller, 1998, p. 86.
7. historicengland.org.uk/listing/the-list/list-entry/1085515 (11/3/2018).
8. Barham-with-Kingston W.I., 2005, p. 36.
9. Wilson & Woodman, 2012, p. 138.
10. Cox D., 1983, p. 63.
11. Borrowman, 1910, pp. 170-1.
12. issuu.com/chislehurstsociety/docs/cockpit_summer_2016_final_draft (6/2/2018).
13. PP, 1844, p. 2.
14. Cox D., 1983, p. 89.
15. Peckham & Humby, 1999, p. 11.
16. *Illustrated London News*, 7 November 1846.
17. Hitchcock, 1985.
18. Nicholls, 2017, p. 125.
19. Hitchcock, 1985, p. 267.
20. Anonymous, 1732, p. 126.
21. Porteus, 1984.
22. historicengland.org.uk/listing/the-list/list-entry/1064246 (17/12/2017).
23. Hasted, 1792, pp. 417-18.
24. Repton & Loudon, 1840, p. 598.
25. *Kentish Gazette*, 6 May 1808, p. 1.
26. Hasted, 1799, p. 125.
27. Jones, 1907, p. 357.
28. *Kentish Gazette*, 12 March 1811 advertisement for provisions.

29. *Bell's Weekly Messenger*, 21 January 1822, p. 6.
30. Griffin, 2013, p. 40; Auction particulars, *Kentish Gazette*, 25 April 1837.
31. *Canterbury Journal and Farmers' Gazette*, 25 April 1885, p. 3.
32. Downes, 2000, p. 64.
33. www.eastkenthistory.org.uk/article:the-poor (3/2/2018).
34. Gardiner, 1954, p. 318.
35. Hasted, 1799, p. 277.
36. Gardiner, 1954, p. 319.
37. www.nonington.org.uk/the-nonington-poor-houses-in-church-street-and-easole-street/ (16/2/2018).
38. *Kentish Gazette*, 31 May 1808, p. 1.
39. Igglesden, Volume 4, p. 66.
40. *Hull Daily Mail*, 7 January 1921.
41. Igglesden, Volume 3, p. 54.
42. Igglesden, Volume 10, p. 58.
43. Stevens, 2002, p. 4.
44. *ibid.*
45. *ibid.*, p. 32
46. Hiscock, 1972, p. 12.
47. *Chelmsford Chronicle*, 9 June 1786, p. 1.
48. Allinson H., 2002, p. 126.
49. PP, 1867, p. 506.
50. Bolton, 2016, p. 151.
51. www.margatelocalhistory.co.uk/DocRead/Before%20seabathing%20Chap%204.html (21/2/2018).
52. Mockett, 1836, p. 300.
53. Walker, 1981, p. 94.
54. Gilham, 1991, p. 23.
55. *ibid.*, p. 61.
56. 2 Thessalonians 3:10.
57. *Kentish Gazette*, 13 May 1778.
58. Vaux, 2006, pp. 60-1.
59. yaldinghistory.webplus.net/page30.html (6/2/2018).
60. Melling, 1964, p. 81.
61. Anonymous, 1732, p. 130.
62. Denne & Shrubsole, 1817, p. 232.
63. Anonymous, 1732, pp. 125-6.
64. Baldwin, 1998, p. 181.
65. HEA 100687.
66. Clancy, 2007, p. 34.
67. Allinson, 2005, pp. 43-5.
68. Ewing, 1926, p. 190.
69. www.kentphotoarchive.com/kpa/eden/thumblarge. php?startnumber=97&edenbridge=2 (5/3/2018).
70. *West Kent Herald*, 13 February 1836.
71. theromneymarsh.net/blueplaques (7/11/2017).
72. historicengland.org.uk/listing/the-list/list-entry/1231597 (7/11/2017).
73. *Kent Weekly Post*, 5 March 1822.
74. Clarke & Stoyel, 1975, p. 174.
75. Chevening Parish History Group, 1999, p. 112.

76. Clarke & Stoyel, 1975, p. 196.
77. HEA 100952.
78. Judge, 1987.
79. historicengland.org.uk/listing/the-list/list-entry/1350241 (7/11/2017).
80. *Kentish Gazette*, 7 February 1794, p. 1.
81. Rogers, 1928, p. 209.
82. www.discovergravesham.co.uk/northfleet/the-hill.html (11/2/2018).
83. historicengland.org.uk/listing/the-list/list-entry/1070851 (11/4/2018).
84. *Kentish Gazette*, 20 August 1814, p. 1.
85. Igglesden, Volume 5, p. 78.
86. Anonymous, 1732, p. 141.
87. *Pembury Contact* No. 802, October 1986.
88. *British Medical Journal*, 1895, pp. 1102–4.
89. Pearman, 1868, p. 141; Ruderman, 1994, p. 34.
90. Rogers, 1928, pp. 207–8.
91. *ibid.*, p. 212.
92. *ibid.*, p. 209.

CHAPTER 6

1. brentfordandchiswicklhs.org.uk/publications/the-journal/journal-8-1999/the-chiswick-workhouse/ (23/2/2018).
2. www.british-history.ac.uk/vch/middx/vol3/pp155-157 (5/3/2018).
3. www.british-history.ac.uk/vch/middx/vol7/pp144-147 (14/11/2017).
4. Rogers, 1928, p. 240.
5. www.british-history.ac.uk/vch/middx/vol3/pp119-122 (25/2/2018).
6. Aungier, 1840, p. 180.
7. Pottles were small containers for measuring and selling fruit etc.
8. Cassell, 1971, pp. 178–83.
9. www.british-history.ac.uk/vch/middx/vol7/pp30-32 (5/3/2018).
10. www.british-history.ac.uk/vch/middx/vol5/pp241-243 (15/11/2017).
11. King & Gear, 2013, p. 152.
12. *Hertford Mercury and Reformer*, 15 August 1837, p. 1.
13. Lloyd, 1888, p. 99; Hitchcock, 1985, p. 273.
14. www.british-history.ac.uk/vch/essex/vol5/pp162-170 (14/11/2017).
15. Robinson, 1840, p. 213.
16. Richardson, 1971, pp. 57–8.
17. Graham, 1974, p. 7.
18. www.british-history.ac.uk/vch/middx/vol4/pp237-249 (5/3/2018).
19. Evans, 1890, p. 282.
20. www.british-history.ac.uk/vch/middx/vol4/pp237-249 (5/3/2018).
21. www.british-history.ac.uk/vch/middx/vol5/pp102-104 (5/3/2018).
22. Sherwood, 1999.
23. www.british-history.ac.uk/vch/middx/vol3/pp25-27 (16/11/2017).
24. www.british-history.ac.uk/vch/middx/vol3/pp59-61 (16/11/2017).
25. www.british-history.ac.uk/vch/middx/vol3/pp1-12 (5/3/2018).
26. www.british-history.ac.uk/vch/middx/vol3/pp45-46 (16/11/2017).
27. *Yorkshire Evening Post*, 1 September 1898.

28. Wingfield, 2003, pp. 12-15.
29. historicengland.org.uk/listing/the-list/list-entry/1080239 (16/11/2017).
30. historicengland.org.uk/listing/the-list/list-entry/1080264 (16/11/2017).
31. www.british-history.ac.uk/vch/middx/vol4/pp49-50 (16/11/2017).
32. www.british-history.ac.uk/vch/middx/vol4/pp31-33 (16/11/2017).
33. www.british-history.ac.uk/vch/middx/vol4/pp117-119 (17/11/2017).
34. www.british-history.ac.uk/vch/middx/vol3/pp200-202 (17/11/2017).
35. www.british-history.ac.uk/vch/middx/vol4/pp105-106 (17/11/2017).
36. PP, 1867, p. 580.
37. Gray, 1963, p. 10.

CHAPTER 7

1. Anonymous, 1732, p. 162.
2. Surrey History Centre Ref. ZS/24/b.
3. Rogers, 1928, p. 322.
4. www.chobham.info/workhous.htm (23/11/2017).
5. Schueller, 1989, pp. 164-5.
6. Crosby, 2003, p. 61.
7. www.pyrford.com/history/pyrford.html (2/5/2018).
8. HEA 101618.
9. McInnes & Sparkes, 1980, p. 14.
10. www2.merton.gov.uk/lower_mitcham_heritage_map_leaflet.pdf (12/12/2017).
11. Bentham, 1923, p. 30.
12. bournesoc.org.uk/bslivewp/wp-content/uploads/Old-Coulsdon-Trail.pdf (201/5/2018).
13. McInnes & Sparkes, 1980, p. 39.
14. Bax, 1891.
15. www.dorkingmuseum.org.uk/poverty-and-the-workhouse/ (30/11/2017).
16. O'Kelley, 2011, p. 5.
17. O'Connor, 1973, p. 41.
18. archaeologydataservice.ac.uk/archsearch/record?titleId=1188088 (9/5/2018).
19. www.epsomandewellhistoryexplorer.org.uk/WorkhouseEpsom.html (29/11/2017).
20. Rogers, 1928, p. 316.
21. *Morning Advertiser*, 30 June 1824.
22. www.epsomandewellhistoryexplorer.org.uk/EwellParishWorkhouse.html (30/11/2017).
23. Abdy, 1992, p. 42.
24. www.elmbridge-online.co.uk/cobham/korea.html (1/2/2018).
25. Heath, 2000, p. 83.
26. HEA 100904.
27. Rogers, 1928, p. 319.
28. Shave, 2017, p. 151.
29. Rotherham & Handle, 2014, p. 29.
30. Walters, 1970, p. 22.
31. *The Lancet*, 19 October 1867, p. 496.
32. PP, 1868, p. 165.
33. *St Peter's Limpsfield Parish News*, Aumtumn 2016, pp. 13-14.
34. www.ifootpath.com/display-ifootpath-walk?walkID=4097 (19/5/2018).
35. Packham, 2004, p. 5.

36. *Surrey Mirror*, 30 July 1907.
37. Davies, 2004, p. 7.
38. Noyes, 1996, p. 21.
39. *ibid.*, p. 16.
40. Crosby, p. 62.
41. *Nottingham Evening Post*, 28 November 1906, p. 7.
42. Macpherson, 1921, p. 81.
43. Shave, 2017, p. 71.
44. Research by Messrs Seymour and Warrington (personal communication from Cranleigh Local History Group).
45. Sampson, 1993, p. 4.
46. Stevens I. D., 1966, pp. 47-8.
47. c18thgirl.blogspot.co.uk/2013/07/part-5-parish-workhouse-in-eighteenth.html (17/5/2018).
48. Baker, 1986, p. 60.
49. Sampson, 1993, p. 5.
50. *ibid.*
51. Dulake, 1977, p. 80.
52. www.reigate-banstead.gov.uk/download/downloads/id/380/view_the_list_of_ buildings_of_architectural_and_historic_interest/ (30/11/2017).
53. Fookes, 2002, p. 83.
54. www.horleyhistory.org.uk/smallfield (17/5/2018).
55. Rogers, 1928, p. 321.
56. *Surrey Mirror and County Post*, 25 April 1930.
57. historicengland.org.uk/listing/the-list/list-entry/1378121 (30/11/2017).
58. *Surrey Mirror and County Post*, 25 April 1930.
59. *ibid.*, 2 May 1930.
60. *The Local Government Manual*, 1908, p. 282.
61. Butler, 1969, p. 4.
62. *ibid.*, pp. 6-7.
63. www.richmondhistory.org.uk/wordpress/history-of-richmond/selwyn-family-development-richmond/ (17/12/2017).
64. Anderson, 1983, pp. 65-7.
65. Macpherson, 1921, p. 82.

CHAPTER 8

1. www.british-history.ac.uk/vch/sussex/vol5/pt1/pp10-101 (25/3/2018).
2. nebula.wsimg.com/2d83fde3f223403b0b2539aea6ed0f6e?AccessKeyId=EDEFA4D7343 7EA30BB23 (5/6/2018).
3. Bartley, 1971, p. 40.
4. PP, *PLC First Annual Report*, p. 21.
5. Lucey, 1978.
6. Gardner, 2012, p. 4.
7. *ibid.*, p. 10.
8. Erredge, 1867, p. 54.
9. *Brighton Patriot*, 16 April 1839, p. 4.
10. Diggle, 1979, p. 15.
11. Dangerfield, 1938, p. 134.

12. *ibid.*, pp. 135-6.
13. *ibid.*, pp. 251-3.
14. www.british-history.ac.uk/vch/sussex/vol6/pt3/p185 (4/4/ 2018).
15. www.slaughamarchives.org/picture/number902.asp (12/6/2018).
16. Holgate, 1925.
17. www.hurstpierpointsociety.org.uk/newsletters/2013_autumn_2014-01-04.pdf (5/4/2018).
18. historicengland.org.uk/listing/the-list/list-entry/1025426 (4/4/2018).
19. historicengland.org.uk/listing/the-list/list-entry/1025460 (4/4/2018).
20. Leppard, 2001.
21. Sutton, 1902, p. 142.
22. www.rh7.org/factshts/workhse.pdf (5/4/2018).
23. HEA 101606.
24. Wright, 1902, p. 106.
25. books.google.co.uk/books?id=N4AYAQAAIAAJ p.560 (22/5/2018).
26. www.westsussex.gov.uk/media/1714/alfriston_eus_report_maps.pdf (6/4/2018).
27. stjamestrustseaford.co.uk/history.html (5/4/2018).
28. HEA 100906.
29. Salzman, 1901, pp. 9, 59.
30. www.westsussex.gov.uk/media/1730/heathfield_eus_report_maps.pdf (7/4/2018).
31. historicengland.org.uk/listing/the-list/list-entry/1183954 (5/4/2018).
32. historicengland.org.uk/listing/the-list/list-entry/1284874 (5/4/2018).
33. www.westsussex.gov.uk/media/1728/hastings_eus_report_maps.pdf (7/4/2018).
34. hastingschronicle.net/features/old-town-workhouses/ (4/7/2018).
35. Valentine, 2000, p. 6.
36. Morrison, 1999, p. 61.
37. *ibid.*, p. 211.
38. rusperchurch.org.uk/history (23/5/2018).
39. www.british-history.ac.uk/vch/sussex/vol6/pt2/pp99-100 (7/6/2018).
40. www.british-history.ac.uk/vch/sussex/vol6/pt3/pp41-42 (7/6/2018).
41. Hickman, 1944.
42. Morrison, 1999, p. 211.
43. Young, 1808, pp. 448-9.
44. HEA 101611.
45. Gordon, 1877, p. 203.
46. www.westsussex.gov.uk/media/1739/petworth_eus_report_and_maps.pdf (7/4/2018).
47. HEA 101612.
48. HEA 101613.
49. www.ryemuseum.co.uk/rye-workhouses/ (17/5/2018).
50. PP, 1835, PLC First Annual Report, p. 340.
51. Hodson, 1920, p. 36.
52. HEA 100995.
53. historicengland.org.uk/listing/the-list/list-entry/1027385 (7/3/2018).
54. www.british-history.ac.uk/vch/sussex/vol6/pt3/pp41-42 (8/4/2018).
55. Bishop J.G., 1892, p. 405.
56. *Brighton Gazette*, 17 September 1835, p. 3.
57. White, 1990, p. 9.
58. Hothersall, 1985, p. 18.
59. Saunders-Jacobs, 1965, p. 29.
60. www.british-history.ac.uk/vch/sussex/vol6/pt1/pp247-259 (8/4/2018).

61. www.westsussex.gov.uk/media/1748/storrington_eus_report_and_maps.pdf (15/5/2018).
62. www.british-history.ac.uk/vch/sussex/vol6/pt2/pp30-34 (8/4/2018).
63. 1851 census entry for Sarah Searle and family.
64. www.westsussex.gov.uk/media/1741/robertsbridge_eus_report_maps.pdf (9/5/2018).
65. Barkshire, 2000, p. 59.
66. www.westsussex.gov.uk/media/1750/wadhurst_eus_report_maps.pdf (9/4/2018).
67. HEA101603.
68. www.westsussex.gov.uk/media/1735/mayfield_eus_report_maps.pdf (9/4/2018).
69. Pullein, 1928, pp. 257-8.
70. Russell, Parker, & Chidson, 2000, p. 42.
71. HEA 101605.
72. www.djbryant.co.uk/westbourne-workhouse/ (9/4/2018).
73. historicengland.org.uk/listing/the-list/list-entry/1026424 (9/4/2018).
74. Shave, 2017, p. 258.
75. HEA 100999.
76. yaptonhistory.org.uk/history/workhouse/ (22/5/2018).

BIBLIOGRAPHY

Abdy, C. (1992). *A History of Ewell*.

Allen, T. (1826). *The History and Antiquities of the Parish of Lambeth*.

Allinson, H. (2002). *Hollingbourne: The History of a Kentish Parish*.

Allinson, H. (2005). *Life in the Workhouse: The Story of Milton Union, Kent*.

Anderson, J.E. (1983). *A History of Mortlake*.

Anonymous. (1653). *Poor Out-Cast Children's Song and Cry*.

Anonymous. (1725). *An Account of Several Work-houses for Employing and Maintaining the Poor*.

Anonymous. (1732). *An Account of Several Work-houses for Employing and Maintaining the Poor*.

Anonymous. (1841). 'A Few Weeks from Home: Visits to Workhouses'. *Chambers's Edinburgh Journal*, pp. 29-30.

Anonymous. (1841). *Clapham, with its Common and Environs*.

Arnold, F. (1886). *The History of Streatham*.

Arthur, A., Boreham, P., & Porteus, G. (1984). *Crime and Poverty in the Dartford Area 1400–1900*.

Aungier, G.J. (1840). *The History and Antiquities of Syon Monastery, the Parish of Isleworth, and the Chapelry of Hounslow*.

Ayers, G.M. (1971). *England's First State Hospitals 1867–1930*.

Baker, R.G. (1986). *The Book of Molesey*.

Baldwin, R.A. (1998). *The Gillingham Chronicles*.

Barham-with-Kingston WI. (2005). *The History of Barham*.

Barkshire, J. (2000). *Burwash: Domesday to Millennium*.

Bartley, L.J. (1971). *The Story of Bexhill*.

Bax, A.R. (1891). 'The Church Registers and Parish Account Books of Ockley, Surrey'. *Surrey Archaeological Collections*, 20-78.

Bellers, J. (1695). *Proposals for Raising a College of Industry of All Useful Trades and Husbandry*.

Bentham, T. (1923). *A History of Beddington*.

Bishop, C.H. (1973). *Folkestone: The Story of a Town*.

Bishop, J.G. (1892). *A Peep Into the Past: Brighton in the Olden Time, with Glances at the Present*.

Black, M. (1993). *West Middlesex University Hospital – a History*.

Blaug, M. (1964). 'The Poor Law Report Re-Examined'. *Journal of Economic History, 24* (2), 229-245.

Blincoe, R. (1832). *A Memoir of Robert Blincoe, an Orphan Boy*.

Bolton, M. (2016). *St Laurence in Thanet*.